An Introduction to Scripture for the
Occasionally Biblically Embarrassed

HOLY TALK

HAROLD "JAKE" JACOBSON

Lulu Publishing Services rev. date: 07/17/2018

Contents

New Testament

Dedication

This work is dedicated to Dr. Edwin Freed, Dr. Carey Moore and Dr. Thomas Ridenour, the three teachers who first opened the Scriptures to me in a way that made my heart burn and to the Rev. Neil Harrison who inspired me to share the wonder and mystery of this story. Each of them is deeply embedded in the pages of this work.

Acknowledgements

I am indebted to Gettysburg College for teaching me to think critically about myself, the world and God. I wish to thank not only my professors of religion but those of the other disciplines that made my liberal arts education a rich and life-changing experience.

I wish to thank Emanuel Lutheran Church in Bradford, PA and Grace Lutheran Church in Clarion, PA for providing a safe and forgiving environment that allowed for exploration and growth.

I wish to thank all my students over the course of the years. Their curiosity and conscientiousness continued to push me to continuing my own growth. I especially wish to thank those recently who endured the conception and writing of this book. Their review, critique and suggestions were invaluable.

I wish also to thank my colleagues who pushed me and supported me into the writing of this book. Their confidence in my abilities kept me going when I was ready to quit on the project.

Finally, I wish to that those who were willing to share their candid embarrassment and frustration of feeling that the Bible was at times a confusing and foreign land they got lost in. To be able to share my love of the scriptures with them is the ultimate motivation for this book.

Preface

In a conversation with a friend of mine they confessed that they had recently purchased a copy of the book, *"Bible for Dummies."* They then went on to share with me how embarrassing it felt as an active churchgoer to walk up to the counter and check out. "Shouldn't I know more about the Bible and not have resort to such a book? What does it say about me that I am this ignorant of the Bible that I need such a book?"

I was stunned by the level and intensity of their embarrassment. What a disservice we have done to such people. Their comment was, "I need a book that helps me be able to approach the Bible without feeling embarrassed about being a Biblical novice". "I also want something substantial that will help me as I grow in my knowledge and understanding of the Bible." "I want a 'help me grow' book that will continue with me as I grow."

I have searched for that book for my friend and countless before them and have not been able to find such a book. I was recounting this story and expressing my frustration with several colleagues when two of them blurted out, "Write it!"

So that is how we got here!

Introduction

THE BEGINNING

It was *that* day, that great and terrible day, September 11, 2001. The events of the day had left me mentally and physically drained. I went to my place of refreshment in those days – my swinging chair on the front porch. One of the characteristics of my neighborhood is that we all have front porches and use them often. On that night all the front porches of the neighborhood were occupied. It seemed that we were being driven into community. In what I've called the blowing of the Divine Dog Whistle we all began to migrate one by one to Peg's front porch. Peg was the matriarch of the neighborhood and regularly entertained the neighborhood conversations from her porch.

We all gathered there including the college students next door. The conversation quickly settled in on the day's events. We took turns rehearsing where we were when we first heard the news, when we saw the footage of the plane crashing into the towers, and when we realized that we were not witnessing an accident but an act of terror. We then began to talk about those friends and loved ones we had not heard from… those in harm's way… we wondered what it would mean for our children… Peg's son-in-law was working in the Pentagon and my boys were of an age that conjured up vivid memories of the draft of the Vietnam era.

What I noticed was that before long the language being used in our conversation was faith talk. It was as if the only language strong enough to hold the content of that day was the language of faith. During this evolving conversation one of the college students (who had earlier admitted that he never darkened the door of a church) chimed up with, "I only have one question that I want an answer for and that is, 'Where in the hell was God this morning?'"

For the next several hours there on the front porch we engaged that question in holy conversation. This was not a time for pious platitudes or trite religious answers… it was a roll up your sleeves and get down and dirty in practical theology. As I reflected on that night several months later I realized that we were beginning to do the work of post-9/11 hermeneutics. What does this all mean in light of our faith?

We have discovered that the events of that day changed much more in our world than the skyline of New York, the Pentagon and the terrain of Southwestern Pennsylvania. It changed the fabric of our lives. It is my contention that we cut off the "front porch conversation" after that great and terrible day. Hermeneutics gave way to an unchallengeable patriotism. The hard questions were prohibited. The conversation aborted. Communities of faith soon experience a nose-dive of attendance. Fear and suspicion now forms the syntax of all conversation over a decade removed from the events of that day.

I am writing this book to open up a particular conversation of faith. It is my hope to not only offer an introduction to scripture that is practical and functional but also to provide an arena where questions of faith can be openly explored. This is not an answer book but rather an invitation to a conversation.

It is my contention that this conversation is not a new conversation but one that weaves in and out of the Jewish and Christian scriptures. I would argue that it is events like 9/11 in the life of God's people that gives rise to much of the content of our scriptures (especially in the gathering and compilation of the material). It is my opinion that these two major life/faith-changing events are the destruction of the Jerusalem Temple and subsequent Babylonian Exile in the Sixth Century B.C.E. and then the destruction of the Second Jerusalem Temple at the hands of the Romans in 70 C.E. I believe these two major events and the surrounding events raise particular conversations among God's people that give rise to the conversation we know as the Old and New Testaments.

This conversation has as its tenor both lament and the apocalyptic. While both elements are to be found in the Hebrew and Christian Scriptures it is my opinion that the primary response to the crisis in the Hebrew Scriptures is lament and in the Christian Scriptures it is apocalypticism. This may also explain the tensions within the Judaism/ Christianity in the 1ˢᵗ Century. Neither of these conversational threads were made available to the Christian community or the nation following 9/11. Most critically absent was the call and ability to lament in the biblical sense. I also believe that while the opportunity to lament may have been missed the apocalyptic thread still may open a new conversation that calls us to move forward even as we look back, which is what biblical apocalypticism does.

It is also my opinion that it is an *open* conversation that scripture invites us into and not a closed collection of belief posturing. As such I hope to raise as many questions as I provide answers in the following pages. I believe that the "life" of the scriptures is in the ongoing conversation and not the words confined between its covers.

Finally, it is my opinion that scripture, particularly the Hebrew Tanakh, (Tanakh refers to the title of the Hebrew Scriptures) was intended to open a conversation. Unfortunately, today we use scripture to cut off conversation. What once was a book that invited questions of faith has become an answer book that does not allow for new questions to be asked of these holy words.

THE CONVERSATION

If we believe that the conversation with scripture is a "live" conversation, then the traditional way of engaging that content leaves much to be desired. Most of Biblical scholarship approaches the task with a methodology akin to an autopsy. (Unless we are Ducky on NCIS few of us have meaningful conversations with a corpse). That is not to say that the tools of Biblical scholarship are not highly useful but more critical is *how* we use them to assist us in a conversation with a dynamic Word?

I prefer to begin with the Biblical material using an inductive rather that deductive methodology. Rather than beginning with the question, "What does the text mean?" I suggest we begin with "What is the text saying to me?"

To that end I encourage the following process as a starting point for engaging the scriptures whether for devotional use, sermon preparation or serious study of the Bible:

- Read the text. Preferably out loud.
- Read the text a second time paying particular attention to words or phrases that attract your attention. Pay special attention to questions that may arise as you listen to the text. I keep a pad of paper beside me when I am doing this and write the notes down as I go.
- If I was using this exercise for devotional reading I would use these notes as a beginning point for my meditation and prayer.
- For our purposes I suggest we use these notes, especially the questions, as an entry point into our conversation with the text.

In this way I would argue that we begin with the assumption that the text has something to say to us today as well as having had a word to say at the time of its first offering. Now we are prepared to bring the tools of our scholarship to bear as we begin to explore the mysteries of this centuries-long conversation.

The second part of the conversation is to recognize that it is intended to be a tri-part conversation between ourselves, the text and the community. The Lutheran program *Word and Witness* talked in terms of My Story, God's Story and Your Story. One of the struggles that pastors and Bible study leaders have with scripture study is that we tend to do our work in isolation from the community so that when we gather the community we and they often assume we are the "expert." This is contributed to also by the Western reading of scripture that seeks the meaning of the text rather than the text as conversation starter which was the traditional Jewish way of approaching scripture (Rabbi so and so says this about the text and rabbi such and such says something a little different... Now, how do we hear the text today?).

The textual conversation then if it is to be truly a living conversation is not simply between me and the text but also must include the community (however we define that). As Martin Luther once is reported to have said,

"Those who read the Bible alone read it to their own damnation." Maybe he understood the conversation.

A note on "story": My preaching tends to be anecdotal and every so often someone (often one of my children) asks, "Was that story you told really true?" My answer is always, "Yes, but that doesn't mean that if the others in the story were asked to tell the same story it might not be different. Truth does not always demand factuality. It has only been since the age of Enlightenment that we have been concerned by factuality and accuracy of scripture. This has spilled over into our study of God's Story. The search for the historical Jesus that began around the turn of the 20th Century has given way to the Jesus Project of the turn of the 21st Century. Neither movement has provided satisfactory answers to those who wish to verify scripture.

Behind this insistence on verification is a cultural movement from authority to evidence. Increasingly ours is a culture that seeks evidence over and against accepting authority outright. For centuries biblical authority has been unquestioned, but ever since the Age of Enlightenment and more recently the advent of the historical critical methods that authority has been eroded. The Bible's truth is not in its factuality but in its witness to the living God. It is a truth that shapes us as God's people as we strive to live together. The authority of the Bible is also not in its factuality but given to it by that same community gathered by its witness.

I have chosen to use Ha Shem *(It is common Jewish practice to restrict the use of the names of God word to use in a liturgical context. Therefore in casual conversation, some Jews, even when not speaking Hebrew, will call God "HaShem", which is Hebrew for "the Name" (cf. Leviticus 24:11 and Deuteronomy 28:58). Likewise, when quoting from the Tanakh Jews will replace God's name Adonai by "HaShem". In deference to my Jewish brothers and sisters I will maintain this practice and use HaShem to designate the God of Abraham, Isaac and Jacob, the God of the Tanakh)* and Abba (The name which Jesus uses to refer to his Father. It literally translates "Daddy") in place of the generic "God." My reasoning for doing this is not only to make a distinction between how the Divine is viewed differently in the Hebrew and Christian Scriptures but also because the term "God" has been overlaid with philosophical baggage such as omnipotence and omniscience which are not scriptural attributes.

Before we begin I would be remiss if I did not say a word about **trust.** As I've completed the survey of Scripture have come to realize that the theme which consistently runs through the chaos and catastrophe is that of trust in HaShem and the Triune God. The word "trust" in Hebrew and Greek is often translated "faith." I find this unfortunate because in post-Reformation church language faith is often interpreted as a noun: I *have* faith. I *need* faith. I have *enough* faith. I have *more* faith than you. In this case faith is often the subject of our conversations. By its very nature the word trust requires an object: I trust HaShem. There is also a much more active element to the word trust than to that of faith.

It is the failure of the people to trust HaShem and later the Triune God that continually gets them into trouble. It is the failure of our primordial parents to trust that HaShem means what HaShem says in the garden that leads them to eat of the fruit and eventually be expelled from the garden. It is the failure of Abraham to trust in the promises of HaShem that leads he and Sarah to involve Hagar in trying to force the issue of offspring. It will be the failure to trust in HaShem's providence that will lead some of the Israelites to pocket the manna. It will be the Kings failure to trust in HaShem that will lead them into a web of political intrigue that will eventually lead to exile.

We find similar breaches of trust in the New Testament particularly from the disciples but also from the later Christians under persecution. I would go even so far to say that it is Jesus' willingness and ability to trust the Father completely, and not his so-called sinlessness, that separates Jesus from the rest of humanity.

THE CRISIS

"Zaydeh (Yiddish for Grandpa) tell me the story again!"

"What story?"

"The story of the Great and Terrible Day. Please, Zaydeh, please."

"Alright, but then it is off to bed with you, Jakob."

"I was but a young boy myself… not much bigger than you. There was much fear. Stories were being remembered and retold on the streets of Jerusalem about what happened to the Northern Kingdom ages before. Prophets came from the HaShem[2] warning of a similar fate if they did not change their ways. But the political experts were advising drastic deals to be cut with neighboring countries in face of the great and terrible threat of Babylon."

"One day crazy young Isaiah stormed into the King's court and pointed to the young girl in the corner… 'King, you see that girl there… yeah, the pregnant one… before that child is old enough to eat solid food this whole mess will have blown over… sit tight and trust the Lord.' But he couldn't… and deals he cut, promises were made and promises broken… just like old times."

"Now let me see…where did I put that scroll? Ah! Found it… mmmm…here is the part you are looking for…"

"A long time ago, Zedikiah, king of Israel, managed to royally tick off old Nebuchadnezzar, king of Babylon. Nebuchadnezzar was so enraged he laid siege to Jerusalem for two years. The siege and famine eventually wore down the resistance and Nebuchadnezzar and his troops attacked and captured the city.

In those days the Temple, the king's palace and all the houses of Jerusalem were burned to the ground. The contents of the Temple, the holy things, were taken as booty back to Babylon. The people of Jerusalem, including the king and his family, were dragged off into exile by Nebuchadnezzar. That, my dear Jakob, is how our people ended up in Babylon."

This type of conversation very well may have been happening in Babylon in the decades that follow the destruction of Jerusalem (586 BCE) and the subsequent deportation and exile of much of the population of Judah. The Babylonian Deportation is not only a political crisis, it is a religious or faith crisis for the people as well. There is great speculation that HaShem has left the building. This pondering is also encouraged by the Babylonians who as conquerors tout the superiority of their god, Marduk, over the claims of HaShem.

A key issue in this conversation is the question of broken promises or broken covenant. Judah has clung to several inviolable promises made by *HaShem* to the people namely that they were inheritors of the Promised Land and that a king like David would sit on the throne in perpetuity. In addition, the Temple in Jerusalem is considered *HaShem's* residence. Now the people are faced with no land, no king and heaven knows what has happened to *HaShem*.

This crisis leads to a conversation among the faithful that I believe centers around four basic questions:

1. Who is our god? Is *HaShem* dead? Has *HaShem* abandoned us?
2. Who are we without our promises?
3. How do we live in community here in Babylon?
4. What does *HaShem* want us to do with our lives?

I believe this conversation drives the community to begin to formulate a response that plays out in the gathering of materials both written and oral into what becomes the Tanakh. This conversation is open ended and continues for centuries.

As this conversation develops several more general concerns spin out from these:

- What a mess we are in!
- How did we get in a mess like this?
- When were we in a mess like this before?

It is my opinion that these shape the structure of the conversation.

- *When were we in a mess like this before?* Leads us to Exodus and the Torah
- *What a mess we are in!* and *How did we get in a mess like this?* Lead us to the prophets (both pre-exilic and exilic)
- *How do we now live day to day in this new world?* Leads us to the Writings

I will use these three aspects of the conversation to move our discussion of the books of the Tanakh forward looking first at the Torah and then the prophets. Following that we will look at the Writings which really don't develop fully until around the time of Jesus. Finally, I will invite us to use these insights to open a conversation about our 9/11 crisis especially as to where the church may find itself being led into the future.

Hebrew Scriptures

(Old Testament)

All Scriptural citations in this section (Hebrew Scriptures) are taken from the **JPS Hebrew-English Tanakh, 2nd Edition.** (The Jewish Publication Society: Philadelphia, 1999).

When Were We in this Mess Before?

As God's people begin to contemplate their fate as exiles in Babylon the thorny questions about HaShem's faithfulness arise, "Have we ever been in a mess like this before?"

"What did HaShem do?

"How did we respond?"

The answers to these questions become the foundational theology for the exiles namely, the Torah. The Torah or Law is contained in the first five books of the Tanakh: Genesis, Exodus, Leviticus, Numbers, and Deuteronomy. Some scholars also refer to this collection of works as the Pentateuch, literally, Five Books.

Why the Torah? Why start here as a response to the crisis of exile? It can be well documented that over the centuries as communities of people are thrust into crises involving identity and/or their relationship with their deity there is often a reactive movement to "legislate" behavior, morality, and ethics. It serves as an attempt to gain control of the chaos. For the people of HaShem, Torah lies at the heart of the crisis and its eventual resolution.

The religion of Ha Shem's people prior to the exile, like most of their neighbors, is a sacrificial cult centered in (but not exclusive to) Jerusalem. Sacrifice offerings are an attempt to appease and manipulate the deity either to restore a broken relationship or to exact a blessing for oneself or the community. Sacrifice is both individual and communal.

With the destruction of the Temple by the Babylonians the central sacrificial cult site is negated. Crisis ensues in exile because there is no

Temple to practice/restore one's relationship with HaShem. Torah study which appears to be practiced alongside the Temple cult now becomes the dominant form of religious practice. I would envision it as the study and practice of Torah becomes the "meatless sacrifice" to preserve the relationship with HaShem.

One of the most important pieces of scholarship with regards to Torah study is the identification of various strands of material from various times in the history of God's people. These strands are traditionally referred to as:

J (Yahwist)	c. 900 BCE
E (Elohist)	c. 750 BCE
D (Deuteronomist)	c. 600 BCE
P (Priestly)	c. 550 BCE

The important part of this discovery is that it reveals that the material in the Torah has a rich and varied history of compilation and editing. This also explains why there are duplicate stories and awkward repetitions at points as well as flat out inconsistent and contradictory material.

The Torah and the historical books constitute the primary narrative of ancient Israel. It becomes the corpus of material that shapes how they see themselves in the past, present and future. It gives the instruction and guidance which will become normative for Judaism. Finally, it tells the story of a distinctive people who are always at risk (if not at the moment, soon). This risk is often from internal as well as external threat.

> *"Zeydah, to think about the Great and Terrible Day makes me scared."*
>
> *"It was a very scary time in many ways. Jakob."*
>
> *"How so, Zeydah?"*
>
> *"Many, many things changed for us as a people. So many things we thought would never change. It has been hard to adjust."*

"Did we ever face a time like that before?"

"Once, a long, long time ago, and far, far away from this place."

"What was it like?"

"Our people were kept as slaves."

"What happened, Zaydeh?"

"HaShem sent a deliverer to set us free."

EXODUS

I imagine that this may be the only introduction to scripture that begins with Exodus rather than Genesis. I hold that there is a straight line from Exile to Exodus addressing the central crisis of faith that is being experienced in the exile. Exodus serves as the story of a particular people and HaShem who claims them and embraces them in a covenantal relationship. It is also the central story of hope for the Exiles. If HaShem can deliver this people from the hands of Pharaoh, then certainly HaShem can also deliver them from the hands of their Babylonian captors. Exodus also lays the groundwork for the central element of that covenantal relationship – Torah.

As the drama opens we learn that the resident aliens, the Israelite people, have greatly multiplied in the land of Egypt and are now a threat to the stability of the Egyptian military industrial complex. There is now in Egypt a pharaoh who did not know Joseph. (More on Joseph later - for now wrap him in his Technicolor dream coat and put him on a shelf). In an effort to limit "production" of more Israelites this pharaoh places taskmasters over the Israelites. The Israelites are now the forced labor of the pharaoh's massive building campaign. "*The Egyptians ruthlessly imposed upon the Israelites the various labors that they made them perform. Ruthlessly they made life bitter for them with harsh labor at mortar and bricks and with all sorts of tasks in the field*" (Exodus 1:13-14) When this fails to reduce the increasing population the pharaoh resorts to various levels of genocide culminating in the decree that every male child be thrown into the Nile.

Our story now becomes more intimate as we encounter a certain Levite man and woman who give birth to a son. (The Tribe of Levi is one of the twelve tribes of Israel and they become the assistants to the priests in the Temple). The boy so beautiful that his mother could not kill him and so puts him on the doorstep of the Pharaoh (not literally, she floats him in a basket down the Nile to where the daughter of the Pharaoh bathed). Long story short, the daughter "adopts" the boy and names him Moses ("I Drew Him Out of the Water"). She employs Moses' mother to serve as his wet nurse so we may assume that as he grows up he is aware of his true identity.

This idyllic arrangement turns south when Moses turns into a young adult. One day while inspecting a work site he witnesses an Egyptian task master beating a Hebrew laborer. In a fit of rage Moses kills the Egyptian. It becomes obvious over the course of the next few days that there are witnesses to this murder. Moses' life and station are in jeopardy. Moses flees to the land of Midian (located on the east shore of the Red Sea in the Arabian Peninsula). There Moses encounters and rescues the daughters of Jethro, a priest of Midian. His reward is to be given one of the daughters, Zipporah, as a wife. Moses settles in tending sheep for his father-in-law, Jethro.

"A long time after that, the Pharaoh dies. The Israelites are groaning under the bondage and cry out; and their cry for help from the bondage rises up to HaShem... HaShem hears their moaning, and HaShem remembers his covenant with Abraham and Isaac and Jacob, HaShem looks upon the Israelites, and HaShem takes notice of them" (Exodus 2:23-25).

One day Moses drives Jethro's flocks out into the wilderness all the way to Mount Horeb, the mountain of HaShem. (Note! Geography is important. Such things as wilderness, rivers and mountains are theological as well as geographic markers. The wilderness is a place for encountering HaShem. Mountains likewise, because of their height, are places closer to HaShem and always fair game for a miraculous encounter or theophany [a visit from HaShem]). It is there that Moses notices a bush that appears to be burning but not consumed.

What ensues is an encounter with HaShem. The content of this encounter is the announcement that HaShem has heard the cries of his people languishing in Egypt, that he will rescue them, and take them to a new land in the region of Canaan. (*So far so good*) Then HaShem informs Moses that he, Moses, is to be his agent of liberation. (*Not so good*) When Moses complains about the lack of adequate education, experience and credentials, HaShem informs him that he will be by Moses' side and that when he rescues his people he is to bring them to this mountain to worship him (*Did I say pay attention to geography?*).

Since this is Moses' first encounter with HaShem he decides he better find out who it is he's talking with so that when asked the "On whose authority?" question he might have an answer. Ha Shem answers, "Ehyeh-Asher-Ehyeh" (the Hebrew is uncertain but it is usually translated as YHWH (Yahweh) – "I Am That I Am" or "I Am Who I Am" or "I Will Be What I Will Be" (*you get the point*) – (this is often read as Adonai or "the Lord" rather than speaking the proper name of HaShem out loud). With that HaShem instructs him to report to the leaders of Israel and take them to talk with the Pharaoh.

By this point Moses is accumulating excuses for not being the one whom HaShem should send. In response HaShem presents him with a magic stick and assorted parlor tricks to impress the opposition leadership. When he complains about his lack of public speaking skills (perhaps even being a stutterer) HaShem suggests that maybe his brother-in-law, Aaron, who is also a Levite, could do the talking. Having run out of excuses Moses goes back to Egypt with a word for Pharaoh, "Let my people go! Or there will be consequences!"

Well, as one might imagine, Pharaoh doesn't roll over and release his work force to Moses. The request to allow the Israelites to go out into the wilderness to worship HaShem meets rather with an increased work load and deteriorating working conditions ("Produce more bricks," and then "Try making them without straw!"). So far Moses is just making things worse for his people. Needless to say, this does not win Moses any popularity contest among his people.

HaShem then commissions and authorizes Moses to speak for him before Pharaoh and his court. We are told at this point that HaShem will also "harden Pharaoh's heart" so that HaShem may multiply the signs and wonders. This has been a troubling concept for many scholars and readers over the centuries. While I will not go into the debate here I believe it points to a radical concept that Ha Shem is not just a god of the Israelites but is willing to manipulate other peoples, nations or kings as well that his power might be made known. Remember where HaShem's people are sitting and listening to this story – as exiles in Babylon. There is a sense that to the victor not only goes the spoils but also the ability to claim the superiority of their god. So Marduk reigns supreme! Over and against this claim is that of HaShem who reveals that he can mess with whatever god he so choses. In short, Babylonians beware!

This all leads to a rather lengthy pissing contest between Pharaoh, his priests, and Moses (other descriptive images may also include: Gunfight at the OK Corral, Luke Skywalker vs. Darth Vader, or John Cena vs. the Undertaker). After the preliminary bouts, a series of requests and refusals ensue, only to be followed by plague and devastation. These include: the Nile is turned into blood, frogs, lice, swarms of insects, livestock pestilence (boils), hail, locusts and three days of darkness. After each plague is the request, "Let my people go." HaShem follows each request with a hardening of Pharaoh's heart which leads to a subsequent reply, "No!"

HaShem saves one final shot for the end, a kind of *coup de grace* of plagues. This will be a killer plague (quite literally) but first the people need to prepare for their exodus. They are told to "borrow" gold and silver from their Egyptian neighbors. Then they are to prepare a final ritual/covenantal meal. A lamb "without blemish, a yearling male" is to be slaughtered for each household. The blood is to be painted on the two doorposts and lintel as a sign. The lamb shall be roasted and eaten with unleavened bread (no time for the yeast to work) and bitter herbs.

The reason for the elaborate and hurried preparation is that the final plague will be the death of the first-born in the land. The blood on the door posts will be a sign for the angel of death to "pass over" that house. The meal – a last supper of sort before the arduous flight from Egypt.

This day will be a day of remembrance, an institution for all time. Elaborate details of what this celebration should look like are included here in the midst of the drama. I believe it's safe to assume that the Passover celebration meal was a critical part of the cultic practice among the Babylonian exiles when the Exodus material was collected.

In the middle of the night death strikes down the first-born of Egypt including Pharaoh's first-born. As the cry of lament arises across Egypt

Pharaoh summons Moses and Aaron and informs them, "Get the (expletive deleted) out of here now!" Prepared to leave, the Israelites, some 600,000 men along with women and children, get out of Dodge and don't look back (*at least not yet*).

HaShem does not lead them out of Egypt by the traditional trade route through Philistine territory lest they be engaged in battle with the Philistines and decide Egypt was a better fate than war, slavery or death. Rather he leads them roundabout by way of the wilderness to the Sea of Reeds (*Yom Suf*). They take with them the bones of Joseph. HaShem goes with them as a pillar of cloud by day and a pillar of fire by night, an early GPS system.

In the meantime, Pharaoh has a change of heart (hardened heart) and taking his chariots pursues Moses and the Israelites. When the Israelites catch a glimpse of Pharaoh's pursuit they panic. Caught between the sea and Pharaoh's army (the proverbial rock and a hard place) they lash out at Moses, "Were there not enough graves in Egypt that you brought us out here to die?" (Moses then cries out in complaint to HaShem. HaShem replies, "Why are you whining?" "I've got this one in the bag".

This Conversation: the Israelites complain to Moses then Moses complains to HaShem becomes a sub-plot throughout the narrative often referred to as the Murmuring Motif. From the very beginning of the relationship the people of HaShem have difficulty with his agenda. Complaint seems to be imbedded into the relationship between HaShem and his people. As we shall see, in time this Conversation becomes the bedrock of an acceptable genre of conversation with HaShem known as the lament.

HaShem causes the Egyptian forces to stall in their pursuit. He uses this lull in the action to instruct Moses to raise his staff over the sea. When Moses does as HaShem directs, the waters part allowing the Israelites to cross dry-shod to the other side. When Pharaoh and his army of charioteers try to follow, the waters close back leaving Pharaoh and all his mighty army doing the Dead Man's Float. (Geographic note: Water is almost always a sign of chaos. HaShem demonstrates his dominance even over the chaotic power of water. While this is less of an issue in the geography of Israel or even Egypt when you are dangling your tootsies in the Tigris and Euphrates Rivers the chaotic flooding is a force to be reckoned with).

As the victory cries ascend to HaShem's ears, Moses lifts his voice in song with a little number from Handel's *"Israel in Egypt."* Miriam, Aaron's sister, and the other women join in on the chorus as well as dance and provide appropriate instrumentation.

The adulation of HaShem lasts only three days into the wilderness. By the time they reach Marah ("bitter") they run out of water. The Conversation commences once again – solution? HaShem brings them to Elim and its twelve springs and seventy palm trees.

They arrive next at the wilderness of Sin (between Elim and Sinai) and now they are hungry. My favorite way to talk about the Exodus journey is to imagine a carful of kids (before personalized technology) crammed into a station wagon for a long vacation. In addition to the standard conversation one might imagine also a few, "Are we there yet?" as punctuation.

HaShem promises meat to eat and bread from the sky each day. Quail in the evening appear and each morning a strange bread-like stuff covers the ground. The Israelites ask one another, "What is it?" or in Hebrew, *"Manna?"* They are to gather enough of the manna each day to satisfy (one *omer* per person). Some gather a little less and others a lot more and yet when the measuring is done those with a lot have no excess and those with a little no deficiency. HaShem's economics – everyone gets what they need.

HaShem promises to provide enough each day. The exception is the Shabbat. One cannot work on the Shabbat so they are to collect enough for the Shabbat the day before. The Israelites are human after all though: "What if HaShem doesn't show up tomorrow?" "What if there isn't enough tomorrow?" Or the biggie, "What if someone who doesn't deserve it comes along and takes my portion?" So, they pocket a little extra as a hedge against tomorrow's uncertainty. What do the find the next day? They find they have stinky pockets because you cannot horde HaShem's generosity. The horded manna all goes bad. HaShem's economic is that there is always enough. Moses ordered the people to place an *omer* (one tenth of an *ephah)* into a jar, seal it, and take with them into the Promised Land as a reminder of HaShem' providence and their failure to trust/believe. The Early Church will continue to deal with this issue – sic. 1 Corinthians).

They leave the wilderness of Sin by stages and camp at Rephidim and once again find themselves without water... you guessed it... the

Conversation starts again. Moses receives instruction to strike the rock with his magic staff and lo, and behold, water flows from the rock. They name the place Massah and Meribah because they quarrel there and try HaShem's patience.

On the third new moon after the Israelites go forth from the land of Egypt they come to the wilderness of Sinai and encamp in front of the mountain (Sinai/Horeb). On the third day HaShem calls Moses up the mountain for a summit conference to lay out the terms of covenant relationship between himself and the Israelites.

The meat of the covenant agreement included the following terms:

1. You shall have no other gods before me
2. You shall not make for yourself a sculptured image of a god
3. You shall not swear falsely using the name of HaShem
4. Remember the Sabbath day and keep it holy
5. Honor your father and mother
6. You shall not murder
7. You shall not commit adultery
8. You shall not steal
9. You shall not bear false witness against your neighbor
10. You shall not covet what is your neighbor's

These become known as the Ten Commandments. What follows then is the remainder of the covenantal agreement. One of the difficulties for 21st Century Americans as they approach Torah or Covenant is that it is all too often seen as punitive or restrictive rather than life-giving. We tend to use the Ten Commandments to enforce behavior rather than to shape living together in community. One of the images ancient Israel uses to talk about Torah is that of a fence. The Torah is that which gives shape (provides boundaries like a fence) to life in community as this particular covenantal people of HaShem. As Robert Frost reminds us, "fences make good neighbors." The psalms open with "Blessed are they who take delight in the Torah of HaShem." That delight is when the community is able to recognize Torah as gift. Like us, that is not always the way Torah or covenant get used over the course of their history so they/we are hauled back to the mountain of HaShem from time to time for a refresher course.

Following a covenantal worship service including the blood of a bull being dashed against the altar as a sign of sealing the deal (Note: Leonard Bernstein uses this image in his **Mass** in referring to the New Covenant) Moses is summoned up the mountain once again to receive all this now in writing – literally, written in stone.

"The Presence of the Lord abides on Mt. Sinai, and the cloud hides it for six days. On the seventh day He calls to Moses from the midst of the cloud. Now the Presence of the Lord appeared in the sight of all the Israelites as a consuming fire on the top of the mountain. Moses went inside the cloud and ascended the mountain; and Moses remained on the mountain forty days and forty nights." (Exodus 24:17-18)

The summit conference commences with HaShem asking for gifts from the people of precious stones and metal with which to fashion a portable sanctuary so that HaShem might dwell among them. He then lays out in considerable detail the building of the Tabernacle and the Ark of the Covenant in which the Tabernacle would be carried. Sacred furniture and vestments are also described. Aaron and his sons shall be ordained priests with the ordination ceremony also carefully outlined. Bazalel (it is not just "religious" figures called by HaShem) is also appointed to carry out the building of the Tabernacle, Ark and its furnishings. The summit finishes with a reminder to keep Shabbat and the giving of the two stone tablets of the Pact/Covenant to Moses and the people.

The focus on Shabbat already in the beginning of the story points to Shabbat-keeping as the primary identifying characteristic of the people of HaShem in Exile. In the midst of the 24/7 military industrial complex of Babylon the Jews were those who kept Shabbat. Shabbat becomes a visible sign in Exile of the reliance on HaShem for sustenance and resistance against their Babylonian captors. As such it becomes the definitive identity for Exilic and Post-Exilic Judaism. (Is it any wonder Jesus is always getting in trouble for messing with Shabbat Laws)?

In the absence of Moses (after all 40 days is a long time) the people get anxious. They go to Aaron and ask him to fashion a god for them – one that is a bit more user-friendly than HaShem. Using the jewelry and precious metals meant for HaShem's sanctuary Aaron fashions a molten calf and declares a festival to celebrate.

HaShem notices what is going on down the mountain and alerts Moses. He informs Moses that he has had it. Enraged, he contemplates destroying this stiff-necked people. Moses intervenes on behalf of his people (a new role for Moses – usually he is complaining about "this people" that HaShem has burdened him with) and talks HaShem down. Moses descends the mountain carrying the two tablets of stone. Upon seeing for himself what is going on in the camp he hurls the stone tablets against the base of the mountain (remember the blood on the altar?). He melts down the calf, pours it upon the water and forces the Israelites to drink it.

HaShem pronounces sentence on the Israelites for their unfaithfulness. Their offspring will be able to enter the Promised Land but not so them. They will not be allowed to cross over… and that includes Moses!

HaShem re-calls Moses up the mountain and he is to bring with him two new tablets of stone. The Lord comes down upon the mountain and announces, *"The Lord! The Lord! A Lord compassionate and gracious, slow to anger, abounding in kindness and faithfulness, extending kindness to the thousandth generation, forgiving iniquity, transgression and sin"* (Exodus 34:6-7). This will become the identifying mark of HaShem well into the future (recalled by more than one prophet before and during the Exile). HaShem then restates the terms of the covenant and the necessary festivals and celebrations.

Moses comes down the mountain and recites the terms of the covenant to the Israelites and commences the building of the Ark, Tabernacle and all their furnishings. When all was finished HaShem instructs Moses how they are to use these ritual furnishings and appointments.

> *"When Moses finishes the work, the cloud covered the Tent of Meeting, and the Presence of the Lord filled the Tabernacle… As the cloud lifts from the Tabernacle, the Israelites will set out on their various journeys; but should the cloud not lift, they would not set out until such time as it did lift. For over the Tabernacle a cloud of the Lord rested by day, and fire*

> *would appear in it by night, in the view of the house of Israel throughout their journeys."* (Exodus 40:34-38)

Exodus is often referred to as a three-act drama: Act 1 – Deliverance; Act 2 – Presence; Act 3 – Covenant. This drama plays out throughout the Hebrew Scriptures, into the New Testament and into the lives of the faithful. It will be powerfully restaged in Babylon, as well as during the subsequent return of the exiles and the rebuilding of Jerusalem (but alas I'm getting ahead of myself).

Rather than the three-act play image I prefer to look at Exodus as a trilogy of movies: The action movie complete with cosmic battle scenes between the forces of light and dark (á la Star Wars); the angst-filled road drama where the characters over time begin to come to know themselves and some cosmic higher power; and finally, a love story with seduction and intrigue, passion and betrayal, boundary setting and reuniting. If we use this image of Exodus as the Trilogy Movie: *"HaShem and the Lost People of Israel"* then the book of Genesis stands as the prequel to the trilogy.

GENESIS

If Exodus is the Trilogy Movie: "HaShem and the Lost People of Israel" then the book of Genesis stands as the prequel to the trilogy: "Beginnings".

The best way to understand Genesis is to imagine the author being interrogated by an inquisitive four-year-old and their incessant question, "Why?" Much of Genesis is what is called etiological myth -why things are the way they are? Genesis is first, and foremost, a story of a particular people at a particular time in history trying to make sense out of their world using the information/story at their disposal. If we were asked today how the world was created, we too might affirm HaShem as creator but then might use words like "Big Bang" and "Evolution" in our explanation. If asked to respond to evidence of a great flood, we would be able to talk about glacier melt. The question, "Why are there so many languages?" would today draw on linguistic development and migratory patterns. Genesis is not an attempt to explain phenomena for all time but to try and make sense out of it in a time-conditioned and information-limited way. There is nothing to say that given the information at our disposal the author(s) of Genesis might not write a very different story that still bears witness to the power of HaShem. Genesis also is not in the business of explaining the "How?" question but rather the "Why?" question. Genesis is all about the relationship of things to HaShem, the creator.

"So, Zaydeh, tell me the story again!"

"What story?"

"The story of the Beginning…. How we got here!"

In the beginning…the genesis!

The Tanakh, unlike the Christian Old Testament is bookended by exilic material. It begins with a cosmic creation narrative and ends (in 2 Chronicles) with the destruction of the Temple, the exile and then a promise (but again I get ahead of myself).

The first of the creation stories (Genesis 1:1-2:4) is written during the Babylonian Exile. It portrays a cosmic god, a god of the whole world. This picture of a universal god frames the entire Tanakh. This is the story of the One-Universal God and his particular people; we should note that just because he chooses a particular people to bless does not mean that he is any less a god over the entire universe. The name for HaShem in Genesis is typically the generic *Elohim* (Lord).

The creation narrative is consistent with the ancient global terrain. There is a Firmament/Dome above and a watery chaos below. The mountains are holy places because they reach to the heavenly realm (same reason churches have steeples)… HaShem is often referred to as El Shaddai (sometimes translated as "god of the mountain").

Creation in this first story is orderly and good…. wait, no, very good. It is the work of a cosmic and powerful god that needs only speak. This is in sharp contrast to existing creation stories of the period which speak of creation in terms of great chaotic battles or sexual unions.

When theologians refer to this story they often use the word *ex niliho* (creation "out of nothing") but HaShem's creation is order out of watery chaos… *tohu wa-bohu*. This chaotic and powerful water reflects the

Babylonian landscape... flooding on the Tigris and Euphrates rivers was not like that of the Nile or the Mississippi rivers but was dictated by the water flow from high in the mountains. This meant that often the raging flood waters were unpredictable and devastating – chaotic.

Humanity is created in the image of HaShem – "male and female they were created" as such there is no hierarchy of genders. The call of humanity is to fertility (Remember the opening lines of Exodus?). They are also called as creation's stewards. Note HaShem never hands over creation... nowhere does he sell the farm. Instead he places humanity in creation as resident caretakers/stewards. There is in this act a responsibility to creation and HaShem.

A key piece of this creative act is the institution of Shabbat (this is not to be seen as, "Oh yeah, creation is finished, I think I'll take a nap."). It is an integral part of HaShem's creation... even HaShem takes/requires a Shabbat. Shabbat keeping becomes the distinctive identity mark of the Jewish people during the Exile. In the 24/7 world of the Babylonian military industrial complex HaShem's people set aside a time to be non-productive because they knew their god will provide (Remember the Exodus lesson of the manna?).

"Zaydeh, if things were so very good why is it so hard today?"

This question brings us to the second of our creation stories (Genesis 2:3-3:24) which is actually the older of the two coming from the Yahwistic tradition, approximately 900 BCE. It is characterized by an anthropomorphic description of HaShem - as having human characteristics... hands, mouth, breath etc.... Creation in this story revolves around the creation of humanity. The rest of creation flows out of the creation of *adam*/man.

HaShem plants a Garden (Humanity at this point in history has become an agricultural society so why shouldn't HaShem also have a garden). In the middle of the garden are the Tree of Life and the Tree of the Knowledge of Good and Evil. The tree has in many cultures also been a holy object or an object of worship (Celtic oak groves or the Norse Yggdrasill for instance). Perhaps that is because in the ancient cosmic geography the tree not only reaches to the heavens but its roots also grow down into the abyss.

HaShem places humanity in the Garden to till and care for it - farm it... This is the original vocation - *Adam* (Earth Man) is taken from the *adamah* (soil) and called to till and care for the *adamah.* Creation is for humanity's pleasure and sustenance but leave the Tree of the Knowledge of Good and Evil alone – it's curse is: If you eat of its fruit you shall die!

HaShem recognizes that *adam*/man is a communal creature. The attempt to create a helpmate for him leads to the creation of all the animals, birds and aquatic beasts which *adam* subsequently names. *Adam* finds the eel positively repulsive and is unable to cozy up to the porcupine. HaShem needs to do some more work. From out of *adam* he takes a rib and fashions a new creature and when *adam* beholds her he exclaims, "Whoa man! This at last is bone of my bones and flesh of my flesh. She shall be called woman because she was taken out of man.

The natural state of paradise is naked, vulnerable and transparent.

[*Stage left* - enter the Serpent]. The serpent (who sounds a great deal like the later Satan – the accuser) raises questions about HaShem's motives and behavior with the couple. The serpent claims that the restriction regarding the Tree of the Knowledge of Good and Evil is because HaShem does not want humanity to be like himself. Seeing that the tree was a delight to the eye and a source of wisdom the woman takes the fruit and eats it and gives some also to the man.

Their eyes are opened and they perceive that they are naked and their first act is to hide their nakedness from each other and HaShem.

Years ago, I oversaw a youth group reenact this chapter of the creation drama as a courtroom scene where *adam,* the woman and the serpent were put on trial before the High Tribunal of Judges. It was fascinating to watch the young people wrestle with the material. A crisis developed, however, when the judges did not arrive at the same verdict as the Scriptures. While all three were found guilty they pardoned the man and woman. Their argument was that the knowledge of good and evil was punishment enough! Moral of the story: Sometimes HaShem really does know what's best for us!

[*Stage right* in strolls HaShem] Perceiving a disturbance in the creation HaShem asks for humanity to show themselves. The man and woman disclose that they recognize their new condition of nakedness which in turn betrays their infidelity. When interrogated a flood of blaming ensues. This is then followed by the judgment/curse (why things are the way they are).

HaShem clothes them (providential care) then kicks them out of the Garden - they become wanderers (exiles). Eden is closed for business... It now becomes HaShem's sole abode.

There is no concept of Original Sin in Jewish theology. It will take Augustine in the Fourth Century to develop this doctrine. Ironically it may have been Augustine who understood the nature of the story best, "My soul hungers until it finds its completeness (shalom) in HaShem." The creation story explains this hungering after the Divine. The story also points to the predilection of humanity to desire to replace god... to control our own destiny...to know what is best for us... to push the boundaries of curiosity and new thinking. The Broadway musical, *Children of Eden*, captures this understanding and tension of creation, HaShem and humanity better than any theological treatise. To live in this tension, one needs the bounds of Torah/Law. It will be Torah that will keep us safe from further self-inflicted damage and preserve the proper relationship with HaShem.

"Zaydeh, why do I fight with my brother?"

A rabbi once told me that the Genesis narrative could be used to explain the brokenness between all familial relationships. It makes for an interesting lens to read the book through.

The Cain and Abel narrative not only reflects the tension between siblings but also the brokenness between farmers and ranchers/shepherds. Abel is a keeper of sheep while Cain is a tiller of soil. It is here where the problems surface. HaShem accepts Abel's offering (animal sacrifice) but ignores Cain's (grain offering)... Cain becomes jealous and this sets off the first fratricide. Again, HaShem shows up asking questions to which Cain replies with that famous line, "Am I my brother's keeper?" The punishment meted out is for Cain to be a perpetual wanderer/exile. Cain is marked so that no one may exact revenge or violence upon him. (There were cities designated in Israel for those guilty of manslaughter or accidental death to protect them from blood feud and revenge by the families of the victim).

Cain marries and we are introduced to his grandchildren:

Jabaal, whose line will issue shepherds and nomads
Jubal will give forth the line of musicians
Tubal-Cain's progeny will be blacksmiths

Chapter 5 details the generations of Adam through Seth (third son) created and blessed by HaShem... (Seth will become the preoccupation of the later Gnostic tradition that develops in the 2nd Century CE). The genealogy runs from Adam to Noah. Genealogies in scripture are not meant to be historical but are used to establish legitimacy and pedigree as well as to move the action forward.

"Zaydeh, where do giants come from?"

At another point in history a similar child (or even a pious adult) will ponder that same question with regards to the Vikings… the answer that time was up North or from Helheim.

The biblical answer given in 6:1-4 is problematic for those who like a nice tidy, factual and inerrant reading of scripture.... the Nephilim are depicted as a race of heroes of old that are the offspring of the gods and the beautiful women of this earth. This section forms the interlude between Adam cycle and the Noah Cycle. These literary interludes become a common feature in the Genesis narrative.

"Zaydeh, what happened to the giants? Where are the huge beasts that once roamed the earth?"

The old Irish Rovers', Song *of the Unicorn*, captures a bit of the flavor of this etiological narrative:

"The Ark started movin', it drifted with the tide, Them Unicorns looked up from the rock and they cried, And the waters came down and sorta floated them away, That's why you'll never see a Unicorn, to this very day."

Flood stories are a consistent narrative throughout the cultures of Middle East and beyond leading scholars over the centuries to speculate on the presence of a great cataclysmic flooding of the earth.

We are told that HaShem is having second thoughts about this whole creation business and contemplates its complete annihilation. (This is but the first of many such provocations). Noah, however, finds favor in HaShem's sight. HaShem declares he is to send a great Flood and instructs Noah to start working on an ark. This must have been quite the scene in the dry and arid Middle East. Noah is told that the ark is to become a floating zoo. He is to take seven pairs of every clean animal and two pair of non-kosher animals.

Once loaded the rains come and the primordial waters of chaos rise from the bowels of the earth and the sky is ripped open releasing its torrents. For forty days and nights it rains. As the water rises everything left on earth drowns, leaving only Noah and those in the ark. The waters swell on the earth for 150 days. Finally, HaShem remembers about old Noah (oops!), and begins to blow the waters back. After ten months the tops of the mountains appear and the ark eventually comes to rest on Mount Ararat.

After forty more days Noah sends out a raven (traditional "messenger-of-the-gods" bird in many cultures) on a reconnaissance mission. He follows this with a series of doves until one returns with an olive leaf so that Noah knows that there is dry land.

Finally, HaShem calls Noah forth from the ark. Upon exit Noah builds an altar and offers an appropriate burnt offering to HaShem. HaShem likes the smell and promises a redo of creation and makes a covenant to never again do such a thing. He blesses the creation again and makes the rainbow a sign of the promise that he will never destroy the earth with a Flood again.

Noah gets drunk at the post-covenant party and passes out in his tent naked. One of his boys sees him and calls his brothers to have a look at their father. But instead of engaging in a bit of sophomoric voyeurism the other two brothers back into the tent holding a blanket up and cover their father's nakedness. When Noah finds out what his younger son, Ham has done he curses him and his offspring – Canaan. The race of Canaan (the

Canaanites) is cursed to be slaves to HaShem's people (now you know the rest of the story).

The Noah cycle ends with another lengthy genealogy.

> *"Zaydeh, why can't we always understand one another? Why so many languages?"*

The story of the Tower of Babel (another name for Babylon) is an etiological myth to describe the existence of the many languages of the earth. There is a tension, beginning in the Garden and continuing throughout Genesis, between HaShem and humanity. The perception is that we would really like to audition for the role of god. As the story goes HaShem confuses the language to quash the attempt by humanity to storm the heavens and play the role of the usurper. The last line of this story, "The Lord scattered them over the face of the whole earth," sets up the call of Abraham and is also an interesting line given the historic reality of the Jews in Babylon who would be scattered in the great diaspora.

> *"Zaydeh, how did we become HaShem's people?"*

Chapter 12 begins the Abram (Abrahamic) Cycle as well as the particular family drama that will culminate with the residency of the "Israelites" in Egypt. The stories of Abram/Abraham, Isaac and Jacob are rather stock stories found in a variety of cultures of their day. In our culture they would be like Paul Bunyan, Davey Crockett or Joe Magarac, perhaps based on actual characters but adorned with a variety of trappings from other cultural stories. Like those of our day these narratives carry with them the overarching notion of promise in the ancestral narratives.

We are told Abram is from the city of Ur which is south of Babylon. [*Ur is a very important archeological site revealing much about the culture of that area prior to 500 BCE including human sacrifice and evidence of a significant flood*]. It was in Ur as Abram and Sarai are settling into their retirement years that HaShem shows up beside the shuffleboard court and calls them to leave this life behind and go to a yet unnamed land that he will reveal to him. (A land that Golda Meir, former Prime Minister of Israel, reportedly pointed out is the one strip of land in the Middle East without oil). The gift of the land comes with further promises: HaShem will make Abram's name great, he will father a great nation, and he will become a blessing to all the families on earth. So, at age 75 Abram, his wife, Sarai and his brother's son, Lot pack up and head for Canaan.

When they arrived, Abram builds an altar to this god who has appeared to him (note he is still at this point a nameless god). He pitches his tent near Bethel and Ai. There is a famine in the land that necessitates Abram going down to Egypt (exiled). Afraid that the Egyptians will see the beauty of his wife, Sarai, and want her, he passes her of as his sister. The ruse is revealed and Pharaoh politely escorts Abram and Sarai to Egypt's door. (This movement to Egypt in times of crisis only to be disappointed or thwarted is a reoccurring theme in the history of HaShem's people. It forms a cautionary tale for future generations and all who remember the story).

From Egypt Abram journeys up into the Negeb. We are told that Abraham is a very rich man. Lot is also to have amassed great herds so that the land could no longer support both. Lot chose the Jordan Valley near Sodom while Abram remained in Canaan, in Hebron, near the oaks of Marmre.

Abram, despite his vast fortune, rails at HaShem that if he dies childless a foreigner, Eliezer Dammesek (Eliezer of Damascus), the steward of his household will inherit everything. HaShem's response is for Abram to look into the heavens and count the stars, "so numerous shall your decedents be." In chapter 15:7-17 we have a covenant ratifying ceremony which ends with the blessing and land grant of all the territory between the Nile and the Euphrates Rivers.

Still barren, Sarai concocts a scheme whereby Abram should try to have a child with her handmaid, Hagar (the Egyptian). Hagar becomes pregnant. Now one must truly believe in fairy tales to believe that there is a happy ending with this household arrangement. Soon Sarai is demanding that Abram do something about the situation – his solution is to drop it back in her lap, "she's your handmaid, you deal with it." Sarai begins to abuse her to the point that Hagar runs away.

The angel of the Lord intercepts Hagar and instructs her to return to the abusive situation. The angel then pronounces a blessing upon Hagar that includes great offspring, the news that she will bear a child (big news!?!), and that this child will be a son and will be named Ishmael (God has Heard). He will be a "wild ass of a man." Hagar returns and gives birth to Ishmael (Abram is 86).

With the birth of Ismael, the Abrahamic promises extend beyond Israel. There is a cosmic/universal claim to these promises. Hagar serves to keep the horizon of HaShem's blessings open to "the other" nations who through him now also have a legitimate claim on HaShem's promises. This is good news to those living in exile for even Babylon is in line to be blessed by HaShem. The Babylonians can rightfully claim access to HaShem through the lineage of Ishmael. I believe this is also good news for those of us living in exile today. As we wrestle with the Post 9/11 world, particularly the religious world, it is Ishmael that may hold the key to substantive conversation among Jews, Muslims and Christians. We share the one claim to the Abrahamic promises and that blood claim acknowledges our familial bond, strained as it may be.

When Abram is 99, HaShem shows up again and addresses himself as El Shaddai ("God Almighty") renews the covenant agreement despite Sarai's barrenness. A new sign/mark of this covenant will be the rite of circumcision. As a sign of the new reality both Abram and Sarai are given new names, Abraham ("God Heeds") and Sarah ("Princess"). The promise of a child is reiterated this time also including gender and name, Isaac ("Laughter"). Ishmael's blessed status is also re-covenanted (Ishmael is included in the circumcision rite). El Shaddai, however, announces clearly that the original covenant will be valid through Abraham and *Sarah* as well as Isaac, the child to be born.

Barrenness becomes an ongoing metaphor in the Tanakh and even into the Christian scriptures to remind the faithful that even when human resources have been exhausted HaShem fulfills his promises. This becomes a promise to cling to in times of exile.

In the next chapter HaShem shows up at Abraham's tent, which is pitched by the oaks of Mamre, in the guise of three strangers. Abraham is quick to practice Bedouin hospitality to traveling strangers. (Hospitality is not politeness in this Bedouin culture but survival. At any moment you may be the wanderer in need of hospitality). Over a meal of curds, milk and beef the three strangers reveal the purpose of their visit – an announcement! Before this year is out Sarah will give birth to a son – at the news Sarah laughs – hence, the name Isaac for her son, "Laughter".

Our delightful natal cycle is rudely interrupted by the destruction of Sodom and Gomorrah. The scene opens with HaShem and Abraham negotiating the terms under which Sodom might be spared – if HaShem finds ten faithful in the city he will not destroy it – oops! The other two travelers have gone ahead into the city and are greeted by Lot and offered hospitality in his home. That evening a mob shows up at his door demanding that he send out the two strangers that they might rape them. Lot refuses but offers his daughters in their stead. What seems to us as absolutely horrific behavior by Lot reflects the sanctity of hospitality at this time. It is a far greater transgression to break hospitality in this case than it is to offer up your daughters. We need to recognize that the issue is not about sex or homosexuality but about violence to the stranger. They want no part of hurting Lot and his family they wish to rape the two foreign strangers.

The two strangers demonstrate super powers keeping the mob at bay while informing Lot and his family of an exit strategy. *"Flee for your life! Do not look behind you, or stop anywhere in the Plain; flee to the hills, lest you be swept away"* (Exodus 19:17). Lot does not wish to flee into the hills so negotiates relocation in the little town of Zoar. A sulfurous fire rains down from heaven and annihilates Sodom and Gomorrah and all the Plain (sounds a lot like a volcanic eruption). Lot's wife looks back and is immediately turned into a pillar of salt. The smoke rises from the Plain like the smoke of a kiln.

Lot and his two daughters relocate to Zoar. It is there the daughters contemplate their future. Recognizing there are no men who have survived, they engage in incest with their father (while he is asleep) and conceive and bear two sons: Moab, from which come the Moabites and Benjamin, the father of the Ammonites.

After another "let's pass my wife off as my sister" scam involving King Abimelech, HaShem gives a newborn son to Abraham and Sarah and they name him Isaac ("Laughter") because the joke was on them. Once again Sarah has had enough of Hagar and her son so she commands Abraham to send them away. He sends them out into the wilderness where they may have died were it not for the intervention of the angel of the Lord. They end up living in the land of Paran and Hagar procures a wife for Ismael from Egypt.

HaShem then puts Abraham to the test by commanding him to sacrifice the child of promise, Isaac, on Mt. Moriah. This seems to abrogate all the promises that HaShem has made concerning Abraham's future. At the last instant HaShem provides a scape goat to sacrifice in Isaac's stead. The issue of human sacrifice turns our sensitive stomachs but was common among cultures of this time. Many scholars have pointed to this story as a statement that HaShem's people would not participate in such sacrifice.

At age 127 Sarah dies. Abraham in his old age decides that Isaac will not marry from among the Canaanite women so sends a servant back to his homeland to procure a wife. With a plot line worthy of a Harlequin romance the servant finds Rebekah and brings her back for Isaac to marry. Abraham lives to the age of 175 (marries a second time and sires six more children). When he dies, Isaac and Ishmael see that he is buried with Sarah in the tomb that he had bought from the Hittites.

If Abraham is viewed as model emigrant/faithful follower, then Isaac's story is that of benign stupidity. In many ways Isaac's cycle of stories forms a brief interlude between the major stories of Abraham and Jacob.

This narrative begins again in barrenness with Isaac's wife, Rebekah. HaShem answers Isaac's prayer and Rebekah conceives twins. From conception these twins are at odds with each other struggling violently in the womb. When they are born, the first, Esau, comes into the world covered with a mantle of red hair with his twin brother, Jacob, hanging onto his heel. Esau grows to be a hunter while Jacob proves to be a real momma's boy. Because of Isaac's craving for game he favors Esau.

One day while Jacob was cooking stew, Esau came in from an unsuccessful hunting trip famished. Desiring some stew in the worse way he negotiates away his birthright for a bowl of the red stuff (therefore he was named "Edom" or red).

There is a famine in the land (like the one in the days of Abraham). Isaac goes to Abimelech, king of the Philistines because HaShem told him not to go to Egypt for relief (a command that will be made again in the days leading up to the Exile). Not having learned anything from dad, Isaac tries to pass his beautiful wife off as his sister. When Abimelech finds out he is enraged. While in the land of Gerar, Isaac's fortunes continue to flourish. He gets richer and richer to the point where the Philistines retaliate by filling in all his wells. The tensions continue to escalate and eventually Abimelech demands that they leave. Isaac's sojourn/exile in the land continues to be a contentious one over land and water rights with those he encounters. Eventually an official treaty is made between him and Abimelech.

When Isaac is old and his eyesight failing, he calls Esau in to offer him his parental blessing but first he asks Esau to go out hunting and bring back dinner. Rebekah overhears the arrangements and dupes her husband by passing Jacob off as Esau. In the end Isaac inadvertently, awards Jacob the parental blessing. Recognizing that Jacob's life is now in danger at the hands of Esau, Rebekah sends Jacob into exile with her brother Laban in Haran (Syria).

On the way, while Jacob stopped for the night, he dreamed of a stairway to heaven (cue Led Zeppelin) with angels ascending and descending upon it. HaShem renews the covenant that he had made with Abraham and Isaac to now include Jacob. Jacob erects a stone and calls the place Bethel ("House of God").

Reaching the land of the Easterners, Jacob discovers that his mother's penchant for duplicity and deception is a family trait. His Uncle Laban cons Jacob into marrying his oldest daughter (she had a nice personality) before he can marry the beautiful Rachel with whom Jacob had fallen in love. Not only does Laban get both daughters married off but procures 14 years of free labor from Jacob.

Jacob loved Rachel more than Leah but it is Leah who proves fruitful bearing Reuben, Simeon, Levi and Judah. Rachel who is barren becomes envious of her sister. As with Jacob's grandmother, Rachel offers her handmaid to Jacob who bears two sons, Dan and Naphtali. Leah, not to be outdone offers her handmaid, Zilpah to Jacob and she bears sons, Gad and Asher. A high-level negotiation involving mandrake root between Leah and Rachel puts Leah back in Jacob's bed producing Issachar and Zebulun (son's number 5 and 6 if you're counting) and a daughter, Dinah. Finally, HaShem blesses Rachel and she gives birth to a son, Joseph.

After Joseph is born Jacob seeks release from his uncle to return to his homeland. This leads to full scale deceptive animal husbandry on the part of both parties. Eventually Jacob packs his household up (including

Laban's idols) and leaves in the middle of the night. When Laban discovers the deception, he follows and overtakes Jacob. After a tense confrontation, Jacob and Laban make nice and seal a covenant agreement with the erection of a pillar. Jacob continues his journey to his homeland.

Jacob seems to remember as he gets close to his homeland that he left amid death threats from his brother, Esau. He sends messengers to Esau and finds that Esau is on his way with a small army to meet him. Jacob divides his camp into two and begins to pray to HaShem in earnest. The next day he sends Esau an expensive gift basket. That evening he sends the remainder of his household across the Jabbok River.

Alone, Jacob settles in beside the river Jabbok. During the night he is encountered by "a man" who wrestles with him all night until the break of dawn. He wrenches Jacob's hip so that the hip socket becomes strained as they wrestle. The man asks to be released but true to form Jacob demands a blessing first. Jacob receives a new name, Israel, because he had strived with HaShem and prevailed. Jacob names the place Peniel for there he had seen HaShem face to face and had been preserved. As the sun rises he can be seen limping in the direction of his brother, Esau. The returning exile has been marked for life. He is not the same man that left. He will bear the marks of his exile for the remainder of his life.

The reunion could not have been more pleasant. The two brothers and their entourages leave together. Esau returns to Seir while Jacob journeys on to the land of Succoth and the city of Shechem where he sets up an altar and calls it El-elohe-yisrael ("El, God of Israel").

The rape of Jacob's daughter, Dinah, by Shechem, the son of the local Canaanite lord, Hamor, seeks to explain the ongoing enmity between the Israelites and the Canaanites. Following the rape, Jacob and Hamor reach an agreement to allow Shechem to marry Dinah on the condition that all Hamor's males are circumcised. Hamor readily agrees to it seeing the economic advantage to such an arrangement. Three days after the mass circumcision while the men were still in pain Simeon and Levi, Dinah's brothers, entered the city and slay all the males. The rest of Jacob's sons follow and plunder the town. I think you can see why there are issues between the two peoples.

HaShem steps in and instructs Jacob to move on to Bethel. Jacob is told that this move also means leaving all the alien gods behind. They bury these and the rings from their ears under the oaks at Shechem. HaShem causes a terror to fall on the cities around them so that no one follows them. When they reach Bethel, Jacob erects an altar and names the site El-bethel (the God of Bethel) because it was there that HaShem had revealed himself to Jacob.

HaShem greets Jacob and his family at Bethel with a blessing and a covenant. Then Jacob sets out from Bethel and goes towards Ephrath. Rachel dies in childbirth along the way and is buried on the road to Ephrath (now Bethlehem) but not before birthing the youngest of Jacob's sons, Benjamin. Jacob had twelve sons: Six born to Leah – Reuben, Simeon, Levi, Judah, Issachar, and Zebulun; two born to Rachel – Joseph and Benjamin; two to Bilhah (Rachel's maid) – Dan and Naphtali; and two to Zilpah (Leah's maid) – Gad and Asher.

Jacob reaches his father's home in Mamre (now Hebron). Isaac was 180 years old when he died. Jacob and Esau buried him. Jacob settles in the land of his father, Canaan.

The Jacob/Esau cycle is important for the Exile dwellers in that what you see is not always what you get: a dirty rotten scoundrel becomes Israel; you can go home again and despite an historical meltdown and exile there is hope for deliverance and return.

The Joseph cycle of stories is the final section of Genesis. We meet Joseph (of Technicolor Dream Coat fame), the favored son of Jacob, when he is seventeen. Already hated by his other brothers, Joseph fuels the fire by retelling one of his famous dreams whose transparent interpretation infers that the days are coming when all eleven of his brothers will bow down to him in homage.

The brothers plot to kill the Dreamer. Soon the opportunity presents itself and they prepare to kill him and tell his father that he was killed by wild beasts. Reuben intervenes and instead suggests that they stick with telling their father the story of Joseph's being killed by wild animals but instead of killing Joseph they would sell him into slavery to the Ismaelites for twenty pieces of silver. The Ishmaelites in turn sell him in Egypt to Potiphar, a courtier of the Pharaoh.

Chapter 38 provides an interesting interlude and serves to heighten the suspense in the Joseph drama. The story of Judah and Tamar has been used by many generations of parents to warn their sons about the evils of masturbation. In reality it is a story about failing to perform the duties of Levirate marriage where it is the duty of the brother to take his brother's wife at the time of his death and produce offspring for her in honor of her now dead husband. When Judah fails to enforce the Levirate code Tamar, his daughter-in-law, uses deception to produce offspring from Judah himself.

Back to Joseph. Joseph proves himself a valuable asset to Potiphar becoming chief steward of Potiphar's household in no time at all. Now we are told that Joseph is well built and handsome (do you hear the music take on a sinister tone?). Potiphar's wife tries to seduce Joseph but Joseph out of loyalty to his master refuses her advances. After several attempts she accuses Joseph of attempting to rape her. Potiphar, in turn has Joseph put in prison.

Joseph's organizational skills become evident in prison and soon the jailer puts him in charge of all the prisoners. While in prison Joseph demonstrates a predilection for interpreting dreams so that when Pharaoh is beset by troubling dreams Joseph is brought in for a consultation. Joseph interprets the dreams as portents of the future: seven years of plenty followed by seven years of famine. Impressed by Joseph's acumen Pharaoh puts him in charge of all the lands of Egypt. Supplies are stored during the seven years of plenty so that when the seven years of famine come Egypt is sitting pretty. The famine proves to be severe and world-wide resulting in the whole world coming to Joseph and Egypt seeking relief.

When Jacob hears that there was food to be found in Egypt he sends his sons, minus Benjamin, to procure food for the land of Canaan. They appear before their brother Joseph (who they do not recognize although he recognizes them) and ask for rations. Joseph accuses them of being spies. Deception and intrigue become the plot line once again. In the end they are sent on their way instructed not to return unless they bring with them their youngest brother, Benjamin.

The famine is so great in Canaan that Jacob sends his sons back to Egypt for more food. They take Benjamin this time and go - this time they are received well. When they go to leave they are generously ladened with supplies. Joseph, once again proving to be his father's duplicitous son, places his silver cup into Benjamin's bag. Needless to say, they do not get far before the authorities overtake them and the "theft" is discovered.

When hauled before Joseph they plead their innocence "this time" and eventually tell the story of selling their brother, Joseph, into slavery. If they cost their father another son it will certainly kill him.

Finally, Joseph comes clean with his brothers and reveals his true identity. He instructs them to return and bring his father and their households back with them. When Pharaoh hears of the story he sends moving wagons and servants to assist with the relocation. HaShem sanctions and blesses the relocation effort and so Jacob and all his household journeys to Egypt and settles in the land of Goshen.

Jacob lives seventeen years in the land of Goshen. On his deathbed he calls his sons before him and blesses each individually. Jacob finishes his blessings with the request that he be buried in Canaan with his kin. Joseph has his father's body embalmed and transported to Canaan with Egyptian burial entourage and ceremony.

After Jacob's death the brothers worry that with dad dead, Joseph will now exact revenge upon them. So once again they go and plead for their lives. Joseph rebuffs them and delivers a line that will weave throughout all of scripture, "You intended evil for me but God intended it for good."

Joseph and his brothers settle in the land of Goshen. Joseph was 110 when he died. He was embalmed and laid in a coffin in Egypt until burial in Canaan could happen.

The figure of Joseph demonstrates how to live in a foreign land. Despite the circumstances that Joseph faces early in the story, as Dr. Daniel Sandstedt (Chair of Contextual Education at the Lutheran Seminary at Gettysburg) was oft heard to say, "Even a bad experience can be a good experience." Even this dysfunctional family can be the carrier of God's blessing.

The themes of barrenness, famine, wandering and deception will be carried through the Torah narrative. The first three point to the vulnerability of the people of HaShem both in this narrative and the condition of Exile. The theme of deception is identified with the human attempt to manipulate situations and at times appears to be an attempt to usurp HaShem's role.

Walter Brueggemann has called Egypt the epitome of "Empire" in scripture (and that is not flattering). It appears that when things go south for HaShem's people they turn south to Egypt. This will be a major issue leading to the Exile. Despite Egypt always failing to fulfill its promises Israel returns again and again causing HaShem's people to be forever going down and coming out of Egypt.

"So that's how we got to Egypt!"

LIFE WITHOUT A TEMPLE:
EXODUS, LEVITICUS AND NUMBERS

"Zaydeh, how can we worship HaShem if we don't have a Temple?"

What do you do if your religious life is built around a sacrificial cult centered in a temple and suddenly that temple is destroyed and you have no ability to rebuild it? That is the dilemma that the Exiles now face. This answer is to create a priestly tradition that does not require a temple for authority or validation.

We find the beginnings of this in the latter section of the book of Exodus. From chapter 25 to the end of the book (apart from chapters 32-34 which deal with the Golden Calf incident and the redo of the tablets of stone) the groundwork is already being laid for this priestly tradition. The material in this section deals with the Tabernacle and the Ark of the Covenant, as well as the furnishings and attendant rites of this mobile temple.

This brings us to the book of **Leviticus**. Leviticus is a creation of the Priestly Tradition that develops during the Exile as a response to the crisis. It is concerned with the issues of holiness and purity which are reflected more specifically as the exiles seek to redefine themselves as distinct people of righteousness and justice. When there was a Temple cult the priests needed to be ritually pure to perform the appointed sacrifices. In the post-Temple era that holiness/purity is now to be the state of the whole people. It is very clear that their holiness derives from the holiness of HaShem. Because HaShem is holy therefore his people must also be holy. Holiness connotes a sense of distance and separateness. This is especially important as a minority in a foreign land. As a result, there is a need for ritual to prepare and bridge any encounter with HaShem and their new neighbors.

As I mentioned earlier the Temple cult was built around the concept of sacrifice. Animal, grain and sometimes human sacrifices were an ancient tradition to maintain a relationship with and on occasion appease, atone or thank the gods. Burnt offerings could be partial with the remainder of the sacrifice retained for a ceremonial meal among the offerors. A portion of the sacrifice was often retained by the priest cult as their "cut". In Leviticus we are also introduced to the concept of a holocaust offering which is a total sacrifice, "wholly burned". We are told that it is the smell of the offering that is what is pleasing to HaShem. It is this understanding that lies behind the use of incense in ritual down to this day. The first seven chapters of Leviticus deal with the various kinds of sacrificial offerings.

Chapters 8-10 deal with the consecration or ordination of priests. This consecration is already attested to in Exodus 29 with the discussion of the Tabernacle. The rite of consecration is laid out in chapter 8 in great detail. Of special note was the anointing of Aaron and his sons. This signifies and reinforces the idea that this priesthood is of divine authorization and derives its power from HaShem. In ancient Israel the king was also so anointed, but after the exile, when there was no longer a monarchy, the term "Anointed One" (*mashiach/messiah*) was used to designate the future messianic king. At the same time a priest could be viewed as *mashiach* after the exile pointing to the messianic hopes and dreams of Israel. This leads to a belief in some circles that there will be two *mashiachs,* a priestly and a royal one.

With chapters 11-15 we enter a discussion of the purity laws. In this section details of what might render a person impure as well as the ritual actions required to restore one to a pure state are outlined. Impurity is not to be confused with sin. The state of impurity is not in and of itself sinful but rather prevents one from being able to approach the altar. There is a movement following the exile and the rebuilding of the temple to expand the need for purity beyond worship life and into daily life (kosher laws).

Chapters 17-26 are most often designated as the Holiness Code. Its language and style point to a separate author from the rest of the Levitical material. The content of the Code revolves around slaughter and sacrifice as well as improper relationships. There is strong evidence that the Code is an attempt to upgrade the priestly material. In the priestly tradition holiness was defined primarily in terms of ritual requirements whereas in the Holiness Code material we move into the realm of ethical behavior towards one another.

Chapter 23 outlines a detailed cultic calendar again upgrading that found in Exodus. Instead of three there are now six cultic festivals: Passover, Unleavened Bread, Weeks, Tabernacles (Sukkoth), Rosh Hashanah and Yom Kippur. The festivals Passover and Unleavened Bread are celebrations of the exodus and deliverance from Egypt. Shavvu'ot (Weeks) commemorates the first fruits brought to the Temple. It is also tied to the giving of the Torah on Sinai. Sukkoth (Tabernacles) is the harvest festival where booths were built in the fields to guard the harvest. It also served as a time to remember the wandering in the desert. Rosh Hashanah, the New Year's festival, is marked by rest, a holy convocation. The observance of Yom Kippur, or the Day of Atonement, is outlined in chapter 16. This festival is a day of sacrifice for the forgiveness of sins. The "scapegoat" serves as a sin offering for the penitent. Leviticus 25 includes and older practice that of a Sabbatical Year where slaves were to be released after six years and fields lay fallow every seventh year. In addition to this a Year of Jubilee is introduced where every fifty years there would be a general emancipation of the land and forgiveness of indebtedness. The reminder of Sabbot keeping is thereby extended from a weekly individual observance into a communal practice which strikes at the heart of economic life.

The book closes with a series of blessings (if the purity laws are observed) and curses (if they are not). The idea of curses and blessings are an integral part of Near Eastern treaties and agreements. Leviticus 26:44-45 clearly points to the Babylonian exile (*Yet, even then, when they are in the land of their enemies, I will not reject them or spurn them so as to destroy them, annulling My covenant with them*).

Since by the time of the Babylonian exile the Temple has been reduced to ashes and no sacrifice can be offered there the book of Leviticus should not be viewed as a "How-To Manual" but rather as a liturgical remembrance and rehearsal of obedience and sacrifice to HaShem. As such it reminds me of an old rabbinic tale told by Elie Wiesel:

> *When the great Rabbi Israel Baal Shem-Tov saw misfortune threatening the Jews it was his custom to go into a certain part of the forest to meditate. There he would light a fire, say*

a special prayer, and the miracle would be accomplished and the misfortune averted.

Later, when his disciple, the celebrated Magid of Mezritch, had occasion, for the same reason, to intercede with heaven, he would go to the same place in the forest and say: "Master of the Universe, listen! I do not know how to light the fire, but I am still able to say the prayer." And again, the miracle would be accomplished. Still later, Rabbi Moshe-Leib of Sasov, in order to save his people once more, would go into the forest and say: "I do not know how to light the fire, I do not know the prayer, but I know the place and this must be sufficient." It was sufficient and the miracle was accomplished.

Then it fell to Rabbi Israel of Rizhyn to overcome misfortune. Sitting in his armchair, his head in his hands, he spoke to God: "I am unable to light the fire and I do not know the prayer; I cannot even find the place in the forest. All I can do is to tell the story, and this must be sufficient." And ...it was sufficient.

... and telling the story was sufficient.

The book of **Numbers** is a retelling of the wilderness wanderings of Moses and his people now told from the point of view of the Priestly tradition. Israel is presented as a purified community that is kept ritually clean in order that it might host the presence of HaShem. As such the focus is on a discipline of holiness and ritual cleanness.

Numbers opens with a genealogy which is a favorite inclusion in the Priestly material. Genealogies provide order, establish relationships and place people in their appropriate place in the social hierarchy. Such genealogies become very important after the Babylonian Exile as a way of reestablishing continuity and order.

The journey from Egypt in Numbers is described as an orderly journey with a distinct focus on the Ark of the Covenant (HaShem's RV). Aaron is also seen not as much as Moses' brother-in-law as he is the priestly leader of the community. This is reinforced with the Aaronic Benediction

(6:24-26) which presents *Shalom* as a blessing of peace and holiness. This benediction is preserved through the centuries and is still used in many Christian communities today. In contrast to Leviticus, chapters 8-10, where we had the consecration of Aaron, here in Numbers, chapter 8, we have the consecration of the Levites. The relationship between these two over the course of Israel's history is very complicated. The Levites are the "un-landed" tribe of Israel deriving their sustenance from the other eleven. They are traditionally seen as subordinate to the Aaronic priests in their Temple duties.

This tension may also in some ways lie behind the material in chapters 11-14 which presents the crisis of being in the wilderness without adequate life support and the open rebellion that ensues. This crisis is not at all unlike the one that the exiles face in Babylon. Israel may be in alien Babylon but HaShem's blessings remain in force through the office of Aaron. Following this interlude, we return to the ritual Priestly material as a reminder of how the relationship with HaShem is to be preserved. The murmuring motif, however, continues at Meribah (chapter 20) and again with the story of the bronze serpent (chapter 21). In short, life in the wilderness/Exile is always beset by complaint.

Numbers contains material other than the Priestly tradition. Numbers presents one of the more humorous pieces (as long as you're not a donkey) of older Yahwistic material in the story of Balaam and his ass. As with much of the material coming out of the Exile this story reveals HaShem's predilection for using "foreigners/aliens" to do his bidding.

In chapter 27 Moses appoints Joshua his successor. The narrative then proceeds with the entry into the new land. The entry (or re-entry in the case of the exiles) into the land is a gift of HaShem and is undertaken with confidence. Numbers makes it very clear that the only way the holy land of a holy god can be securely entered is by a holy people.

THE HISTORIAN: DEUTERONOMY AND THE DEUTERONOMIC HISTORY

The book of Deuteronomy is the final and transitional book of the Torah. While composed of several layers of tradition it is clearly the work of a single editor or school of editors written in the time of the Babylonian Exile.

Chronologically, the Deuteronomy narrative is positioned between Numbers 33-36 and Joshua 1-4. Here our journey to the Promised Land pauses "beyond the Jordan in the land of Moab." There is a reflective tone to this book and a clarifying as to what is important for keeping covenant with HaShem as they enter the next stage of their journey.

For Deuteronomy, the goal of creation is the settlement of Israel in the Land of Promise. For a modern version of this we need only look at the conquest of the Americas by the Europeans and the development of the doctrine of Manifest Destiny that excused the destruction of whole civilizations.

The two central themes of Deuteronomy are that the commands given to Moses on Sinai are central to the covenant with HaShem and that these commands are about holiness and purity. The Priestly perspective on the Exile is that it was caused by profaneness and impurity on the part of the people. This will be made clear in our next section of the Prophets as we look at the Deuteronomic version of history leading up to the Exile.

The content of the book revolves around three main speeches by Moses:

1. 1:6-4:49 provides general instruction about entry into the Promised Land. Above all else DO NOT FORGET SINAI!!!! This is especially true of the commandments and particularly, "You shall have no other gods and no idols".
2. 5:1-28:68 comprises the central speech of Moses. In 5:6-21 the Ten Commandments are reiterated. Then in chapters 6-11 we read of the *shema "Hear, O Israel, the Lord is our God, the Lord alone. You shall love the Lord your God with all your heart and with all your soul and with all your might"* (Deuteronomy 6:4-5). which forms the creedal baseline for the people of HaSem. The call is for HaShem's people to derive their purpose and identity from adherence to the commands from Sinai. Chapters 12-25 form the legal corpus of Deuteronomy. This section serves as a commentary on the Decalogue (Ten Commandments).

3. The final speech (29:1-31:29) serves as a transition for the people of HaShem. The people move from the generation of Moses (the Man from Sinai) to the generation of Joshua (the Man for the Land).

Chapter 32 offers us *The Song of Moses* which is a recital of what HaShem will do in the event of his people once again succumbing to idolatry and worship of other gods.

In chapter 33 Moses offers his blessing upon each of the twelve tribes individually. When he finishes, Moses goes up to Mount Nebo where HaShem shows him the Land, a land that he will never enter. Moses dies there and is buried in Moab.

In the book of 2 Kings Chapter 22 we read of the discovery of a book of the law during a spring housecleaning of the Temple which when taken to King Josiah (621 BCE), becomes the basis for Josiah's religious and political reforms. In the early 1800's a young German scholar by the name of W.M.L. deWette identified the discovered "book of the law" as being that of Deuteronomy (or at least portions of it).

The reforms outlined in the book are both political and religious. There is a great centralization of control particularly with the religious reforms. All shrines and temples outside of Jerusalem are torn down. This effectively eliminates the practice of worshipping to local gods and their traditions. The Levites who operated these country shrines are put out of business. Their arrival in Jerusalem produces a glut of religious professionals and sets up tensions between priests and Levites.

In politics (particularly with regards to the king) there is a reconstitution of things political in a way that they now reflect the terms of covenant. In 1 Kings 8:1-22, which is part of the Deuteronomic History, we are told of the people's request for a king, HaShem's initial refusal and finally, his acquiescence. It will be the failure of the king to keep the terms of the covenant made through Moses that will ultimately spell the doom and destruction that leads to exile.

Scholars have identified great similarities in form and content between these covenants and those of the Assyrians who occupied Judah at that time. As such Josiah's reforms make the claim that despite what seems contrary evidence, HaShem is still calling the shots… even though they are occupied in the present (and may be so again).

Deuteronomy/The Book of the Law plays a great role in the Babylonian Exile. As mentioned earlier, the exiles are faced with the lack of a temple in which to practice the sacrificial terms of the covenant. They do, however, have a book. As such they move from the people of the Temple to the people of the book. Study of the Law takes the place of sacrifice. The synagogue would develop as a place for this study and a new class of leaders would develop called the Scribes (Men of the Book). These are learned men who keep the teaching of the Law scrolls available through the careful management of the scrolls. As such they are early religious librarians. Their task is to maintain the books/scrolls so that they continue to be the interpretive authority in Israel (over and against the priests). This class of leaders will also be responsible for the Deuteronomic History of Joshua through 2 Kings and probably the final editing of Deuteronomy itself.

The books of the Deuteronomic History will comprise the first six books of the next major section, the Nevi'im, or Prophets. Along with the Major Prophets it is this section that will probe the question, "How did we get into the mess called the Exile?"

How Did We Get into This Mess?

As we begin to probe the answer to the question of causation with regards to the Exile the writings of the Tanakh are daring in their discourse. They posit the blame solely on the shoulders of the religious and political establishment of Israel and later Judah. In contrast, when the Christians wrestle with this question after the destruction of the Second Temple in 70 CE the blame is laid at the feet of the Jews and their failure to accept Jesus as Messiah which is seen as part of God's apocalyptic plan. The response to 9/11 moves even farther away from this answer as it denies any complicity of the culture or judgment of God that might have prompted such action on the part of the Islamic terrorists.

The biblical writings that focus most directly on this question are collected under the heading of the Prophets. If the Torah is the articulation (in story and commandment) of the norms of faith and the obedience commensurate with the rule of HaShem then the prophetic literature is that which articulates Israel's faith and practice in the rough and tumble of historical reality. If Torah is the ideal then the Prophets are the real, the place where faith hits the road.

The Prophets (Nevi'm) are comprised of three sections: The Former Prophets (Joshua, Judges, 1&2 Samuel and 1&2 Kings), the Latter Prophets (Isaiah, Jeremiah and Ezekiel) and the Twelve (Hosea, Amos, Micah, Nahum, Habakkuk, Zephaniah, Haggai, Zechariah, Malachi, Joel, Obadiah and Jonah).

THE FORMER PROPHETS

The Former Prophets, referred to more accurately as the Deuteronomic History, comprise the historical books of Joshua, Judges, 1&2 Samuel and 1&2 Kings. These books provide the main account of the history of ancient Israel, albeit in a biased way, theologically speaking. They draw their theological perspective from the book of Deuteronomy and as such provide a smooth transition from the Torah to the Prophets. The identity of the prophet in these books is that of one who interprets "political" life according to the rule of HaShem as laid out in the Torah (and most explicitly the book of Deuteronomy). According to Deuteronomy there are four major divisions of Israel's history: The Age of Moses, the Conquest, the Judges and the Monarchy. For decades it was assumed that this material all shared in a single editor collecting at the time of the Exile. More recent scholarship has opened the door for a second period of editing which may have come after the Exile.

Joshua

As Deuteronomy provides us with the account of the Age of Moses so now Joshua opens the door to the Conquest of the Promised Land. While the biblical account purports that this was to be an extensive conquest, from the wilderness in Lebanon to the Great River, the Euphrates, and up the Mediterranean Sea (1:4) the drama of the conquest described in chapters 2-10 present a much more limited conquest from Bethel on the south to Taanach on the north (just south of Megiddo). Scholarship has hotly debated the veracity of the narrative. This is reinforced by the failure of archeological evidence to corroborate the story. Out of this debate have arisen four theories to explain the Conquest: Immigration, Conquest, Evolution and Revolt. Both the immigration and evolution theories point to a gradual process of assimilation. The former originating from outside of Canaan and the other from inside. In this case a nation of Israel emerges over time in the land of Canaan. The conquest theory, which given our treatment of the Native Americans was the preferred American theory, has failed to be supported by archeological evidence. While the revolt theory (that it was a liberation movement to overthrow the rule of Egypt in Canaan) has archeological evidence it is hardly supported by the biblical account.

Regardless of which theory you adhere to, there are a couple of episodes in the conquest material worthy of our attention. In chapters 3-5 we have material highly reminiscent of previous stories: the crossing of the Jordan River (a redo of the crossing of the Yom Suf), a second circumcision, and the celebration of the Passover. This material surrounds the conquest of Gilgal and serves as prelude to the Battle of Jericho. The siege of Jericho is introduced by an encounter with HaShem (5:13ff) that reinforces the understanding that this conquest is not solely a human endeavor but has "holy" support (hence ritual purity is of utmost importance). The priests and the army circumnavigate the city walls seven times with ram's horns blowing and as the Spiritual tells us, "De walls came a tumblin' down."

The remainder of the book concerns the Twelve Tribes and the allotment of land to each except for the Tribe of Levi which receives no land. The book ends with a Covenant renewal ceremony (24). It includes a rehearsal of the past and a call for undivided loyalty to HaShem. The final act is to lay the bones of Joseph (that have been brought from Egypt) to rest at Shechem marking the end of an era.

Judges

"Zaydeh, what's a judge?"

The period of the Judges picks up following the death of Joshua. The time of the Judges reflects a period before Israel has a king and consists of twelve loosely affiliated tribes. The term translated in the title of the book "judges" is elsewhere translated "chieftain" or "leader". The "judges" were charismatic military leaders who would be chosen in times of crisis within the Tribes. After the crisis, however, the judge would continue to rule for the rest of their lifetime at which time they might resemble a more typical judge-type rendering verdict on critical decisions or controversies. One of the unique features of the judges was that they were not gender biased so that their ranks also include the likes of Deborah. The judges are by and large ruthless, tribal chieftains, mercenaries or bandits. The crises that provoke the judges are mostly inter-tribal and not international in nature. There appear to be two themes running through these characters that reflect its Deuteronomic editing namely, kingship and the continual apostasy of the people. There is great pressure often put upon these judges to become kings. This points to a seeming tension between the rule of HaShem and that of the earthly king. At this point in the history they decline or are thwarted from becoming such kings. Secondly, it appears that when a judge dies it is not long before the people fall away from keeping Torah and end up in another crisis that necessitates the choosing of another judge. This pattern prefigures the ongoing script that will eventually justify the Assyrian and Babylonian conquests. The most famous of the judges were: Gideon, Abimelech, Jephthah and Samson. High on violence, intrigue, and machismo their narratives read more like a *Rambo* movie plot than a biblical narrative. Most appear to be stories of local color of folk heroes that have been lightly sprinkled with Deuteronomic piety.

The final four chapters of the book of Judges foreshadow the ensuing books that will pick up the story of the monarchy. These chapters are framed by "In those days there was no king in Israel; everyone did as he pleased" and clearly send the message that without a judge anarchy soon reigns. In the end the verdict of Judges is that humanity, especially the Israelite version of it, left to its own devices is corrupt and cannot exist without divine guidance.

1 Samuel

While 1&2 Samuel were originally one book, what is now known today as 1 Samuel provides us with the transition between the period of the Judges and the institution of the monarchy. It also introduces us to the first of the minor prophets, Samuel. We are introduced to Samuel's mother, Hannah, in the opening verses of the book – Hannah is barren (sound familiar?). We are also told that his father was a devout man offering sacrifices at the shrine at Shiloh where the sons of Eli were priests. After prayerful intercession (ok, negotiation, "If you grant me a son I will dedicate him to you and he will be like Sampson, a nazirite") and sex with her husband, Hannah conceives and bears a son, Samuel ("I asked the Lord for him").

When Samuel is weaned, Hannah takes him to the temple along with the appointed offerings. She lends him to HaShem (the verb "to lend" is from the same root as "to ask" so there is a play on words in that the one asked for is now lent). Hannah breaks out in song which bears a striking resemblance to Mary's Magnificat in Luke's gospel. Samuel grows in stature and reputation, "All Israel from Dan to Beer-sheba, knew that Samuel was trustworthy as a prophet of the Lord."

It is revealed through Samuel (following a somewhat comic divine revelatory conversation) to Eli that his sons were running afoul of the Torah in performing their priestly duties. It is prophesied that a faithful priest will be raised up and that Eli's sons will meet with an appropriate fate.

We pick up the action in chapter 4 as Israel wages battle against the Philistines but are routed, the Ark of the Covenant is captured, and the sons of Eli killed. The Philistines take the captured Ark and place it in the temple of their god, Dagon. In a somewhat humorous story HaShem and Dagon engage in nightly battle with the statue of Dagon ending up on its face every morning. (Walter Brueggemann has a marvelous treatment of this episode in his book, ***Ichabod Toward Home)***. After attempts to pawn it off on neighboring towns with disastrous results they send the Ark back to the Israelites. Armed with the Ark once again the Israelites rout the Philistines.

Shortly after this it becomes obvious that the administration of the judges is not working. The people come to Samuel and demand a king like all their neighbors have. HaShem takes personal offense at their rejection of him as king. Samuel relays HaShem's response with an essentially, "be careful what you ask for" speech. The people insist, HaShem responds, "Let them have their king!"

> *"Zaydeh, how do you choose a king?"*

> *"That's a good question. When HaShem's people sought out their first king they looked for someone who would stand out from the crowd."*

> *"So, he was a mighty warrior, a wise man, a gifted leader?"*

"No, he was tall! And handsome."

Tall Saul. Hardly the portrait of a king. But then again.…

In a playfully ironic narrative, Saul (from the Tribe of Benjamin) is led by his father's lost asses to Samuel the seer/prophet who will anoint him king over HaShem's people. Samuel summons the people at Mizpah and denounces them for having forsaken HaShem and demanding a king. While HaShem provides the king, he does not approve of the new arrangement. The institution of king is not divinely ordained or approved. (Is it any wonder Saul is hiding among the baggage when they go to make him king?). While most seemed to accept Saul, there are scoffers who question his credentials and his ability to "save" them. Saul leads a military force against the threat of the Ammonites defeating them convincingly. This seems to silence his critics for now and Saul proceeds to Gilgal to be coronated.

Samuel, upon the ascension of Saul to the throne, announces his retirement as leader over the people. Gathering the people, he takes one last shot at the monarchy. He recites the mighty act of HaShem concluding with, *"you said to me, 'No, we must have a king reigning over us… Well, the Lord has set a king over you! Here is the king you have chosen, that you have asked for"* (1 Samuel 12:12). In short, you've gotten what you've asked for so don't blame me.

During a critical battle with the Philistines, Saul becomes anxious and impatient because Samuel has not yet arrived to entreat HaShem for a favorable outcome, so he takes it upon himself to offer the appropriate burnt offering. When Samuel arrives, he condemns Saul for overreaching the bounds of his authority and breaking covenant. By committing this royal *faux pas* Saul has now jeopardized his dynasty. HaShem will seek elsewhere for the next king. (This confusing of the roles of king and prophet/priest will again come into play during the reign of John Hyrcanus in the 1st century BCE). In chapter 15 Saul and Samuel resume their conflict when Saul fails to carry out the *harem* (total annihilation) of King Agog of Amalek saving the best of the spoils for himself and his men. While *harem* was the common military practice of the day in all cultures, here it is viewed as a divine mandate and so Saul is portrayed once again standing over and against the covenant.

This "final straw" leads HaShem to call upon Samuel to go and anoint a new king who will rule after Saul. In cloak and dagger fashion Samuel travels to the home of Jesse the Bethlehemite in search of the once and future king.

Under the guise of participating in a sacrificial feast Samuel goes to Bethlehem and there invites Jesse and his sons to join him in the feast. He is certain that HaShem has chosen Jesse's son, Eliab because of his stature and looks (he's been down this road before with Saul) but HaShem has other ideas. Seven sons of Jesse are presented to Samuel with HaShem turning each down in turn. Finally, Samuel asks Jesse if he has any more sons and is informed that there is one younger son out tending the flock (shepherd tending flock… mmm…file that one away for later). He is brought in from the fields and HaShem instructs Samuel to anoint this one and we are told that HaShem "gripped" this one from that day on. David is described as ruddy-cheeked, bright-eyed and handsome.

We are told that Saul's mental health goes south about this time (the spirit of HaShem has departed from him) and he is beset with fits of depression. Saul determines that what he needs is a good lyre player. Ironically, it is David who is recommended. David enters Saul's service, for when David plays, Saul finds relief.

Soon after this the Philistines engage Saul's army once again this time putting forth a "champion" by the name of Goliath, a mountain of a man. The very sight of this giant causes Saul's army to wet their britches.

David's brothers are in Saul's army and his father sends David to them with supplies. On one of his trips to the camp David engages some of the men in conversation about the Goliath situation. His brother becomes irate that he is talking with the soldiers and wonders why he has left the sheep alone in the wilderness (did I say something about kings and shepherds?). In the end David volunteers to engage Goliath in battle.

As the encounter begins there is the prerequisite taunting where Goliath points out that David comes minus the recommended armaments. David's reply is that he has bound the name of the Lord of Hosts to himself and that this Lord will deliver the day (a similar sentiment is captured centuries later in St. Patrick's Breastplate, "I bind unto myself this day the strong arm of the Trinity" not to mention Deuteronomy 6 and the binding of the Torah). We know how the story plays out, David fells the giant with a stone from his slingshot and beheads him with the giant's own sword. The Philistines are routed and run for their lives all the way back to Gath.

David is taken into Saul's household and becomes a close friend of the king's son, Jonathan. David also is made head of Saul's army and becomes an overnight sensation and hero: *"Saul has slain his thousands; David, his ten thousands."*(1 Samuel 18:7). Saul's jealousy boils. Saul actually tries to kill David at this point but David eludes him. Saul tries a new tack by proposing a marriage between David and his daughter, Michal. The catch was that David's bride price was to be a hundred Philistine foreskins (Saul is hoping that the Philistines would be the end of David once and for all). However, David returns triumphant from his quest producing not one hundred but two hundred trophies. Saul's fear and envy of David reach epic proportions and he repeatedly tries to have David killed but thanks to Jonathan and Michal he escapes.

A grand cat and mouse game ensues as Saul seeks to track David down and kill him. David gathers around him a band of mercenaries and continues to battle the Philistines. On many occasions David is delivered from the hand of Saul through the efforts of those called by HaShem to sustain David and his men: Abbithar, the priest, gives David consecrated bread to eat (which will cost him and his fellow priests their lives when Saul finds out). When Abigail's husband, Nabal, refuses to help David, Abigail takes matters into her own hands and provides for David and his men out of Nabal's stores. (When Nabal drops dead, as a result of apparent punishment, David takes Abigail as his wife.)

Twice David is presented with opportunity to kill Saul as he sleeps but refrains from doing so (such a cowardly murder hardly complements the heroic David). After the second episode David and Saul have a confrontation that ends with Saul returning to his home and David going on his way.

Following the death of the prophet Samuel, Saul bans all spirits and ghosts from the land (remember we are dealing with a psychotic king in old Saul). At this time the Philistines resume war against Saul. As the enemy force masses against Saul he seeks to engage HaShem in conversation but HaShem is silent. So, Saul disguises himself and seeks the aid of the witch of Endor (hints of Macbeth) to conjure up for him a ghost, preferably, Samuel (Yes, Saul has banned all spirits and ghosts from the land). The witch does, Saul seeks the ghost of Samuel for guidance, and Samuel announces the curse of HaShem, *"Saul, the kingship has been torn from your hands and given to your countryman, David"* (1 Samuel 28:17). If that is not enough, Samuel informs Saul that tomorrow he and his sons will join Samuel.

At this point David has been hired as the personal bodyguard for Achish, the king of the Philistines. There is concern amongst the other Philistines about David's loyalties so Achish sends him packing before the great battle. Upon returning to his encampment in Philistia (Ziklag) David finds it burned and his wives taken captive by the Amalekites. Sustained by the aid of an Egyptian and his offerings of fig and raisin cakes David overtakes and defeats the Amalekites in a daring dawn raid. Meanwhile, back at the ranch, the Philistines are closing in on Saul at Mount Gilboa. The battle rages and Saul is wounded by enemy archers. He asks his arms-bearer to run him through with his sword but the young man refuses. Saul then falls on his own sword. When the Philistines discover Saul's body the next day they strip him of his armor, behead him, and impale his body on the wall of Beth-shan. Loyalists come and retrieve Saul's body and those of his sons, burn them and bury them under the tamarisk tree in Jabesh and then fast for seven days.

2 Samuel

"Zaydeh, does David get to be king?"

"You're getting ahead of yourself, Jakob"

News reaches David of Saul's death in his camp at Ziklag. David offers a beautiful requiem in tribute to Saul which will later be called the Song of the Bow in the Book of Jashar. Following this HaShem instructs David to go up to Hebron where David is anointed king over the House of Judah.

Abner, Saul's commander in chief, takes Saul's son, Ishbosheth, over to Gilead and sets him up as king of Israel. A long drawn out war between the House of Saul and the House of David ensues. After a dispute between Abner and Ishbosheth over a woman Abner seeks to make peace with the House of David. Terms are decided upon. On his way back to the enemy camp, Abner is encountered by Joab, David's general, and killed. When Ishbotsheth hears of Abner's death he loses the heart for war and flees to the land of Benjamin.

All the tribes of Israel come to David at Hebron and make a pact with him before HaShem. David then becomes king over all Israel. He is thirty years old when he becomes king and he rules for forty years. David seizes the Jebusite city of Jerusalem and renames it the City of David.

The Philistines once again rise up against David and Israel and this time David routs them, driving them all the way to Gezer and recapturing the Ark of HaShem. In a grand parade with singing, dancing and much cavorting, as well as some full frontal nudity, David brings the Ark of HaShem into Jerusalem.

After David is settled into his new palace he decided that HaShem needs an equivalent house so inquires of his prophet Nathan about the issue. At first Nathan gives the go ahead but then is confronted by HaShem who questions why all of a sudden he should go from being a mobile god to one locked up in a house.

This serves as the backdrop for the keystone passage of 2 Samuel: *"Your house and your kingship shall ever be secure before you; your throne shall be established forever"* (2 Samuel 7:16). HaShem promises to raise up offspring for David and this son will build HaShem a house even as HaShem establishes a house (dynasty) for him. HaShem will be like a father to him and he like a son to HaShem.

David continues to subdue enemy after enemy in an almost regular season of war. It is during one of these seasonal campaigns, while his army is campaigning, and David remains in his cozy palace that he has an affair with one of his general's wives. The torid affairs goes south in a hurry when the woman in question, Bathsheba, is found to be pregnant. Since Urriah, her husband, is serving at the front there is little doubt as to what she has been up to.

David brings Uriah back from the front in the hopes that he will sleep with his wife and the child can be passed off as his. Unfortunately, Uriah practices the disciplines of combat and refrains from intercourse with his wife choosing instead to sleep outside like his men. Recognizing how long an army would last if it was discovered that the king was sleeping with their wives while they were off fighting for him, David takes drastic measures.

When Uriah is sent back to the fighting orders accompany him. Joab, the commander, is to put Uriah in the front lines, charge the enemy, and when the enemy is engaged, they are to pull back leaving Uriah holding the proverbial bag. Uriah dies a hero's death and after an appropriate period of mourning Bathsheba marries David and bears him a son… and everyone lives happily ever after… well…not quite.

It seems that HaShem is not at all pleased with David's behavior and sends Nathan, the prophet, to talk with David. Using a parable of a poorman and his little ewe lamb, Nathan leads David down a path of self-incrimination and self-judgment. David stands before Nathan (and HaShem) naked in his guilt. The punishment is threefold: since David resorted to the sword (killing Uriah) his household will be in perpetual conflict, his own wives will be taken from him and another will sleep with them, and finally the child shall die.

The remainer of the book is a playing out of these curses upon David and David's continual attempts to unify the twelve tribes into the semblance of a nation. Chapter 22 is a beautiful hymn composed by David to honor HaShem. This is then followed by the "last words of David" in chapter 23. Somewhat surprisingly, David does not die after his final words and the fighting and killing continues to rage through to the end of the book.

1 & 2 Kings

"Zaydeh, is there anyone left to be king?"

"Yes, Jakob, the wisest of kings is yet to come. His name is Solomon."

With the opening chapter of 1 Kings we can begin to see that the divisions between the books of the Deuteronomic History are somewhat artificial and arbitrary. One "book" spills into another. This is true of the movement from Samuel to Kings. Instead of picking up with Solomon's reign we must deal with David's death first.

The beginning of 1 Kings brings to a close what is often refered to the Court or Succession Narrative that begins in the later chapters of 2 Samuel. We pick up the narrative being told that David is old and cold (a very different picture from that of the virile warrior). He gets progressively older throughout the first chapter as well.

Chapter one describes the struggle for David's throne by the two remaining sons of David (by different mothers) Adonijah and Solomon. Adonijah proclaims himself king but without the backing of the royal court. Nathan, the prophet, colludes with Solomon's mother, Bathsheba, in a plot to ingratiate her son before King David, and to recall for David the "promise" that he made to her that Solomon would be king (not all that unlike Rebekkah and Jacob). Nathan, the prophet; Zadok, the priest; and Benaiah, the army commander back her testimony. David proclaims Solomon king and asks that he be brought to the royal court. He is crowned king and the party commences.

Word is delivered to Adonijah at the his own coronation feast that he has thrown for himself, that David had crowned Solomon King. The next thing we know Adonijah is hugging the horns of the altar and wetting his proverbial pants in fear. Solomon arrives and simply tells him to, "Go home!" Unfortunately for Adonijah he cannot go quietly and continues to seek favor. It turns out to be the final straw and Solomon has him killed.

David by now is quickly approaching his deathbed. He lays out for Solomon his marching orders: stay faithful to the Mosaic covenant (the Deuteronomic ideal for a king) and take care of the unfinished business (a couple of timely executions of Abner and Shimei should do the trick). With this David enjoys the sleep of his ancestors and Solomon is firmly established on David's throne. (An inciteful, entertaining, if not a bit irreverent treatment of David's reign is captured in Joseph Heller's novel, **God Knows**).

With the ascension of Solomon to the throne, Israel enters into its golden years (aka "The Good Old Days"). We are told that Israel and Judah in these days are as numerous as the sands by the sea (hearkening back to the original promises made to Abraham in Genesis). Solomon consolidates his power through a succession of royal marriages to the daughters of foreign powers.

Solomon is also renowned for his wisdom. Tradition attributes to him the book of Proverbs as well as the Wisdom of Solomon. When asked by HaShem what gift he desired, Solomon responded, wisdom. This wisdom is demonstrated in 1 Kings 3:16-27 where two prostitutes bring a maternity suit to Solomon for judgment. Offering to cut the infant in half the real mother is revealed and Solomon is heralded as possessing the divine wisdom necessary to execute justice.

Solomon was also a prodigious builder erecting many new structures in Jerusalem and engaging in extensive urban renewal in places like Hazor, Gezer and Megiddo. His most famous effort, however, is undoubtedly the Jerusalem Temple. Completing what his father, David had dreamed of building, Solomon erects a house for HaShem. As was customary in the ancient Near East a temple was the place where the god dwelt, and so Solomon orders the Ark of the Covenant (HaShem's RV) to be brought into the new temple and we are told that the presence of HaShem filled the House of HaShem. This sense of the Temple as the dwelling of HaShem will be reflected later in Ezekiel when we are told that the presence/glory of HaShem left Jerusalem before it is destroyed by Babylon ("HaShem has indeed left the building!").

One of the downsides of having a bevy of foreign wives is that they tend to bring with them their foreign dieties. Not only is it reported that Solomon offers sacrifices at the high places (shrines outside of Jerusalem) but he erects temples for his wives' dieties and worships there as well. While this points to a tolerance towards the gods and goddesses of neighboring countries it does not sit well with the Deuteronomic editors.

It is this crucial point that the editors point to as the reason the united monarchy cannot be sustained. As a result, HaShem sends enemies against Solomon because he has worshipped Ashtoreth the goddess of the Phonecians, Chemosh the god of Moab, and Milcom the god of the Ammonites. One of those opponents was Jeroboam who oversaw Solomon's forced labor.

Following Solomon's death civil war breaks out between Jeroboam and Rehoboam (Solomon's son) and the northern ten tribes secede from the union leaving only the Tribe of Benjamin in the Kingdom of Judah. The issue which motivates the ten tribes does not appear to be the worshipping of foreign gods but rather the forced labor practices instituted by Solomon. Prior to Solomon's death and encouraged by the prophet, Ahihah, Jeroboam flees to Egypt. This highlights a connection within the narrative between Solomon's practices and what Moses and the people experienced under the hand of Pharaoh.

After Solomon dies, Jeroboam returns from Egypt and is crowned king of the north, Israel. The kings of the north, beginning with Jeroboam, adapted a charismatic leadership style that closely resembled that of the "judges" from an earlier day.

The exodus event becomes the central religious focus of the cult sanctuaries at Bethel and Dan. This theme is largely ignored in the south until the refoms of Josiah. The Deuteronomist is appalled by the construction of two shrines, one in Bethel and the other in Dan. Jeroboam is branded an idolater by the editor for setting up two golden calves (ahha, sound familiar?). The setting up of shrines outside of Jerusalem will be refered to in the future as "the sin of Jeroboam."

While the succession in the southern kingdom proceeds smoothly fulfilling the Davidic promise, the reign of the kings in the north is marked by repeated coups and uprisings. It is not until Omri (885 BCE) that we have anything in the north resembling a dynasty. Omri is responsible for setting up Samaria as the capital of Israel. As one might expect the Deuteronomist editors are not impressed and brand Omri as displeasing to HaShem worse than all those preceeding him.

The introduction of the prophet Elijah (chapter 17) marks a distinct transition in the narrative. The focus now is on the prophetic ministries of Elijah and Elisha. The stage is set: Omri's son, Ahab is now king of the north. Ahab takes Jezebel, daughter of Phonecian King Ethbaal, as his wife. To please her Ahab builds a temple to the god, Baal, erects an altar to Baal in the temple and sets up a sacred post (a bit phallic to say the least). Guess what? This angers HaShem. In fact we are told that Ahab did more to vex HaShem than any of those who had preceeded him... and that's doing something.

The prophet Elijah, shows up with news of HaShem's displeasure with Ahab. The consequenses of Ahab's idolatry will be that HaShem will shut the heavens up and there shall be neither dew nor rain until he says so. The drought is on!

After delivering the message HaShem comes to Elijah with a word, "Get out of town fast because your life won't be worth much if old Jezebel gets a hold of you. Head east and hide out in the Wadi Cherith". He goes to the Wadi Cherith, east of the Jordan, and holed up there while HaShem sends ravens with bread and meat every morning and evening and he drinks his fill from the wadi (reminiscent of the bread of the wilderness in Exodus).

Eventually the wadi dries up and HaShem comes with new instructions. Elijah is to go to Zarephath where he will find a widow who HaShem has chosen to care for Elijah. When he arrives in town he finds a widow gathering sticks at the entrance to town. He calls to her, "Bring me some water." As she starts to get his water he calls again, "While you're at it bring me some bread too". Her reply is chilling. "I have nothing baked for I have only a little flour and oil, enough for one last meal for my son and I, and then we are prepared to die." Elijah's response, "Don't be afraid… fix mine first… for HaShem has promised that the jar of flour and the jug of oil shall not run out." She does as Elijah instructs her and the jar of flour and the jug of oil do not run out.

Meanwhile the widow's son falls sick and gets progressively worse until there is no breath left in him. The widow rales at Elijah, "What have I done to you? If you had not shown up at my door HaShem wouldn't have even known that I existed." "Give me the boy," Elijah barks. He takes the boy up to his room and lays across him three times crying, "O Lord, let this child's life return to his body." HaShem hears the prayer. Elijah picks up the child and brings him to his mother, "See your son is alive." To which she replies, "Now I know you are a man of HaShem. Now leave us alone!"

In the third year of the drought Elijah is once again instructed by HaShem to appear before Ahab. On his way he is encountered by Obadiah, Ahab's steward (who is faithful to the cause of HaShem). Elijah tells Obadiah to inform King Ahab that "Elijah is here!" Ahab tracks Elijah down and is instructed by Elijah to assemble all of Israel as well as Jezebel's priests of Baal and Asherah on Mount Carmel.

On Carmel Elijah challenges the prophets of Baal and Asherah to a barbeque cookoff, the winner of which will prove to all which is the true god. The prophets of Baal and Asherah are unable to call down fire from heaven to consume their offering. Elijah, the consummate showman, douses his offering with water and then offers prayer to HaShem. The offering is consumed and in the fury of his zeal, Elijah has all of Jezebel's prophets killed.

Elijah takes Ahab up the hill and points out the cloud on the horizon that portents rain and the end of the drought and famine. When word reaches Jezebel, however, of what Elijah has done she informs Elijah that he will suffer a similar fate. Frightened, Elijah flees.

He runs into the wilderness until he collapses under a broom tree and there begs HaShem to simply take his life. HaShem's response is to send an angel with bread and water. Strengthened he continues for forty days and forty nights until he reaches Mt. Horeb (aka Mt. Sinai).

There Elijah finds a cave which he deems suitable for his retirement condo. While Elijah is settling in HaShem shows up and asks Elijah what he thinks he is doing. Elijah explains that his faithfulness to HaShem has ended up with him being a fugitive and that he is the only one left who is faithful to HaShem in all of Israel (a similar feeling is expressed but the exiles in Babylon).

HaShem calls Elijah to come to the mouth of the cave. Then HaShem passes by in all of his traditional manifestations, earthquake, wind and fire… finally there is a soft murmering sound or crushing silence. HaShem speaks, Elijah what are you doing here? Elijah explains that his faithfulness to HaShen has ended in him being a fugitive and that he is the only one left who is faithful to HaShem in all of Israel.

HaShem takes exception to Elijah's assessment (as well as his desire to hang up his prophetic mantle) and gives him a new itinerary which includes appointing his successor Elisha and anointing a new king in Israel.

Elijah sets out and finds Elisha who is plowing in the field and he places his mantle upon Elisha's shoulders. After offering a sacrifice of the oxen, Elisha arises and follows Elijah as his attendant.

We return to the political exploits of Ahab. It is a time when relationships between Israel and Judah are friendly but Israel is under intermittent attack from Syria (Aram). King Jehoshaphat of Judah and King Ahab of Israel join forces against Syria. Prophets are called in for a consult prior to engaging the enemy. Victory is assured by the prophets. Well, except for the word of the prophet Micaiah son of Imlah. Micaiah predicts doom in the upcoming battle. This story reveals the difficulty with prophesy in that there are often contradictory prophetic utterings. Often it is only as history unfolds that the true prophetic word is disclosed. History rules in favor of Micaiah and Ahab is killed in the battle of Ramoth-gilead.

Following the death of Ahab Elijah resurfaces. Elijah is called by HaShem to confront Ahab's son, Ahaziah about his consultation of foreign gods. When news of this unnamed prophet reaches Ahaziah he asks for a description and is told, "He is a hairy man with a leather belt tied around his waist." Immediately, Ahaziah recognizes him as Elijah (a similar recognition will be anticipated in the gospels when John the Baptist is decribed in similar terms).

The opening of 2 Kings continues then with the transfer of power from Elijah to Elisha and Elijah's assumption into heaven via the whirlwind and fiery chariot. Elisha's prophetic ministry is different than that of Elijah's. Gone are the battles with the prophets of Baal or any hints of a social or moral clean up. Instead Elisha is focused with fulfilling the terms of Elijah's forced reenlistment at Mount Horeb. The story of Naaman, the leper from Syria demonstrates a foreigner's appeal for aid from HaShem. HaShem demonstrates that he is a "God without Borders". Once again, the Deuteronomic theme of outsiders benefiting from Israel's god and HaShem's willingness to use foreigners to accomplish his purposes for Israel are evident in the Elisha material. This story of Naaman as well as the widow of Zaraphat (Elijah) will show up in the gospels to establish this claim as well and that of the ministry to the non-Jew (Gentile).

The narrative that follows with the Elisha cycle of material alternates between accounts of the kings of Judah and those of Israel. With some exceptions the overall movement of the narrative is a swirling down the cosmic commode toward inevitable destruction.

Due to the strong Davidic dynastic presence in Judah the sucession of kings goes pretty much smoothly but in the Northern Kingdom succession is marked with coup, assassination and intrigue. This weakened the Northern Kingdom at a much faster rate than that of the Southern Kingdom making it a tempting prey for outside harassment.

One of those taking advantage of Israel's situation is Assyria under the leadership of Tiglath-pileser. While Israel has been paying heavy tribute to Assyria for some time Tiglath-pileser is interested in the expansion possibilities as well as monetary gains. He captures much of the northern part of Israel and deports the peoples to Assyria. In the end it is the attempt by Hoshea (the last king of Israel) to withhold payment as well as to conspire with Egypt (nothing good ever comes from conspiring with Egypt) that spells doom for Samaria. The rebellion is squashed and the nation of Israel/Samaria is destroyed in 722 at the Battle of QuarQuar (Dr.

Freed [Gettysburg College] would be impressed that I still remember that date). Assyria assumes control of the territory. The biblical material lays the blame for this destruction on Israel's sins against HaShem. These are primarily cultic infractions: "They rejected all the commandments of the Lord their God; they made molten idols for themselves – two calves (sound familiar?) – and they made sacred posts (phallic symbols) and they bowed down... and worshipped Baal." They also practiced human sacrifice, Black Magic and other sundry offenses. (2 Kings 17:16-18).

Attention both from the Deuteronomic Historian and the Assyrians now turns to Judah. While Judah appears to be on the same trajectory as the North there are two kings that receive favorable press: Hezekiah (who was already on the throne at the time of the Northern destruction) and Josiah. Hezekiah reportedly attempts to institute reforms aimed at stamping out the worship of foreign deities and eliminating the high places of worship but with little if any success.

During Hezekiah's reign (701 BCE) Assyria's king, Sennacherib invades Judah (2 Kings 18:13 ff). Sennacherib sends envoys to Hezekiah laying out Judah's situation. First, they had relied, once again, on help from Egypt, in an attempt to hold Assyria at bay (obviously unsuccessfully). Secondly, Hezekiah does not have sufficient military assets to do battle with the Assyrians or a god powerful enough to protect them so Hezekiah's only real option is to make peace. A struggle between the prophet Isaiah, who advocates sitting tight and trusting HaShem and Hezekiah ensues. In the end Jerusalem is spared destruction because of the heavy tribute Hezekiah agrees to pay the Assyrians.

At age twelve, Manasseh succeeds Hezekiah and reigns for 55 years. We are told (2 Kings 21:11ff) that because of the things that Manasseh did in his reign (which were worse than that of the Amorites) HaShem decrees that he will bring disaster upon Jerusalem and Judah.

Manasseh is followed by Amon who is introduced and dismissed in two paragraphs. This paves the way for Josiah, the hero of the Deuteronomic Historian. Josiah is 8 years old when he ascends the throne and reigns for 31 years. His sweeping reforms include a centralization of the religious cult in Jerusalem as well as a centralizing of the government. It is in Josiah's reign that the Book of the Law (Deuteronomy) is discovered during a Temple housecleaning. This book then becomes the basis of his reforms.

Josiah is killed at the battle of Megiddo when he confronts Pharaoh Neco and the Egyptian forces who are rolling their way to Assyria.

With the intervention of the Egyptians, Josiah's son Jehoiakim (originally Eliakim) becomes king of Judah. Like many of those before him he does what was evil in the sight of HaShem. We are told that King Nebuchadnezzar comes up from Babylon and makes of Judah a vassal state. This goes well for about three years and then Jehoiakim turns and rebels against the Babylonians. At this HaShem releases the fury of the surrounding nations upon Judah

Jehoiakim was succeeded by his son, Jehoiachin who ruled in Jerusalem for only three months. Egypt had been soundly defeated by Babylon and so was unavailable to lend support to Judah. As a result, Nebuchadnezzar marched straight to Jerusalem and laid siege to her.

> *King Nebuchadnezzar of Babylon marched against Jerusalem, and the city came under siege, King Nebuchadnezzar advanced against the city while his troops were besieging it. Thereupon King Jehoachin of Judah, along with his mother, and his courtiers, commanders, and officers, surrendered to the king of Babylon... He carried off from Jerusalem all the treasures of the House of Lord and the treasures of the royal palace; he stripped off the gold decorations of the House of the Lord – which King Solomon of Israel had made – as the Lord had warned. He exiled all of Jerusalem; all the commanders and all the warriors – ten thousand exiles – as well as the craftsmen and smiths; only the poorest people in the land were left. He deported Jehoachin to Babylon; and the king's wives and officers and the notables of the land were brought as exiles from Jerusalem to Babylon. All the able men – all of them trained for battle – and a thousand craftsmen and smiths were brought to Babylon as exiles by the king of Babylon (2 Kings 24:11-16)*

King Nebuchadnezzar appoints Jehoiachin's uncle, Mattaniah, as king in his place and then changes his name to Zedekiah. Zedekiah in turn rebels against the king of Babylon. 2 Kings 25 offers a graphic description of the siege of Jerusalem ending with, *"On the seventh day of the fifth month…Nebuzaradan, the chief of the guards, an officer of the king of Babylon, came to Jerusalem. He burned the House of the Lord, the king's palace, and all the houses of Jerusalem. He burned down the house of every notable person."* (2 Kings 25:8-9). The remnant of the people was then taken into exile in Babylon.

THE LATER PROPHETS

Isaiah

The book of Isaiah is one of the more complicated books in the Tanakh. It is the work of at least two but perhaps as many as four or five different authors. It covers a span of time from the incursions of the Assyrian Empire, through the Babylonian exile and the subsequent deliverance at the hands the Persian Empire. As such there is pre-exilic material, exilic material as well as post-exilic material. It is customary to break the book into two and perhaps three major sections depending on the scholarship.

The work of the prophet known as Isaiah, the prophet of the eighth century BCE often referred to as First Isaiah, has traditionally been identified with chapters 1 through 39. This material is seen within the context of Judah's engagement with the Assyrian Empire between the years 742 and 701 BCE. Chapters 40 through 55, referred to commonly as Second Isaiah, is believed to have been written, or collected, by the end of the Babylonian exile and the rise of the Persian Empire. A date around 540 BCE is generally accepted today for this material. Third Isaiah, chapters 56 through 66, deals with the return from exile and the very difficult task of reestablishing a faithful community in Judah. The material in this collection dates probably around the year 520 BCE.

When we look at Isaiah we have not only three bodies of material, written in three different time periods, but we also have three very distinct messages being delivered. First Isaiah is a word of judgment and encouragement to trust in the faithfulness of HaShem. Second Isaiah, written during the exile in Babylon, is a word of hope for the anticipated release from exile and return to Jerusalem. Third Isaiah, written following the return from exile, is a word of encouragement in the face of the conditions that the exiles have encountered in the return to their homeland.

First Isaiah (1-39)

As we turn our attention to First Isaiah (chapters 1 - 39) we find a combination of rhetorical and historical materials interwoven in such a way as to describe the conditions within Judah and Jerusalem that led to the eventual destruction of the Jerusalem Temple and the Babylonian exile. We are told in the prologue that the prophecies of Isaiah span the reigns of four kings of Judah: Uzziah, Jotham, Ahaz and Hezeikiah.

The opening chapter of Isaiah is a lament over the loss of the northern kingdom of Israel at the hands of the Assyrians in 722 BCE under the leadership of Sargon II. This lament changes its tune in verse eight and becomes a word of judgment and warning for Zion (Judah). Jerusalem is compared to Sodom and Gomorrah as a place where right worship and sacrifice to HaShem has not produced the fruits of justice for the widow and orphan.

Chapter 2 contains a collection of prophecies attributed to the prophet concerning Judah and Jerusalem. As the continuing situation with the Assyrians escalates the Jerusalem Temple will become a symbol of security. Many will take comfort in its towering presence as a symbol of HaShem's dwelling with his people. Isaiah claims that this confidence is misplaced as HaShem is already being supplanted by the introduction of foreign worship practices. Rather than looking to the mountain of HaShem for help the people would be better off to dig holes in the ground for themselves. Even now HaShem has set the time for the great and terrible day. On that day only HaShem will be exalted so do not put your trust in mere mortals or temporal structures.

Chapter 3 continues the mood that has been set as it describes the dismantling of the current political, religious and social structure at the hands of HaShem. Chapter 4 uses images from HaShem's encounter with Moses on Mount Sinai to speak of his protection of the faithful from Israel as well as Judah and Jerusalem.

One of the most beautiful, if not a bit disturbing, pieces of poetry in the entire Tanakh is to be found in Chapter 5 in a piece that is often entitled the Song of the Vineyard. The image of Judah as a vineyard established here will become a favorite image not only in the Tanakh but in the New Testament as well. Many of the parables of Jesus will play heavily on the image of HaShem's people as the Vineyard. The opening lines speak of HaShem planting a beautiful Vineyard, caring for and tending it. At the same time these choice vines have failed to produce fruit. This failure to produce fruit (justice) will force HaShem to decisively deal with the Vineyard. The song speaks of impending exile and HaShem's willingness to use a foreign power to execute his justice. The days to come will be filled with distressing darkness.

In the year that King Uzziah died, we are told of Isaiah's call in the temple. In very dramatic and picturesque language we hear of Isaiah's encounter with the divine presence. In the midst of the incense of the Temple sacrifice we hear the song, "Holy holy holy! The Lord of Hosts! His presence fills all the earth!" This brings Isaiah to his knees and the claim that HaShem certainly must have the wrong man, for he is a man of unclean lips, ushers from his mouth. A hot coal from the brazier is taken by one of the attendants and placed on Isaiah's lips with the announcement that his uncleanness is now burned away. This forgiveness is followed by the backhanded call by HaShem which comes in the form of a question, "Whom shall I send?" Isaiah responds with a standard liturgical answer which by now we should recognize as five of the most dangerous words in Scripture, "Here am I; send me." HaShem then outlines the prophet's agenda.

Chapter 7 introduces one of the main themes of First Isaiah, and the major reason for its eventual downfall, namely a failure to trust HaShem and instead rely on political intrigue. A bit of a historical excursus is in need at this point. Tiglath-Pileser II of Assyria turns his attention to the kingdoms to his west including Israel, Damascus, and Judah. In an effort to fend off his advances Pekah, king of Israel, and Rezin, king of Damascus, form an alliance and invite Judah to join. When King Ahaz declines the invitation Pekah and Rezin attack Jerusalem. Ahaz in turn appeals to Tiglath-Pileser II for aid. The rebellion is put down in 722 BCE. Israel (Northern Kingdom) is conquered and crushed. Isaiah then is called to address the situation. Isaiah's words to King Ahaz are essentially, "Chill out, King. HaShem has this one under control. In fact, I'm willing to give you a sign you want." King Ahaz responds with a pious refusal but Isaiah provides one anyway. In one of the most important passages in the Tanakh for New Testament writers, Isaiah points to a young pregnant woman and informs Ahaz that before the child born to this woman is able to eat real food this whole thing will blow over. Just sit tight, Mr. King. But alas, good old Ahaz couldn't sit tight and trust in HaShem. The resulting consequences will be devastating.

In the midst of this gloom and doom judgment and impending darkness comes chapter 9 with a brilliant word of light and hope. It speaks of light in the midst of darkness. It speaks of release in the midst of imprisonment. It speaks of victory in the midst of seeming defeat. The image of the child returns in the form of expectation of one who will reign with justice and equity and be blessed by HaShem. Even in the midst of this flash of light there is a dark note of warning. Beginning with verse seven the chapter turns toward the fate of Israel, the Northern Kingdom. Its fate will not be so blessed. While Judah is spared the wrath of the Assyrians, Pekah and Rezin must pay the full price which Isaiah claims is the fury of HaShem.

In the startling revelation HaShem reveals that Assyria has been the rod of his anger, *his* agent against those who failed to practice justice. However, Assyria would have its day when it to would face the wrath of HaShem. When all had been fulfilled for Jerusalem he would turn his attention to the arrogant king of Assyria. As he had done with the Egyptians by the sea, so would HaShem's anger burn hot against Assyria.

The expectation of a coming king who will bear the mark, if not the lineage, of the great King David is introduced in chapter 11. This will be a king of justice who shall restore Judah to its place of prominence over all the nations of the earth. In those days this king shall gather all those exiles who have already been scattered from their homeland. Like Moses before him he will dry up the Euphrates River and usher his people home from Assyria. There is some speculation that King Josiah was expected to fulfill this role and in many ways, did as the last great King of Judah. Chapter 12 then becomes a bit of a celebratory postscript.

A series of pronouncements or judgments against the nations begins in chapter 13 and continues through chapter 28. These will include indictments against Babylon, Philistia, Moab, Damascus, Ethiopia, Egypt,

Dumah, Kedar, Judah, Tyre, and Ephraim. These graphic and brutal pronouncements are punctuated by HaShem's faithfulness to Judah and the House of Jacob. For them there will be a day when oppression will end (including that of Babylon). A dire prediction for the fate of the world, worthy of Revelation, is unveiled in chapter 24. This chapter ends, as does Revelation, with the revealing of the presence of HaShem on the Temple Mount in Jerusalem.

Chapter 25 introduces a vision of a new Jerusalem that will become the basis for the later image of the messianic banquet. As with the victory over Pharaoh and the Egyptians at the sea which prompts Miriam to break into song, so this day of the Lord will inspire the entire nation of Judah to erupt in the communal thanksgiving of chapter 26. This chapter ends with a reminder that it will be but a moment before all the indignation passes and Judah can rejoice.

Any doubt if this section of Isaiah is apocalyptic is dispensed with in chapter 27 where Isaiah introduces the elusive serpent, Leviathan. Here Leviathan, or the Dragon of the sea, is the embodiment of chaos. Like the watery chaos that covered the earth the creation, the presence of Leviathan bears witness to these forces of evil and that they continue into the present age. In the final days the Leviathan will be slain by HaShem and his vineyard will again become a vineyard of delight, Israel shall sprout and blossom, Jakob's sins shall be absolved and those who have been scattered from Egypt to Babylon will return to the Mount of Jerusalem.

Apocalyptic foreboding returns in chapter 28 with the pending judgment on Israel *and* Judah. Chapter 29 opens, dripping with lament, "Ah, Jerusalem, Jerusalem..." (This same opening line will be used by Jesus in the gospels as he too laments over Jerusalem). Still even in the midst of this judgment there is hope for those who remain faithful - a day of deliverance awaits them.

Chapter 30 returns us once again to one of Isaiah's favorite rants, the refusal to trust HaShem and instead putting their trust in political wheeling and dealing (especially with Egypt). In this chapter they are reminded that since it didn't work the first time (when there arose a Pharaoh who did not know Joseph), why should the leaders of Judah believe that it will work this time? The bottom line is - Egypt cannot be trusted. Only disaster can come out of such an arrangement. Stand fast in the faith, keep the commandments and the people of Judah will be singing. Fail to do this and the stench left will be reminiscent of Sodom and Gomorrah. This lament of judgment continues through chapter 34 when once again the mood changes.

A beautiful homecoming to the Kingdom of Shalom is what we find in chapter 35. In a very familiar passage the image of a desert bursting into bloom changes the bleak landscape, the weak becoming strong, the infirmed are healed, the desert watered and a highway laid out for the exiles to return. In many ways this chapter could easily fit in the material which we call Second Isaiah. Its imagery and message offer hope not only to those already exiled in Assyria but also to those who will find themselves in exile in Babylon.

King Hezekiah is introduced by name for the first time to us in chapter 36. Here we are told of King Sennacherib of Assyria's invasion of Judah. In mocking tones, the king of Assyria picks up the theme of the futility of a Judah/Egyptian alliance. Hezekiah's response to the impending crisis is to fast and pray in the hope that HaShem will deliver them from the hands of the Assyrians. In verse 21 and following we hear in a message from Isaiah to Hezekiah of HaShem's judgment against Sennacherib and his blasphemous tirade: "It's time for you to start packing your bags because I'm gonna put a hook in your nose and drag you back where you came from" We are told that Sennacherib breaks off the siege retreats to Nineveh where he is assassinated by his sons.

Hezekiah falls dangerously ill and Isaiah informs him that the time has come to put his affairs in order for he is about to die. Hezekiah's response is to pray for deliverance and in 38:5 it is revealed to him that HaShem has heard his prayers and will add 15 years to his life. Hezekiah responds to this good news with the beautiful poem in verses 10 – 20.

In the final chapter of First Isaiah an envoy from Babylon arrives at Hezekiah's palace and is given the royal treatment including a tour of the kingdom's riches. When Isaiah hears of this he chews the King out and with dark foreshadowing proclaims, *"The time is coming when everything in your palace, which our ancestors have stored up to this day, will be carried off to Babylon; nothing will be left behind"* (Isaiah 39:6). Hezekiah's response to Isaiah is that all is well for HaShem's word is for another time, not

Hezekiah's time. To quote a popular saying, "Not my circus. Not my monkeys." Not my problem!

[Intermission: 160 years]

We find ourselves in a 160-year intermission between the end of First Isaiah and the beginning of Second Isaiah. This period is marked by the battle of superpowers. Assyria, the bane of Judah's existence throughout First Isaiah, manages to self-destruct in the seventh century BCE and its capital city Nineveh is destroyed. This allows for the rise of the Babylonian Empire under the leadership of Nebuchadnezzar and in 598 BCE he undertakes the invasion of Judah. In the year 587 BCE, Nebuchadnezzar destroys the city of Jerusalem devastating Judah politically, socially and theologically. Not only is the infrastructure destroyed but so too the dynasty and the promises of HaShem. Most of the leading citizens of Jerusalem were deported to Babylon with the remaining population scattered and exiled to other places. In Second Isaiah the demise of the Babylonian Empire is already anticipated and by the end of the book the Persian Empire, under the leadership of Cyrus, is heralded as the new Empire on the block (and the exiles' savior).

Second Isaiah (40-55)

"Comfort" is not only the opening word of Second Isaiah but it is the mood of the book. This is a book of comfort addressed to exiles in Babylon. It opens with the announcement that the exiles' sentence has been served. A prophetic voice from the wilderness announces the building of the highway through the desert that was prefigured in Isaiah 1. This is to be a highway to welcome back the presence of HaShem. If there was a lingering question as to whether HaShem had left the building it is now clear that he is back with his people.

A sentinel is called by HaShem to proclaim the good news. In the ensuing exchange (which will become very familiar language as we talk about the Wisdom literature of the Writings) he ponders what he should cry. His affirmation is that all human life is transient and that the only thing we can count on is the breath of HaShem, the word of HaShem.

In a rather startling announcement that will be echoed in Jeremiah and Ezekiel the sentinel is instructed to announce that HaShem is taking over as Shepherd/King. The remainder of chapter 40 is a question and answer comparison of the status of humanity over and against HaShem. The familiar close of the chapter, verses 28 – 31, uses creator language to speak of the faithfulness of HaShem's promises even in the midst of human weariness and surrender. HaShem is about to deliver.

In chapter 41 we catch a glimpse of how this deliverance is to be accomplished. HaShem is even now raising up a victor from the East, who we recognize as Cyrus of Persia, to release the exiles. In verse eight we have an interesting construction: "But you, Israel, my servant, Jacob, whom I have chosen, Seed of Abraham." What makes this important is the appeal to Abraham and not to Moses. This shifting in Second Isaiah is a major shift in emphasis that occurs during the exile. The appeal to Abraham, over and against Moses, signifies a more universal claim to HaShem's realm. The Mosaic covenant was closely connected to the Temple Jerusalem whereas the Abrahamic covenant could easily be extended to include even the exiles in Babylon. After all Abraham was called out of the land of Ur to establish HaShem's people in the first place. The conclusion of the chapter again plays heavily on the imagery of a desert called into new life, producing an abundance of water and foliage. HaShem declares that all of this is as he has foretold.

One of the unique features of second Isaiah is the incorporation of what are called Servant Songs or references to a suffering servant. The identity of the servant is not clear. Is it the prophet? Is it Judah? Is it the people of HaShem in general? The New Testament writers and the early Church Fathers will identify this servant with the personage of Jesus.

The first of the servant songs is found in Chapter 42. This servant is one who practices passive or nonviolent resistance. The servant has been called by God to rescue the prisoners and those who sit in darkness. The actor in this servant song is not the servant but rather HaShem who will take on the enemy himself.

With allusions to the Exodus, chapter 43 leads the people figuratively into the promised land where HaShem is in charge. This people, called out of exile, are now to be witness to HaShem's power. This witness language is reminiscent of the courtroom rhetoric that we found first in chapter 41.

HaShem's virtues and victories are extolled, not the least of which this is deliverance of the people by making a road through the sea. (Note how the author parallels the image of the road through the sea and the road through the desert. Those returning from exile in Babylon over the road of the desert were prefigured by God's actions in the book of Exodus as the exiles from Egypt escape over the road through the water)

Idols are the topic of conversation in chapter 44. Idols made by hand out of wood, stone, or metal are contrasted with the living HaShem – who can compare? It is HaShem, the creator, who has promised Jerusalem that she will be re-inhabited, that Judah will be rebuilt, that chaos shall be subdued, that Cyrus will be called to lead his people out, that Jerusalem will be rebuilt and that the Temple shall be reestablished.

Cyrus is the one addressed by HaShem in chapter 45. HaShem makes it clear that Cyrus will be duly compensated for doing HaShem's bidding but he must not be mistaken in thinking that any of this is his own doing – "I am the Lord," says HaShem. Those who forget this are destined to end up like so many broken potsherds. The remainder of chapter 45 is a recital of the glory of HaShem that I believe is in response to feedback that perhaps using Cyrus is not that good of an idea after all. The language is reminiscent of the "Whirlwind" speech in Job where Job also is questioning the actions of HaShem. Similar messages are now addressed to the House of Jacob in chapter 46 and to the Babylonians in chapter 47. Remember who is in charge!

HaShem offers to the House of Jacob a locker room speech in chapter 48. A series of "What I have done for you…" and "What I'm about to do for you…" entries are followed by the command to get out of here (Babylon)! This dramatic exit is also reminiscent of the language of the Exodus departure. As they go, however, they are to be proclaiming that it was HaShem who redeemed his servant Jacob!

The coastlands, the nations of the world, are those addressed in chapter 49. However, the servant must be addressed before the nations. The servant is lamenting the fact that his efforts in working with the House of Jacob have been in vain. In typical HaShem fashion the servant is informed that HaShem has underestimated the scope of his task and rather than just being called to the 12 tribes of Jacob he is now to be sent to the whole world – a light of the nations. Having received a new call, the servant is now given the message which he is to proclaim: The nations are to be put on notice that HaShem is the boss. Using the images mother and child as well as bride, HaShem speaks to the House of Jacob of his faithfulness and enduring love.

This faithfulness and enduring love are challenged by claims of HaShem's abandonment of his people. The accusation is met with a question, "When did I divorce you?" Chapter 50 reminds the people that HaShem did not desert them but they were sold off for their sins/crimes. Again, questions of HaShem's potency are answered by the recitation of previous acts of power. The servant song that begins in verse four speaks of one who has been called to sustain the weary with the word of HaShem. There is nothing special about the servant either in appearance or behavior that one should take notice. It will be HaShem who will be the vindicator, leaving no one to pronounce a verdict against the servant.

Abraham and Sarah are again appealed to in chapter 51 as the foundation for the people's claims. HaShem reminds his people that he has brought comfort and has restored them to the veritable paradise of Eden. This promised triumph is at hand and the people should look to the heavens in anticipation. The call is to be awake in preparation, for as it was in the days of creation so now HaShem is about to act. The one who brings comfort also brings deliverance.

We find a wake-up call in chapter 52, a call to shake off the dust, but this time the audience is Jerusalem itself. The exile was once again compared to the sojourn in Egypt and HaShem's deliverance to that of Moses. The message of the day however is that this deliverance is at hand. Welcomed on the Temple Mount is God's messenger who brings the good news. It is a time for the ruin of Jerusalem to rejoice for she is to be redeemed. Soon even the vessels from the Temple shall be returned. HaShem will go before them and protect their flank as he accompanied the Exodus people by a pillar of cloud by day and a pillar of fire by night.

"Who can believe what we have heard?" The end of the exile is incomprehensible to those who spent their life in Babylon. The suffering servant of chapter 53 has borne the guilt of his people and his righteousness will make many righteous, he has borne the sins of many and makes intercession for the sinners. It is no wonder that this servant song is used to describe the salvation made possible in Jesus' life and death.

Barrenness shall give way to fruitfulness, there will be a need for expansion for HaShem is calling his people back to him. As HaShem promised that he would no longer destroy the earth (Noah) so he has kept his promise to restore the exiles. Reconstruction projects lie ahead even as the next generation become a new wave of disciples to HaShem (no longer do they need to worry if their children will have faith). No fear of oppression in the future for no weapon shall succeed against the power of HaShem.

Second Isaiah closes with a "Ya'll Come" invitation to all who are in need. Come to the new Jerusalem and enjoy its fruits free of charge. Nations shall be summoned and will come running. The wicked shall give up their wicked ways. This is all impossible! "My ways are not your ways," reminds HaShem. No, we cannot comprehend the grace and mercy of HaShem. Our task is to witness to it and to raise our voices in songs of celebration.

Third Isaiah (56-66)

The material of Third Isaiah is attributed to a time just after the return and restoration of the community in Jerusalem following the Exile. The dates often given are between 522- 516 BCE, which are the dates for the rebuilding of the Temple and 444 BCE which reflects the restoration of the community under Ezra Nehemiah. Current scholarship pushes for a date somewhere in the early 520s BCE.

The crisis which the returning exiles faced was that the land was not empty (as it was not empty in the time of the Conquest). There were those who were never deported as well as new arrivals from other countries. The question of status among all these peoples becomes a major concern during this time. Are those who were exiled in some ways more faithful than those who remained? Do they enjoy an elevated status in the eyes of HaShem? This is a dominant question.

Walter Brueggemann in his commentary on Isaiah speaks of three distinct units in third Isaiah. The central unit is comprised of chapter 60 through 62 and is highly reminiscent of second Isaiah in both its promises and its mood. The theme of this section is that HaShem will bring forth a new emerging Judaism. Chapters 56 through 59 highlight the disputes that are already dominating this emerging Judaism: Torah obedience shapes the ethical demands of this new community especially around issues of inclusiveness and neighborly needs. Finally, chapters 63 through 66 focus on vision and dispute in the budding Judaism.

The language of the early chapters of third Isaiah is also reflective of the Wisdom literature of the Writings. It addresses a faith in action or "Where is it that my faith hits the road?" Justice is to be the name of the game in this new community. It is a justice for insiders as well as outsiders. Foreigners are welcome.

Sabbath observance becomes highly significant. While in exile Sabbath keeping in the midst of the military-industrial complex that operated on a 24/7 schedule quickly set the Jews apart from the Babylonians. Sabbath keeping became then a hallmark of Babylonian Judaism. What does it mean to be faithful? Keep the Sabbath. This then is carried over into the restored communities of the emerging Judaism. It also explains why Jesus and his disciples get into so much trouble when they challenge the finer points of Sabbath Law.

It seems that in the interim worship life has gone amok. Issues of child sacrifice, foreign deities, incantations and spells have become the bill of fare but these abominations must give way to the laws of HaShem. Do this and the community will flourish; it will be a light like the dawn. HaShem will hear the cries of his people and he will rebuild the ancient ruins.

This first section closes with a covenant renewal. *"And this shall be my covenant with them said HaShem: my spirit which is upon you, and the words which I placed in your mouth, shall not be absent from your mouth, nor from the mouth of your children, nor from the mouth of your children's children – says HaShem – from now on, for all time"* (Isaiah 59:21).

The centerpiece of third Isaiah, chapter 60 through 62 begins with the now familiar "arise-and- shine" call. No matter how dark it gets in the rest of the world the presence of HaShem shines upon his people. Look around and you will see all that the Lord has done and continues to do. Even now foreigners are supporting the work of rebuilding including the rebuilding of the Temple. The close of chapter 60 becomes an image used in the book of Revelation from the New Testament that speaks of the glory of HaShem being such that the sun is no longer needed to light the day or the moon the night.

We have again a servant song in chapter 61 which is a call to herald the good news of HaShem. The comfort which was delivered to the exiles is now to be communicated to all, particularly those in need. Even now HaShem is performing a great reversal of fortune. The actions of HaShem compel the servant to speak, he will not be silent. In typical prophetic form this reversal shall be celebrated or designated by the reception of a new name. No longer shall HaShem's people be called "Forsaken" or their land "Desolate" but rather they shall be called by a new name" I delight in her "and the land "Espoused." The watchman is instructed to mount the walls and to watch for the coming deliverer.

The final section of third Isaiah, chapter 63 through 66 focus on the vision of this new emerging Judaism. The past performance of HaShem is rehearsed as well as a yearning for the return to the good old days. Chapters 65 and 66 return to the theme of correct worship practices in the new Jerusalem.

The close of chapter 66, the book of Third Isaiah, and Isaiah itself returns to an apocalyptic theme. Images of chariots, whirlwinds, fire and sword serve to remind the reader of HaShem's power and rage. The task now before the people of HaShem is to gather the nations for HaShem is the god of nations and not just of the people of Judah. Again, in language that will find itself creeping into Revelation, the book closes on the note of a new heaven and a new earth and a Temple where all the world will come to worship - so says HaShem.

Jeremiah

Like the book of First Isaiah, the book of Jeremiah is a response to the crisis of the last days of Judah and the destruction of Jerusalem in the year 587 BCE. The collapse of the Assyrian Empire opened the door for the Babylonians under Nebuchadnezzar to begin a territorial expansion. Judah became a political football with the Babylonians to the north and Egypt to the south who desires to keep Judah as a buffer zone between themselves and Babylon. After the reign of King Josiah (639 –609) his successors engaged in alliances sometimes with Babylon and other times with Egypt. In 598 Babylon invaded and carried off the son of King Jehoiakim and many of the prominent citizens into exile in Babylon. This would result in growing tensions between those who remained in Judah and the exiles in Babylon. The question becomes who represents the authentic community. In 587 Babylon delivered the crushing and final blow bringing an end to an independent Judah. This final blow was marked by a second exile and the destruction of the Temple in Jerusalem. The crisis was now on.

The prophet Jeremiah belongs to the Northern (Ephraimite) tradition whose roots go back to the Mosaic tradition. Therefore, in Jerusalem, Jeremiah is a political outsider. Jeremiah's reflects a Torah-based political reform which flies in the face of the royal policies of Jerusalem. As with First Isaiah, Jeremiah is concerned with the incipient political brinkmanship which he contrasts with the sovereign power of HaShem.

As we will see, one of the themes within Jeremiah is that of the holy remnant. It envisions the future the faithful Jewish community which will reside as a small and vulnerable community. It will be this community that will carry the future of Judaism. It is not a surprise then that the early Christian community turned to Jeremiah in an effort to frame the life and ministry of Jesus as well as the emerging and fragile Christian community.

In the first chapter we have what should now be a very familiar occurrence, namely the call of the prophet. The form is standard: a call by HaShem, followed by the protest of the prophet (in this case Jeremiah claims to be too young to do the job), followed by HaShem's rectifying of the situation (here he puts his words physically in Jeremiah's mouth himself). The call is not to be a pleasant one for he will be called to uproot and pull down, to destroy and to overthrow, to build and to plant. The call concludes with a series of visionary images: a branch of an almond tree (the word for almond tree is a wordplay that coincides with the watchfulness of HaShem) and a steaming pot tipped southward (disaster will come from the north). HaShem expects Jeremiah to be prepared, but also to know that he will be supported by HaShem in all that he does.

A lament over Jerusalem begins chapter 2. In characteristic language Jeremiah proclaims to Jerusalem HaShem's judgment over them. While HaShem is faithful to the covenant people of Jerusalem, they have failed to keep their end of the bargain. Again, employing the language of the Exodus, Jeremiah condemns the ongoing political wheeling and dealing with first Egypt and then Babylon. The prophet discloses that such behavior will be their downfall.

Using the covenant of marriage as an image, Jeremiah accuses and condemns the nation of whoring with many lovers. Reminding them of the fate of the kingdom of Israel who engaged in similar behavior he lays out the inevitable punishment if they should not turn back to HaShem, their faithful husband and father.

In chapter 4 Jeremiah declares the marks of such a return. If they are willing to repent and return to HaShem then they should proclaim a fast of repentance (even in the face of opposition from the Royal authorities). Upon further reflection HaShem is doubtful of their ability or willingness to return to him. Again, in a long lament over their behaviors HaShem lays out the crimes. HaShem, in chapter 5, again questions why he should forgive this people and not bring retribution to them. For like the house of Israel so the house of Judah has betrayed him. Therefore, HaShem declares that retribution on his part is justified.

Preparations for battle or at least defensive fortifications are called for in chapter 6. The enemy is at hand sweeping down from the north. Yet in the midst of all these preparations the prophet declares that HaShem will take the side of the enemy because of the failure to keep covenant and the perpetuation of their political scheming. No longer are even the sacrifices of the Temple adequate or acceptable to HaShem. HaShem describes Babylon as his appointed refiner. Despite the refining, the end result will be rejected silver, for HaShem has now rejected his people.

The poetic injunction against Judah and Jerusalem now gives way in chapter 7 to narrative. The prophet Jeremiah is instructed to go to the Temple and to call for repentance. In words that will be clearly echoed in Jesus speeches before the Temple, Jeremiah is instructed to point out how easily even these mighty walls can come tumbling down. After all the aberrant behavior the people of Jerusalem still look to the Temple as a place of safety and security. HaShem asks, "Is my house to be a den of thieves?" He reminds them to travel up north to Shiloh and see what happens to temples. In the shadow of the Temple the prophet again returns to the Exodus theme and reminds the people that it was covenant and not sacrifice that preserved HaShem's people in their sojourn.

At the end of chapter 7 and continuing into chapter 8, HaShem announces the impending great and terrible day of judgment. Even in the midst of this time of judgment HaShem demonstrates a compassion and sorrow on behalf of his people. Already in chapter 8 we find strong illusions to the coming deportations and in chapter 9 he definitively unveils the scattering. This exile should usher in a time of lament and morning for nothing can save them from this fate.

In much the same way that Isaiah contrasts man-made idols and HaShem, Jeremiah, now in chapter 10 contrasts the laws of the nations with those of HaShem. In short, man-made laws cannot stand before the Law, Torah of HaShem. Lest they forget what the Torah contains, Jeremiah is instructed to recite the terms of the covenant before the inhabitants of Jerusalem. In a language reminiscent of Deuteronomy, the people are to proclaim these terms throughout all of Judah and Jerusalem. Having heard once again the terms of the covenant the inhabitants of Judah and Jerusalem have had their transgressions revealed in the fate that awaits them will be a disaster which they cannot escape.

Using the language of the courtroom, the doomed inhabitants of Jerusalem dare to present charges against HaShem even though they know that by doing so they will reveal their own guilt. At the end of chapter 12, HaShem responds using the motifs of Shepherd and Vineyard. HaShem's Vineyard (see the song of the Vineyard in Isaiah) has been ravaged by many shepherds/kings. As for these wicked neighbors, HaShem's wrath will uproot them even as it uproots Judah. However, after Judah has been uprooted, HaShem will take them back and restore their inheritance.

In a rather colorful gesture, HaShem in chapter 13 instructs the prophet to go and buy linen underwear. After wearing it for some time the prophet is to take it up north to bury it. After a long time, he is to go back north to get it. What he finds is that the underwear is ruined and not good for anything. HaShem then uses this image to talk about Judah and Jerusalem. They too are ruined and useless. Jerusalem is then referred to as the Queen Mother who will be seized with birth pangs like a woman in labor.

In light of the prophet's indictment it appears that the court prophets are assuring the inhabitants of Jerusalem that these calamities shall not come near them. You can almost hear HaShem's sly laugh as he instructs Jeremiah to tell these prophets they will be left lying in the streets of Jerusalem because of famine and sword with no one left to bury them. This raises the question among the inhabitants of Jerusalem that perhaps

HaShem has indeed spurned them. Again, they ask why HaShem's anger burns hot against them. HaShem's response is to lift up the iniquity of their ancestors and the failure to keep covenant as well has HaShem's superiority over all things (including the nations of the world). This question and claim will be a centerpiece for those living in exile. The twofold question that gets asked is: "What did we do to deserve this?" and "Has HaShem left the building?"

In an apparent reference to the potency of the court prophets HaShem declares in chapter 15 that even intercessors such as Moses and Samuel couldn't change the course of events. The judgment is destined. The fate of Jerusalem will be fourfold: this sword will slay, the dogs will drag, the birds of the sky and the beast of the earth will devour and destroy. Even in the midst of this dire future the prophet speaks of a remnant in 15:11. Then in language reminiscent of the servant songs of Isaiah an unknown plaintiff pleads to HaShem. In return HaShem promises to deliver the faithful (those who produce noble fruits) from the hands of the wicked.

In language that Paul will use later in the New Testament, HaShem announces that this is not a time to be thinking about marriage. In fact, the voice of the bridegroom and the bride, the sounds of mirth and gladness will be silenced. What once was the standard line to describe HaShem's activity during the Exodus as: he brought the Israelites out of the land of Egypt [the mighty arm and an outstretched hand], is now used to describe what HaShem will do in the future when he brings the Israelites out of the north land (Babylon) and out of all the lands to which they have been banished. He will take them back and give them their fathers land. The end of chapter 16 introduces the image of the fisherman. The fisherman will drag the guilty out and the hunter shall hunt them. Once and for all HaShem will display his power and might so that all might know that his name is Lord.

Chapter 17 begins with the image that Judah's guilt has been inscribed upon the tablets of their hearts (no longer stone). This image will again be returned to in chapter 31 where the prophet talks about a new covenant. The wicked and the faithful are contrasted using the images of desert and oasis. The wicked will dry up and wither in the desert heat but those planted by water will send forth their roots into the stream (the fountain of living waters- HaShem). The prophet is now told to go stand by the

People's Gate (the gate through which the kings of Judah enter and leave) and rehearse the Sabbath commandment which it seems the inhabitants of Jerusalem have forgotten.

The image of the Potter is used by HaShem in chapter 18. Jeremiah is to go down to the house of the potter. Watching the potter, he discovers that when the vessel the potter is working on is spoiled the potter is able to rework it to make a new vessel. The question is asked if HaShem can do likewise with the people of Judah. Like clay in the hands of the potter so is Judah in the hands of HaShem. Even as HaShem is devising disaster there is a call to turn. However, once again their actions belie their preference of the plans of humans over those of HaShem.

By the middle of chapter 18 the people of Jerusalem have had enough of Jeremiah. Their first assault will be a war of words. Jeremiah's response is swift. He prays for deliverance even as they are digging the pit. HaShem, please act now! HaShem's response in chapter 19 is to send Jeremiah to buy a jug and then go to the Potsherd Gate and proclaim the word of HaShem. Jeremiah is to lay out HaShem's indictment upon Jerusalem once again and then to smash the pot in the sight of all people. This broken pot attests to HaShem's action regarding the people of Jerusalem; they too shall be smashed and like a clay vessel cannot be mended. Already the dead are piling up until there is no more room. Perhaps the most damning statement is that the city will become unclean.

Following this demonstration Jeremiah goes to bring similar news to the Temple. It is there that he encounters the High Priest, Pashur, son of Emmer, who has Jeremiah arrested and flogged. After his release the next day Jeremiah issues an indictment over Pashur and the religious cult. He announces the imminent exile in Babylon which will sweep up Pashur and all his cronies.

Jeremiah then launches into a rather intense "Why me, Lord?" lament to HaShem for having called him to do this task. He even goes so far as to pray that he wished he'd never been born. As Jeremiah sees it his is calling in life is to spend all his days and shame.

King Zedekiah tries to send Jeremiah as an emissary to Pashur, son of Malchiah and Zephaniah, to see if the priests have any better word about the situation with Babylon than does Jeremiah. If you don't like the word of one prophet you go find one that will match your outcome. Jeremiah's response to Zedekiah is to once again forecast the impending doom at the hand of the Babylonians. Jeremiah also speaks to the people gathered and reminds them of the words uttered by Joshua at the river Jordan before the people cross into the promised land, "I have set before you the way of life in the way of death." If you stay in the city you will die. In his final rant Jeremiah lifts up the primacy of the Torah with its call for justice, a call which the house of the king of Judah has failed to uphold and who will pay the price for his failure.

In chapter 22 HaShem sends Jeremiah to the King to speak with him directly. Zedekiah has failed to practice Torah with regards to justice. Jeremiah's call to the king is to change his behavior. A failure to do so will result in the destruction of the palace.

In perhaps one of the more significant lines in the book of Jeremiah 22:8-9, the prophet projects into the future those who will pass by the destruction of Jerusalem and ask why HaShem would do such a thing to such a great city. The answer given is that they forsook the covenant, Torah. This line encapsulates the message of Jeremiah (as you find yourself bogged down in Jeremiah's continual ranting you may wonder why he simply didn't offer this line in the beginning). Jeremiah continues with similar indictments against successive kings: King Josiah as well as King Coniah.

Chapter 23 reintroduces the image of the shepherd. The shepherd King has not preserved the flock but rather is responsible for scattering them. This image will play heavily again in the book of Ezekiel and later in the Gospels, especially chapter 10 of John's Gospel. HaShem announces that he will assume the position of Shepherd and the task of gathering his people. He would then appoint new shepherds to take care of his gathered flock. In verse five HaShem declares that in the future he will raise up a branch of David's line who will be a deliverer like Moses who brought his people up out of Egypt. The Messiah in the book of Jeremiah is clearly a Mosaic Messiah who will stand in the tradition of both David and Moses and who will be a faithful keeper of Torah.

Jeremiah turns now on the colleagues in his prophetic guild. Essentially these court prophets have been providing the kings the word that the kings want to hear rather than the harsh word of truth. Martin Luther King Jr. centuries after Jeremiah, will use words from this chapter to introduces his famous "I Have a Dream" speech. Here however, Jeremiah uses the image of the dream to refer to the court prophets' fantasies that all would be fine. Jeremiah winds down his tirade against his colleagues as he introduces the term "burden". This term in Hebrew can denote both divine speech as well as a weight that must be carried. The court prophets have assumed that they can speak for HaShem - a claim which Jeremiah vehemently refutes.

Two baskets of figs placed before the Temple becomes the image used by HaShem in chapter 24 – this following the first exile by the Babylonians. The first basket had very good figs, the second basket had very bad figs, so bad that they could not be eaten. HaShem declares that the first basket represents the remnant that he will single out among the Judean exiles in Babylon. This remnant he will bring back from the land of Babylon and will replant them and not uproot them again. The basket of bad figs includes the likes of Zedekiah, his officials and those in Jerusalem who have been left behind. Through violence, famine and disease HaShem will exterminate them from the land.

In chapter 25 we find ourselves in the fourth year of the reign of King Jehoiakim (son of Josiah). Jeremiah addresses the people of Judah first, by calling attention to his twenty-three-year prophetic ministry among them as well as that of many other prophets who called them to be attentive to the Torah. It is their failure to listen to Jeremiah and his colleagues that has left HaShem no choice but to send King Nebuchadnezzar of Babylon in to enact HaShem's justice. HaShem's punishment has limits however. For seventy years they will languish in exile but at the end of 70 years HaShem will bring King Nebuchadnezzar down and Babylon will become a desolation for all time. HaShem then directs Jeremiah to take the word of judgment to all the nations announcing a time of destruction and desolation upon all the nations of the world.

Chapters 26 and 27 take us back to the first year of the reign of Jehoiakim. The mood is hopefulness on the part of HaShem that perhaps after hearing Jeremiah's message the people may repent. We remember from chapter 25 that this will not be the case. Instead of repentance the priests and the prophets revolt against Jeremiah and threaten to kill him. In a line that will be repeated in the New Testament, the priests and the prophets bring charges against Jeremiah saying: "This man deserves the death penalty, for he has prophesied against the city, as you yourselves have heard"(Jeremiah 26:11). Jeremiah claims that he was only speaking the word of HaShem. His argument is found compelling by the officials and he was spared the death sentence. We are told of another prophet, Uriah, who spoke a similar message to that of Jeremiah's but Jehoiakim tracked him all the way to Egypt, dragged him back and put them to death.

In chapter 27 Jeremiah is instructed to put a yoke about his neck and go to the king of Edom and Moab and to pronounce judgment upon them. Like Judah, they too shall fall to King Nebuchadnezzar of Babylon and their religious professionals shall not be able to save them. Using the image of the yoke, Jeremiah speaks to King Zedekiah of Judah, instructing him to submit to the king of Babylon. If he does so he will live, if not all will die. Of special note here is that the vessels from the Temple and from the palace that were not confiscated in the first wave of exile, are to be taken to Babylon and attended to so that they may be brought back by the returning exiles.

Chapter 28 opens with a word from the prophet Hananiah who announces that the exile will be short in duration. In no more than two years HaShem will break the yoke of Babylon. Jeremiah's response is basically, "Oh that HaShem would be so generous… But…. Now hear the word that I've heard from HaShem". In short, Jeremiah says the truth of the prophet's words can only be evidenced in the future. Hananiah, in a power-play, takes the yoke off Jeremiah and breaks it up before the people, announcing that so shall the yoke of Babylon be broken. Jeremiah ups the ante by declaring that Hananiah is not from HaShem and that he shall die (which later that year he does).

A letter sent by Jeremiah to those living in exile is found in Chapter 29. The text of the letter urges the folks to settle into life in Babylon. When the 70 years of exile are up HaShem promises to honor his promise and to bring his people back. This exilic community becomes the remnant from which HaShem will reconstitute the nation after the exile.

In chapter 30 Jeremiah is instructed to take the scroll and write down the words that HaShem will give to him. The text of this scroll is to be about the restoration of HaShem's people to the land of Israel and Judah. HaShem has heard their cries. He will act. He will take from them the yoke and remove their bonds and will establish a new king like David. The people are encouraged not to be dismayed in this time of exile for HaShem will restore the fortunes of the nation. The scroll is continued in chapter 31 with the stacking of images one upon another that proclaim a great reversal of fortune culminating in HaShem gathering his people like a shepherd. For HaShem has heard the cries of Rachel weeping in Ramah, and the lament of Ephraim. As HaShem was quick to uproot and pull down the nation so too will he now build and plant.

In Lutheran circles at least, Jeremiah 31:31- 34, is one of the more famous passages from Jeremiah. It speaks of a new covenant that will be made between HaShem and the house of Israel. It will not be like the covenant that HaShem had made with those whom he brought out of Egypt in the time of Moses. History has shown that they were not able to keep the terms of that covenant. This time the covenant will be written on their hearts and it will be clear to all people that HaShem is their god and they are his people. At that time their sins shall be forgiven and remembered no more.

Chapter 32 finds us in the eighteenth year of the reign of Nebuchadnezzar. Nebuchadnezzar is besieging Jerusalem while Jeremiah is a prisoner in the palace compound. The word of HaShem from Jeremiah becomes a word of judgment of wrath for the city of Jerusalem and its pending destruction. The rest of the chapter details the fate of Jerusalem.

We find Jeremiah is still in jail as chapter 33 opens. The word of HaShem that comes to Jeremiah continues to detail the fate of Jerusalem and Judah at the hands of the Babylonians. However, HaShem promises that after the purge he will pardon all their sins and they will be restored to good fortune. A sign of this restoration will be the raising up of the king from the branch of David, thus restoring the promise of a Davidic dynasty. This new covenant of HaShem cannot be broken unlike the previous covenant. This covenant rose out of the love of HaShem for his people.

Chapter 34 meanders back and forth between prophetic judgment and a word of covenant and restoration. In verse five we hear the institution of the year of Jubilee as a sign of remembrance for HaShem's forgiveness of his people. Every seven years slaves must be set free. Failure to do this will carry a harsh penalty.

HaShem uses the example of the Rechabites faithfulness to their covenant as a model for the faithfulness that he will demand of his people. Because they were faithful to their covenant they now inhabit Jerusalem.

Chapters 36 through 45 comprise a unit of material within the book of Jeremiah often referred to as the Baruch Document. Chapters 36 and 45 provide the book ends with chapter 36 detailing the writing of the document and chapter 45 revealing a special promise to Baruch. The remaining material deals with: the threat of Babylon (chapter 37-40:6); the political intrigue following the destruction of the Temple (40:7-41:8) and the harsh condemnations following the attempts to involve Egypt in the political solution (42:1-44:30).

HaShem instructs Jeremiah to have a scroll prepared to collect the words that HaShem has delivered to Jeremiah. So, Jeremiah calls Baruch to write down Jeremiah's dictation. Because Jeremiah is in hiding for fear of his life, he instructs Baruch to take the scroll to the Temple and to read it before the people. The scroll is confiscated, burned and warrants are issued for the arrest of Jeremiah and Baruch. HaShem hides Jeremiah and Baruch and commissions the writing of a new scroll with further emendations of judgment.

Jeremiah's prophetic utterances concerning HaShem's judgment of Judah at the hands of the Babylonians/Chaldeans lands him in prison for a long time. First in the house of the scribe Jonathan, which has been made into a jail, and later in the prison compound itself. While the officials wish to have Jeremiah put to death because it was bad for morale, King Zedekiah ordered the Jeremiah be put into a pit in the prison compound (somewhat reminiscent of Joseph's fate). We are told there is no water in the pit, only mud. Jeremiah is left sinking into the mud. He is eventually rescued by Ebed-melech, the Cushite. Once again Jeremiah is brought to king. Zedekiah has a question, "Will the Judean defectors hand the king over to the Babylonians?" Jeremiah's response was, "No, so long as you sit tight and listen to the word of HaShem." Jeremiah is returned to prison where he remains until Jerusalem is captured by the Babylonians.

Chapters 39-41 detail the invasion and capture of Judah and Jerusalem by the Babylonians. Jeremiah is among those who are chained and led into exile in Babylon. He is however, released at Ramah by his captors and remains in the land of Mizpah. When Mizapah falls Jeremiah finds himself with a remnant who are heading to Egypt for safety.

In chapter 42 this remnant is warned against going to Egypt, less the same thing that happened with Moses happens to them. In short, you can't trust an Egyptian. Caught between a rock and a hard place, Egypt or Babylon, the remnant opts not to listen to HaShem's orders to return to Judah but rather heads to Egypt, Jeremiah and Baruch among them. This decision will bring judgment upon Egypt as outlined in chapter 43-44. For all his troubles, Baruch is to be spared.

In chapter 46 we embark on a new section of material which continues the judgment against Egypt and the consortium of nations formed to withstand the onslaught of Babylon. This detailed judgment extends all the way to chapter 49.

In chapter 50 Jeremiah's attention turns toward the Babylonians and the exiles to be found in Babylon. Jeremiah announces that the day is coming when the exiles will be set free. When that day comes they are to flee Babylon for Babylon itself is to be destroyed. Babylon, the instrument of HaShem's judgment, will now be treated harshly for their treatment of the exiles. In verse 41 the Persian Empire is alluded to as the instrument of HaShem's judgment upon Babylon. Chapter 51 details the destruction of Babylon. Once read, the scroll which Jeremiah sends to Babylon is thrown into the Euphrates River as a final sign of judgment.

Chapter 52 serves as the dénouement for the book of Jeremiah. In it we have a summary of the final days of Judah, the destruction of Judah by the Babylonians and the exile of over 4,600 Judeans. The book closes on a rather tender note as it reveals that in the thirty-seventh year of the exile King Jehoiachin of Judah is released from prison and regularly dines with the king of Babylon for the remainder of his days.

Ezekiel

In many ways the books of Jeremiah and Lamentations should be prerequisite reading for understanding the pathos of the book of Ezekiel. The political machinations of Jeremiah and the overt angst of Lamentations serve as backdrop for the drama that will unfold in the book of Ezekiel.

Ezekiel is a thirty-something prophet from the Zadokite line of professional priests. When we meet him, he is already in exile in Babylon, the fifth year of exile to be precise. The salient features of the book of Ezekiel are the vivid visions or religious experiences, to use a more modern term, which haunt Ezekiel's ministry. At times they may lead us to wonder if Ezekiel was on an acid trip or perhaps smoking some strong peyote. I believe we are better served by trying to enter the experience rather than to decipher or understand the vision

As we meet Ezekiel he is in the throes of one of these spectacular visions. The images are of a fiery chariot and throne, consistent images of the presence of the divine throughout the Middle East at this time. The sum and substance of the introduction in chapter 1 is to say that Ezekiel and we are standing in the presence of the most high HaShem. It's time to listen.

Chapters 2 and 3 constitute the content of the vision and Ezekiel's call to the prophetic ministry. Some of the features of this vision include: the giving of the prophetic spirit charism to Ezekiel, the reminder that all may not be receptive to what the prophet has to say, the eating of the scroll/word of HaShem and that this call is to the house of Israel who are hardheaded, hardhearted and a rebellious breed. In 3:12 and following we have essentially a vision within a vision. Ezekiel is carried away and finds himself once again in the raw presence of HaShem. He is teleported to the particular exile community that is dwelling by the Chebar Canal. It is there that Ezekiel sits stunned for seven days waiting to hear from HaShem.

HaShem appoints Ezekiel as the watchmen for the house of Israel and he is to warn them of HaShem's judgment against wickedness. If Ezekiel fails to do that the judgment will fall upon him (high-stakes prophet-ing at its best!). As with previous prophets Ezekiel is given a series of object lessons with which to make HaShem's point. The first of these is a brick with the name of the city Jerusalem written on it. In a scene which conjures up images of playing with army men as a child, Ezekiel is to lay siege now to the brick/Jerusalem. He is then to lie on his left side and take the punishment for the house of Israel, a punishment that will last 390 days. He then is to bake bread and eat of this ration for 390 days. This bread is to be baked on human excrement so to make it clear that this is unclean bread. The prophet then is instructed to shave both beard and head as well to take threads from the peoples' garments to use for kindling fires around the miniature Jerusalem. HaShem's announcement is that the fire has now gone out upon the whole house of Israel. Confused yet? Ezekiel essentially is given the ability to see what is going on in Jerusalem while he himself is in exile. While the fire has gone out in Jerusalem, (HaShem has left the building), in the image of the chariot, HaShem is now capable of being mobile even to the point of showing up in Babylon.

The prophet is to remind the people that HaShem has set them up in the midst of the nations as a nation above nations but because of their failure to observe Torah they must now pay the price. The Babylonians will indeed be successful in their siege of Jerusalem. The prophet is also to address those sanctuaries and communities outside of Jerusalem so that they are aware that a similar fate awaits them for their behavior as well. Doom! is the word of chapter 7. Doom is coming! Even now the chains of bondage are being forged by their unfaithfulness.

We are introduced to a second vision in chapters 8-11. Like Ebenezer Scrooge, Ezekiel is visited by a figure while sitting in the comforts of his home surrounded by the elders. The apparition is on fire and has the appearance of amber. He grabs Ezekiel by the hair and spirits him off to Jerusalem. He is made to look at the abominations that are occurring in Jerusalem. Ezekiel finds himself joined by cherubs and the presence of HaShem. Ezekiel must watch as judgment is executed. HaShem's judgment is relentless even in the face of his people's protests.

In chapter 12 Ezekiel is told to prepare himself for exile; pack a suitcase with exile gear and make a spectacle of himself among the people. In this way he is to announce the coming exile to Babylon and that this calamity is a result of their unfaithfulness and the judgment of HaShem. These days will be a time of high anxiety and messing of one's britches. Chapter 13 warns of those prophets who will speak a conciliatory word of comfort… they are misled! Ezekiel announces a call to repentance and return which will be judged on an individual basis but Jerusalem's fate is sealed.

Using the image, the grapevine in chapter 15, reminiscent to Isaiah's vineyard image, Ezekiel announces the fate of Jerusalem. Like grapevines burned in the fire, Jerusalem will become good for nothing.

All the inhabitants of the land originated and are birthed from the land of the Canaanites. HaShem chose them and cared for them as his own people. Chapter 16 outlines his care for this people in the days of their youth. Despite all that HaShem had done for them this nation played the harlot with every Tom Dick and Harry nation around them. How HaShem must have anguished at their betrayal? If there is any doubt how the nation's action affected HaShem? The remainder of chapter 16 makes it clear that they will pay.

Ezekiel uses an allegorical image of two eagles to explain the realities of Jerusalem's fate in chapter 17. The attempt to woo Egypt into an alliance and Egypt's subsequent betrayal of the deal are lifted up as one more sign of Jerusalem's unfaithfulness and prostitution of itself.

Chapter 18 deals with the issue of personal versus corporate unfaithfulness. At issue is the fate of the unrighteous one who repents over and against the righteous one who falls from grace. The fate of the former is life; the fate of the latter is death. This is seen by the community as unfair, to which HaShem replies that he would rather not see anyone die, so therefore repent and live.

A musical dirge forms Chapter 19 and constitutes a summary of the preceding eighteen chapters. In compact form it speaks of the fate of the Lion of Judah and its subsequent relocation. Far from abundant waters, it now finds itself in the Babylon deserts. Chapter 20 then goes on to provide a more detailed description of the relationship between HaShem and his people beginning with their sojourn into Egypt and subsequent deliverance. It is clear in this description that failing to follow the laws of Moses has produced the conditions for Judah's downfall. As HaShem brought his people out of Egypt with a mighty arm and an outstretched hand, he will now lead them into judgment and exile. Chapters 21 and 22 continue a detailed description of this judgment.

We are introduced to two daughters, Oholah [tent] and Oholibah [my tent is in her] in chapter 23. In a rather bawdy "R" rated version the behavior, the fate of the nations of Israel and Judah is graphically played out.

The image of a cauldron is introduced in chapter 24 as an allegory for the rebellious breed of Judah. The prophet is instructed to take a cauldron filled with the choicest cuts of meat, cook the meat thoroughly, remove the meat and place the empty cauldron back on the fire. Even this will not purify the cauldron/nation.

In characteristic fashion of the prophetic office, the prophet's life often becomes a parable in and of itself. In 24:15 Ezekiel's wife dies and he is told by HaShem not to mourn her death. In the same way Jerusalem's death is not to be mourned.

HaShem's judgment will not be confined only to the House of Israel. The nations of Ammon, Moab, Edom, Philistea, Tyre, Sidon and Egypt; all those who would stood and cheered at the demise of Judah, shall meet the judgment of HaShem and his servant Nebuchadnezzar of Babylon (chapters 25-29).

Chapter 30 introduces the Day of the Lord into the discussion. Again, this day of the Lord will be a universal day of judgment encompassing all the known world. No one will go unaffected. This judgment will fall particularly harsh upon the nation of Egypt as the prophet outlines in chapters 31 and 32. In language reminiscent of the Exodus, HaShem promises to strike terror upon the land of the living of Pharaoh and all his army.

The prophetic word changes audiences in chapter 33 back to Ezekiel's countrymen. Ezekiel's call from chapter 1 is reiterated as is a summary of his judgments upon the house of Israel. In verse 21 we are told that in the twelfth year of Ezekiel's exile he received news that Jerusalem has fallen. The fate of Jerusalem's fall will be that of desolation. All of this shall be a sign that validates the word of the prophet, "When these things come to pass - and they will – they should know that a prophet has been among them."

In chapter 34 the audience changes once again to that of the king. Using the traditional image of the shepherd, Ezekiel delivers a harsh indictment against the Royal leadership. The accusation is that instead of tending the flock the kings have been tending themselves and their own needs. This behavior has left a weakened and injured flock who have strayed and gotten lost in the process. The shepherds also have done nothing to rectify the situation. The deportations in Israel at the hand of the Assyrians and the exile of the Judeans to Babylon have resulted in HaShem's people/sheep being scattered all over the face of the earth. HaShem promises not to sit idly by and let this continue. Instead HaShem is prepared to become the shepherd of his flock, to seek them out from where they have been scattered and to rescue them from the jaws of their predators. He will gather them in and return them to the hills of Israel where they shall find good grazing land and an attentive shepherd.

In the latter half of the chapter HaShem turns his attention from the shepherds to the flock. There will be a judgment process among the members of HaShem's flock. Those who have pushed with flank and shoulder to obtain for themselves the best grazing land at the expense of the weaker sheep will be judged and those who have been scattered by such behavior will be returned to the flock. This theme of judgment of the sheep will be picked up by Matthew in chapter twenty-five of his gospel as he uses the image to talk about the final judgment.

The final verses of the chapter attend to the promise of a single shepherd in the image of David who will become ruler among them. A new covenant will be established and blessings shall ensue that will produce a land reminiscent of the Paradise of Genesis.

For their crimes against Judah prior to the exile the Edomites, residents of Mount Seir, will face harsh punishment at the hand of HaShem (chapter 35). The land shall become desolate at which the whole earth will rejoice. This indictment continues into chapter 36. The prophet is instructed to reveal to Israel the nature of Edom's punishment. There will be a reversal of fortunes to the extent that Israel's desolate plains will blossom and flourish and the rich lands of Edom will become desolate. It is very clear however that HaShem's action is not predicated on the righteousness of Israel (they were as unclean as a menstruous woman) but rather that HaShem's holy name might once again be restored. HaShem will therefore cleanse what is unclean, put a new spirit within his people and call them into a right practice of Torah. This accomplished, they shall dwell in the land that he will give them and they shall multiply like sheep. Then all shall know that HaShem is Lord.

Ezekiel's vision of the valley of dry bones (chapter 37) is perhaps the most famous of all of his visions. Addressed in part to the exiles, it reflects their current situation of discouragement and hopelessness. The word addressed to Ezekiel in the vision is that even now HaShem is in the process of rattling the bones of this people with self-identification is: our bones are dried up; our hope is gone; we are doomed. The announcement is that HaShem is about to open their graves, bring them back to life, and return them to their home soil. The prophet is then instructed to use sticks as a visual aid to illustrate how he will bring together the two scattered kingdoms into one. This unified kingdom will have one shepherd like David, and they will faithfully obey Torah. They will be fruitful and multiply there and the presence of HaShem shall dwell once again in his sanctuary.

Chapters 38 and 39 introduce the land of Gog and Magog. This fictional land is often associated with the Scythians of the far north. These chapters detail this land's rise to power, assault on Israel and its utter destruction at the hands of HaShem. The book of Revelation in the New Testament will reference this land as part of an apocalyptic vision.

Chapters 40 through 46 present a vision of the new Temple. In precise detail the layout of the new Temple is disclosed to Ezekiel. This description is punctuated by the highlighting of various rooms for the priests who will serve there as well as the dedication rites that will proceed their use. The selected attire (descended from Zadok) and conduct of the Levitical priests is also described in detail. A liturgical calendar is also to be found in this section outlining the various fees and festivals to be celebrated. Chapter 47 offers a vision of the Temple precinct that also calls to mind the creation found in Genesis.

The remainder of Ezekiel addresses the redistribution of the land, the setting of borders, and the assignment of tribes to inhabit the restored land.

THE BOOK OF THE TWELVE

In the Jewish tradition the remaining 12 prophets in the *Neviim* (Prophets) are collected into what is known as the Book of the Twelve. These 12 prophets include: Hosea, Amos, Micah, Nahum, Habakkuk, Zephaniah, Haggai, Zechariah, Malachi, Joel, Obadiah and Jonah.

The books of Hosea, Amos, and Micah are generally considered to deal with the sins of Israel and are often partnered with the prophet Isaiah. These sins include political promiscuity, economic disregard for the poor and downcast as well as idolatry.

Punishment and divine anger are the themes that unite Nahum, Habakkuk, and Zephaniah. These books are seen as complements to the prophet Jeremiah.

Haggai, Zechariah, and Malachi are prophets of the restoration. Jeremiah 30 – 31, Isaiah 40 – 55, and Ezekiel 40 – 48 would provide similar counterparts to these books.

This leaves the books of Joel, Obadiah, and Jonah as the remaining miscellaneous prophetic books within the collection of the Twelve.

Hosea

In the opening lines of the book we learn that Hosea prophesied during the reign of Jeroboam of Israel as well as during the reigns of Uzziah, Jothan, Ahaz and Hezekiah of Judah. This would put the prophet operating most likely in the years leading up to the destruction of Samaria/Israel in the years 722 BCE.

The book of Hosea is divided into two major sections, chapters 1 through 3 and chapters 4 through 14. The first section contains prophetic material that is illustrated through Hosea's marriage to a prostitute (or a very promiscuous woman at the least). The second section deals primarily with the political and religious life of the Northern Kingdom leading up to its destruction in 722 BCE. These two sections are distinguished from one another by voice – chapters 1 – 3 are recounted in the third person whereas the remaining chapters are first-person narrative.

The prophet Hosea is instructed by HaShem to marry a wife of "whoredom," and Gomer seems to fit the bill. She bears him a son to be named Jezreel as a sign that HaShem will punish the northern kingdom for its deeds in the Valley of Jezreel, where Jehu had slaughtered Jezebel and the royal family. She then bears two daughters. The first is named, "Not Accepted" and the second, "Not My People." Hosea's marriage becomes a metaphor for the relationship between HaShem and the people. Like Gomer, Israel goes whoring after other partners most especially that of Baal. Despite Israel's unfaithfulness and subsequent judgment, HaShem promises to establish a new covenant. In those days the Israelites will turn back and seek the Lord their God and David their king – and they will thrill over the Lord and over his bounty in the days to come.

The remaining chapters of Hosea are comprised of a series of oracles which highlight and indict Israel's unfaithfulness. In chapter 11 we have a soliloquy on the lips of HaShem reminiscing about falling in love with Israel while she was still young which bears witness to the conflicted emotions that HaShem has in dealing with his people. He loves them but is troubled by their behaviors and it will be their behaviors that cause them to be destroyed. Chief among these behaviors is the acceptance of Baal worship in the ongoing reliance on political intrigue with Egypt. In chapter 14, HaShem demands that Samaria/Israel must bear her guilt because of her unfaithfulness to HaShem. It also contains a plea by HaShem to return and to forsake their former ways and return to covenantal life.

Amos

The prophet Amos is identified in the opening lines of the book as a sheep breeder from Tekoa (10 miles south of Jerusalem). It is fairly clear that the locus of Amos' prophetic utterances was that of the sanctuary of Bethel and surrounding sanctuaries (10 miles north of Jerusalem). This means that Amos operated in both the territory of the Northern as well as the Southern Kingdoms. We will find another prophet later in the New Testament operating in a similar manner.

The book of Amos is divided into three major sections: the oracles against the nations (1:3-2:16), a collection of short oracles (3-6) and a series of visions (7-9).

Oracles against the nations were the stock and trade of an Israelite prophet. A prophet who could not conjure up a good oracle against one of Israel's neighbors or Israel itself was not worth his salt. The oracles included in the first section of Amos are addressed to Damascus, Gaza, Tyre, Edom, and then, Moab, Judah, and Israel. The common theme of the oracles' judgment is that of the economic disregard for the poor and needy. This becomes focused in chapter 4 with the introduction of the wonderful image of the cows of Bashan, who lie about on their ivory couches in lavish living and gluttonous eating while all those around them were starving.

The final section of Amos opens with a vision of a plague of locusts, followed by an all-consuming fire and the plumb line. These visions speak to the decisive judgment upon Israel at the hands of HaShem. As a result of his prophesying Amos is driven out of Bethel back to Judah where HaShem summarily sends him back to the north. It is there that Amos receives a vision of a basket of figs. The judgment upon Israel is that they devour the needy and annihilate the poor of the land through the manipulation of economic measurements. Because of this behavior HaShem will send a famine upon the land. Chapter 9 finds HaShem standing by the altar at

Bethel whereupon he strikes the altar so that it quakes. At this the final judgment for Israel is disclosed, there is no place they can go and hide that Ha Shem will not find them. As in previous prophets Amos ends with a note of hope and restoration. A remnant shall be preserved and in time HaShem will mend the breach, build up the ruins and a new vineyard will be planted on the soil that he will give them.

Micah

Micah hails from the small town of Moresheth, which lies about 23 miles southwest of Jerusalem. He prophesies concerning Samaria and Jerusalem during the reigns of Jotham, Ahaz, and Hezekiah of Judah. This would make him roughly a contemporary of Isaiah. Unlike Isaiah however, Micah is not tied to the royal court but is rather a rural prophet.

The general theme of Micah is that of idolatry. The opening chapters highlight the idolatry of the sanctuary at Bethel and the Northern Kingdom but attention is soon turned to the southern kingdom and its own brand of idolatry. Citing that the latter should have known better because it had the North as an example, Micah describes HaShem's judgment as swift and brutal. In the midst of this harsh judgment there are still prophets in the land that are prophesying that all will be well (a reoccurring theme). In contrast Micah's response is that Zion shall be like a plowed field, Jerusalem shall be a heap of ruins, and the Temple Mount itself will be like a shrine in the desolate woods.

Still, amid this judgment there is a note of hope sounded, of days to come when HaShem will restore Jerusalem, they shall turn implements of war and to implements of agriculture, Everyman shall sit under his own fig tree without being disturbed, and HaShem will gather his sheep. In chapter 5 the prophet announces that from insignificant Bethlehem a new king will rise up who will shepherd the remnant of Judah.

The overriding issue for Micah as it is in Isaiah and Jeremiah is that Ha Shem's people fail to rely on his promises to protect his people and instead insist on political and religious wrangling's, alliances, and marriages to protect themselves in times of crisis.

Nahum

Nahum is born in Elkosh (a small Galillean village on the eastern banks of the Euphrates River).

Nahum opens with an oracle against Nineveh. Nineveh was the capital city of Assyria and was destroyed in the year 612 BCE by the Babylonians and the Medes. The tenor of Nahum's oracles is of celebration (you can almost hear the munchkins from the Wizard of Oz providing backup vocals: "Ding Dong...."). Desolation, devastation and destruction is the refrain. Brutal images of annihilation, rape and bloodlust are used to describe the judgment of HaShem upon the Assyrians.

Habakkuk

While there is a superscription to the book of Habakkuk the events described place it at the time of the end of the Assyrian Empire (612 BCE) and the rise of the neo-Babylonian Empire (626 – 605 BCE). Habakkuk is set against the backdrop of the Egyptian/Assyrian alliance, the failed attempt by King Josiah of Judah to halt the Egyptian advance and the subsequent victory of the Babylonians at Carchemish.

In a scene reminiscent of the Mummy film series, the prophet announces the raising up of the ancient, fierce and impetuous army of the Chaldeans (the precursors of the Babylonians). Again, in brutal description the prophet portrays the Babylonian onslaught and destruction of the Assyrians. One of the developing characteristics within the prophetic corpus is the use of foreign powers by HaShem to accomplish the desired results of his judgment.

The final chapter of Habakkuk is a prayer in the style of a psalm of supplication. It is a prayer for compassion on HaShem's part. One can only imagine considering the destructive judgment of HaShem on the enemies of Judah that HaShem is also capable of executing such judgment upon the unfaithfulness of his own people – Habakkuk's prayer most assuredly was prayed with quivering voice.

Zephaniah

Zephaniah also reflects the fall of Nineveh. The book's superscription reveals that Zephaniah is a descendent of Hezekiah and prophesies during the reign of King Josiah of Judah.

Unlike the two previous prophets, Zephaniah's message of judgment is also directed towards Judah as well as Assyria. In classic form Zephaniah provides oracles against the nations including Assyria, Philistea, Moab and Ethiopia. The main concern however for Zephaniah is Jerusalem. Zephaniah uses the image of the Day of the Lord to speak of the impending judgment of Jerusalem. The charges brought against Jerusalem include the consorting with the prophets of Baal and the succumbing to the traditions, trends, and fads of their neighbors (most especially their costuming). Like so many of the preceding prophets, the final editorial process offers a ray of hope HaShem will annul the judgment of the faithful remnant and the fortunes of Jerusalem will be restored.

Haggai

With Haggai we are introduced to the prophets of the restoration and postexilic prophecy. Mentioned alongside Zechariah in the book of Ezra, Haggai and his message are instrumental in the rebuilding process of the Temple following the exile in Babylon. The superscription places us in the second year (520 BCE) of the reign of King Darius. Darius' predecessor, Cyrus, was the Persian king who defeated the Babylonians and emancipated the exiles.

There were many critical issues facing the returning exiles to Jerusalem. It appears from Haggai that there is a dispute over whether it is now appropriate to rebuild the Temple in Jerusalem. The prophecy of Haggai obviously underpins those who wish to rebuild. Without a Temple the risk of defilement of the appropriate sacrifices is heightened. It is clear then that the Temple is necessary to assure the proper worship of HaShem.

Zechariah

Zechariah opens with a plea for repentance, or turning around, *"Do not be rebellious as your fathers were but heed the warnings and decrees of*

HaShem" (Zechariah 1:4). With that the book of Zechariah lays out several night visions received by the prophet.

The first of these is a vision of riders on four horses - two bays, a sorrel, and a white. We are told by the angel (who functions as the visions' interpreter) that these riders are on patrol for HaShem and bring news that the world is at peace and that Jerusalem is pardoned. This may reflect an extensive surveillance force that was present within the Persian Empire that enabled the Empire to subdue any pending disturbances.

The next vision is one of four horns. These are the horns that tossed Judah, Israel and Jerusalem. They now have come to subdue the nations that might revolt against Judah.

The third vision is of a man holding a measuring line with which to measure Jerusalem in preparation for its rebuilding. Unlike the intricate and carefully subdivided new Jerusalem of Ezekiel's visions this, Jerusalem will be a city without walls.

In a fourth vision the prophet is shown Joshua, the high priest and the Accuser/Satan. While the role of Satan will later take on diabolical significance as it is equated the figure of the devil, here the Satan more than likely refers to a prosecutor or perhaps to that person in the royal court to whom all good snitches report. Joshua is found in filthy clothing, connoting unworthiness. Joshua however, is not actually guilty and the accuser takes it on the chin from HaShem for making such accusations. Joshua is then outfitted with a new set of clothes as a sign of his worthiness. Following this HaShem makes two promises to Joshua: first, as long as Joshua adheres to the code of conduct for priests HaShem will make him the high priest and second, HaShem is about to raise up a righteous branch, a legitimate heir to the throne of David.

A golden menorah appears to the prophet in the fifth vision. It has seven lamps upon it. This sign announces that Zerubbabel, who has begun the building project shall be the one to complete the new house for HaShem. The seven lamps are the seven eyes of the Lord watching over the whole earth (HaShem has his own surveillance operation). Two sons of Zerubbabel are represented by two olive trees flanking the menorah. Since both king and high priest serve the anointed one, this is probably a reference to the separation of church and state which was consistent in Israel's history.

The next vision is of a flying scroll which signifies the covenantal curses over those who fail to keep covenant. In another vision wickedness is personified as a woman seated inside a tub which is then transported back to Shinar/Babylon where it will be housed.

The final vision is of four chariots drawn by four horses; bay, black, white, and dappled, signifying the four winds of heaven which again are patrolling the earth and announcing the deliverance of the exiles. The prophet is instructed to take the silver and gold of the exiles and make crowns with which to crown Joshua high priest. This is a rather unusual development in that it should be Zerubbabel who was crowned as king. This may reflect a suppression of Zerubbabel by the Persians, who perceive him as a messianic threat.

The final two chapters of Zechariah shift the focus from the restoration of the monarchy to the faithful keeping of Torah and the promises of a hopeful future. The original book of Zechariah probably concludes with chapter 8. The following five chapters are most likely reflective of a later editor.

Classified as some of the most obscure and difficult passages in the Tanakh these additions to Zechariah may be a totally separate work that was later attributed to Zechariah. Scholars feel that the oracles contained here may either reflect situations whose time and place have been lost or are eschatological in nature.

One of the major themes of this section is that of kingship. Chapter 9 is important with regards to the gospel writers for its description of a (messianic) king in verse nine and following. This humble king, while standing in great contrast to the rulers of the day, is reminiscent of prophetic oracles regarding the restored monarchy. The writer turns once again to the image of Shepherd to talk about the description of the king. Chapter 11 contains a reference to 30 shekels of silver to the one who will attend the sheep and who announces the division between Judah and Israel. This is then followed by the announcement of HaShem's intention to raise up a new Shepherd/King. Chapter 12 raises up the image of the house of David which will be akin to the angel of the Lord and will protect Judah from assault. Chapter 13:10-14 introduce the compassion of the house of David that mourns for the one they have pierced as one mourns for one's only child. The gospel writer John will refer to this passage in reference to the crucified Jesus in chapter 19 of his gospel.

Chapter 13 also points to the end of the prophetic vocation. It is evidence that during the Persian period the prophetic office loses its credibility and authority. There is a shifting of religious authority to the scribes as interpreters of Torah which will become the dominant authority during the Second Temple Period.

The book concludes in eschatological fantasy that describes an apocalyptic battle between the residents of Mount Zion and the invading Babylonians. HaShem will destroy all nations who seek to destroy Jerusalem. The final image of the section portrays Jerusalem as the holy city to which the nations will come year after year to worship HaShem as king at the annual Festival of the Booths (the Festival of the Booths is also the context for the Transfiguration of Jesus in the gospels). This gathering of the nations points to the apocalyptic hope of a time in the future when the kingship of HaShem is fully revealed in all its glory among the nations.

Malachi

My colleague, the late Pastor Earl Runge, often referred to Malachi as the last of the great Italian prophets. (Wait for it. Okay, it wasn't that funny.) However, the name of this anonymous work is probably connected to chapter 3:1 and refers to "my messenger." The Tanakh divides the book of Malachi into three chapters whereas English translations designate four chapters.

This short work is taking advantage of the situation by raping and looting what is left of Judah. The announcement to Edom is that even now HaShem is planning to rebuild Judah and then they will be sorry. The central part of the book is an indictment against the priesthood announcing that HaShem will refuse to accept any offerings of such a corrupt priesthood. Religious infidelity, the breaking of covenant, is also extended to the secular infidelity that appears to be happening in society with men divorcing Jewish wives in favor of foreign wives.

Again, the book ends on a hopeful note for the faithful remnant. A scroll of evidence has been written by HaShem that in the Day of the Lord, he will remember their faithfulness. The book ends with a final reminder to observe the Torah and the announcement that Elijah will return prior to the awesome Day of the Lord. This final note on Elijah will have significance both for Jews and Christians as Jews still await the arrival of Elijah (leaving a vacant seat at Passover for his arrival) and Christians view John the Baptist as the return of Elijah, hence ushering in the Day of the Lord/Kingdom.

Joel

While the book of Joel offers very few clues as to its date most scholars today agree that it is from the post exilic period and in fact may be one of the latest if not the latest of the prophetic books. The book of Joel is a response to a national crisis – a plague of locusts.

The plague of locusts is as if a nation has invaded the land, the devastation is widespread if not total. What is called for by the prophet is a cultic response. First comes the lament. The present situation with its attendant loss must be lamented. The second response is to sound the alarm to announce the enormity of the destruction. The third response to call a fast, a time of repentance in which the nation is called to fast, to weep, and to lament.

This action then rouses HaShem into action. There is the announcement of the promise of new grain and oil and a time of abundance. This is not a time to be afraid but to trust in HaShem's care for his people. It will be a time of great reversal of fortune.

After that HaShem will pour out his Spirit on all flesh, male and female, old and young. There will be prophesying and dreaming as well as visions. All of this is a precursor to the great and terrible day of the Lord. Those who invoke the name of HaShem shall be saved. There will be a remnant on Mount Zion and in Jerusalem in those days and HaShem will restore the fortunes of Judah.

In those days HaShem shall repay the nations for what they have done to Judah and Jerusalem. They will do well to beat the plowshares into swords and their pruning hooks into spears as they prepare for the great battle. HaShem is about to carry out judgment like a reaper swings the sickle.

In contrast, HaShem will shelter his faithful people and Jerusalem will be a refuge for his children. A time of prosperity shall ensue for Judah and Jerusalem while utter destruction is the verdict for the nations of the world. The fortunes of Judah and Jerusalem shall be forever as HaShem shall dwell in Zion.

Obadiah

The book of Obadiah offers us a rare glimpse of the conditions in Judah following the Babylonian invasion. (For you Jeopardy fans Obadiah is the shortest book of the Bible.) The concern for Obadiah is primarily the nation of the Edom.

The first part of Obadiah is a series of oracles against Edom for the wrongs that it has done to Judah and Jerusalem. The fate of Edom shall be the fate of all the nations that are taking advantage of the situation in Judah. Obadiah also announces the restoration of Judah that will follow the execution of this judgment. In later rabbinic literature Edom will become the archetype for the enemies of Judaism and a code word for Rome itself.

The tenor of Obadiah's vindictive vengeance may in fact be one of the harshest executions of justice that we find in the Tanakh.

Jonah

Unlike any of the other prophetic books Jonah is a story about the prophet himself. There is some speculation that this Jonah refers to the Jonah that is mentioned in Second Kings 14:25. If this is so, this Jonah prophesied during the reign of King Jeroboam II of Israel in the Eighth century BCE. However, this Jonah has little in common with the one that is mentioned earlier either in content or character and most scholars believe that he is a fictional character invented centuries after the reign of Jeroboam. The narrative is whimsical, ironic and humorous.

HaShem calls Jonah to go and prophesy judgment upon the city of Nineveh. Unlike the traditional response to a call, Jonah flees the other way to Tarshish. He hires a boat in an effort to escape HaShem's service. Not surprisingly there is a storm and when the sailors discover what Jonah has done they become terrified and offer Jonah as a sacrifice to HaShem. We are told that HaShem provides a huge fish to swallow Jonah and it is there that he spends three days and three nights in the belly of the fish. (This image will be picked up in the New Testament in conjunction with the crucifixion and resurrection of Jesus.) Jonah prays to HaShem for deliverance and HaShem instructs the fish to puke Jonah up on the beach.

There is a renewal of call for Jonah to go to Nineveh and to prophesy's judgment. This time Jonah goes and finds that Nineveh is an incredibly large city. It takes him several days to make the journey across the city. Periodically he stops to announce that 40 days more and Nineveh shall be overthrown. When news reaches the king, he proclaims a fast and calls for national repentance. HaShem witnesses Nineveh's repentance and renounces his punishment upon the city.

We find that this greatly disturbs and displeases Jonah who complains to HaShem, *"I knew you would do this all along, I don't know why I even bothered!"* With this Jonah leaves the city and makes a shelter under which he sits and pouts. HaShem provides a plant that grows up and provides Jonah shade, saving him from further discomfort. This greatly pleased Jonah. However, the next day HaShem provides a worm that eats the plant so that when the sun rises it beats down upon Jonah. He becomes faint and prays to die once again. HaShem questions him as to why he is so concerned about a mere plant. If Jonah was so concerned about a plant shouldn't HaShem be concerned about the people of Nineveh?

THE WRITINGS

"Zaydeh, why does it seem that bad things happen to good people and good things happen to bad people? It doesn't seem fair. Does not the Torah say that the blessed will have good things given to them and those that fail to keep Torah will be cursed?"

Whether it is spurned on by the realities of post-exilic Judah or not the Writings enter into a new dialog with the Torah and the Prophets as well as with the cultural-historical context of her day in wrestling with that question (which Rabbi Harold Kushner turned into a best seller, *Why Do Bad Things Happen to Good People?*). This is true explicitly in the Three Great Books (Psalms, Job and Proverbs) as well as the Five Scrolls of the Megilloth (Song of Songs, Ruth, Lamentations, Ecclesiastes and Esther) and implicitly in the apocalyptic book of Daniel and the history books of Ezra-Nehemiah and First and Second Chronicles. In the Three Great Books the answer is given in hymn and lament. Whereas in the Five Scrolls that voice is drawn into the liturgical calendar that serves to socialize and sustain this distinctive community. In the book of Daniel, hope of HaShem's triumph over all threats to Jerusalem invites courage and freedom as a distinctive Jewish voice emerges. This distinctive voice is then captured in the History Books which bring the Tanakh to a close with an unexpected recovery. In Judaism's preoccupation with the exile it is revealed as a community that is always coming home... returning from exile.

THE THREE GREAT BOOKS

Psalms

The psalms are the ancient mapping of Israel's life with HaShem. They constitute the primary guide for faith and worship in both synagogue and church. As the hymns and songs of faith that I was raised on had a profound, if not subtle, influence on my faith development so too do these songs impact the life of faith of an individual probably more than the other writings.

The Psalms underwent a long editorial process whereby many songs and poems from many sources were formed into collections for usage in a variety of contexts, until finally the several collections were shaped into a grand scheme of the present Psalter of five books 1-41; 42-72; 73-89; 90-106; 107-150 (corresponding to the Torah's five books).

In their present form, there is a distinct Jerusalem accent to the psalms. The images of the Temple, HaShem as creator and king, and the Davidic King contribute to that accent. The psalms that emphasize a Davidic King are those psalms most often accredited to King David as author. By the time of the psalter's present form these psalms constitute a witness to the Messianic King as well as looking back on the Davidic kingship.

The cosmic theme of creation present in many of the psalms speaks to the permanence of the Temple and Jerusalem. This becomes important in the time of the Exile as well as into the future of Judaism in the Diaspora.

The Psalms are comprised of four major genres: Hymn, Communal Lament, Individual Lament, and Individual Song of Thanksgiving. Below is a look at a brief description of each genre followed by a representative psalm.

Hymn: The hymn genre reflects an exuberant act of praise that exalts and celebrates either the person of HaShem or the characteristic actions of HaShem. The hymn can either reflect the thanksgiving of an individual or the community as a whole.

Psalm 117

> *Praise the Lord, all you nations;*
> *extolled Him, all you peoples,*
> *for great is His steadfast love toward us;*
> *the faithfulness of the Lord endures forever.*
> *Hallelujah.*

Typically, as you can see, the hymn is a summons join in thanksgiving followed by the reason for such praise. In this case reason for the praise is HaShem's steadfast love and faithfulness.

Communal Lament: The communal lament usually reflects a public crisis that concerns the entire community. A modern public crisis that would offer an opportunity for communal lament was the terrorist attacks of September 11. As this event certainly affected the whole world community, no such communal lament issued from the mouths of God's people. In fact, any attempt to do so was quashed in the name of patriotism.

Psalm 74

In the opening verses we have the emotional outcry of the community which expresses feelings of rejection, the call for HaShem to remember his promises and the relationship that he established with his people.

Why, oh God, do you forever reject us,
        do you fume and anger at the flock that you tend?
Remember the community you made yours long ago,
        Your very own tribe that you redeemed,
        Mount Zion, for you dwell.
        Bestir yourself because of the perpetual tumult
        all the outrages of the enemy in the sanctuary.

In verses 3-9 we have the description of the disaster.

        Bestir yourself because of the perpetual tumult
        all the outrages of the enemy in the sanctuary.
Your foes roar inside Your meeting place;
        they take their signs for true signs.
        It is like men wielding axes
        against a gnarled tree;
        with hatchet and pike
        they hacked away at its carved work.
They made Your sanctuary go up in flames;
        they brought low in dishonor the dwelling place of your
        presence.
They resolved, "Let us destroy them all together!"
        They burned all God's tabernacles in the land.
No signs appear for us;
        there is no longer any prophet;
        no one among us knows for how long.

Verses 10-12 issuer return to lament.

Till when, O God, will the foe blaspheme,
        will the enemy forever revile Your name?
        Why do you hold back your hand, your right hand?
Draw it out of Your bosom!

One of the hallmarks of lament, either communal or individual, is that it moves from lament to doxology. In verses 12-17 we have such a doxology:

O God, my King from of old,
who brings deliverance throughout the land;
it was You who drove back the sea with Your might,
who smashed the heads of the monsters in the waters;
it was you who crushed the heads of Leviathan,
who left him his food for the denizens of the desert;
it was you who released springs and torrents,
who made the mighty rivers run dry;
the day is Yours, the night also;
it was You who set in place the orb of the sun;
You fixed all the boundaries of the earth;
summer and winter — you made them.

Following the doxology, the psalm closes with a series of imperative petitions on behalf of the community

Be mindful how the enemy blasphemes the Lord,
how base people revile your name.
Do not deliver Your dove to wild beast;
do not ignore forever the band of your lowly ones.
Look to the covenant!
For the dark places of land are full of the haunts of lawlessness.
Let not the downtrodden turn away disappointed;
let the poor and needy praise your name.
Rise, O God, champion your cause;
be mindful that you are blasphemed by base men all day long.
Do not ignore the shouts of your foes,
the din of your adversaries that ascends all the time.

Individual Lament: Whereas the communal lament addresses a crisis that affects the whole community/nation and individual lament concerns personal distress (sickness, abandonment, imprisonment) and asks HaShem to intervene and deliver.

Psalm 13

As with the communal lament the individual lament opens with the complaint/lament:

How long, O Lord; will you ignore me forever?
How long will you hide your face from me?
> *How long will I have cares on my mind,*
>> *grief in my heart all day?*
How long will my enemy have the upper hand?

The complaint gives way to the petition or petitions:

Look at me, answer me, O Lord, my God!
Restore the luster to my eyes,

The lament then moves from petition to a rationale as to why HaShem should honor the petition:

> *lest I sleep the sleep of death;*
> *this my enemies say, "I have overcome him,"*
> *my foes exalt when I totter.*

The lament ends then with a glad resolution and an expression of response but the one in lament:

But I trust in your faithfulness,
> *my heart will exult in your deliverance.*
I will sing to the Lord,
> *for he is done good to me.*

Individual Song of Thanksgiving: unlike the general hymn the individual song of thanksgiving is a direct response to HaShem's intervention in a personal crisis. The psalm of thanksgiving includes both a review of crisis as well as an account of the rescue.

Psalm 30

The psalm opens in doxology:

I extol You, O Lord,
for You have lifted me up,
and not let my enemies rejoice over me.
O Lord, my God,
I cried out to You,
and You healed me.
O Lord, You brought me up from Sheol,
preserved me from going down into the Pit.

All you faithful the Lord, sing to Him,
and praise his holy name.
For He is angry but a moment,
and when He is pleased there is life.
One may lie down weeping at nightfall;
but at dawn there are shouts of joy.

The doxology paves the way for the report of the crisis or unexpected trouble:

When I was untroubled,
I thought, "I shall never be shaken,"
for you, O Lord, when you were pleased,
made me firm as a mighty mountain.
When you hid your face,
I was terrified.

This is followed by a prayer of complaint usually in the past tense:

I called to you, O Lord;
to my Lord I made appeal,
"What is to be gained from my death,
from my descent into the Pit?
Can dust praise you?

> *Can it declare your faithfulness?*
> *Here, O Lord, and have mercy on me;*
> *O Lord, be my help!"*

There is now an affirmation of HaShem's intervention into the crisis:

> *You turned my lament into dancing,*
> *You undid my sackcloth and girded me with joy,*

The psalm then concludes the promise to praise and thank HaShem for his intervention:

> *that my whole being might sing hymns to You endlessly;*
> *O Lord my God, I will praise you forever.*

The psalms are not unlike the "Negro spirituals" that have no author or identifiable place or origin, but simply arise in the life and practice of the community and are found to be recurrently adequate to many different usages over time. They have enjoyed a place in the liturgical life of both Jewish and Christian communities. I believe this is due to their timeless quality and their ability to express the emotions of both individual and community at times when words are not easy to come by. One of my devotional practices is to read a psalm each day. It is uncanny how many days the psalm read has something to say about the day. In the days following my dad's death in 1970 it was a psalm, Psalm 77, that gave voice to the wordless cries of my heart and enabled me to express emotions that were at best confusing and at worst all consuming.

Proverbs

> *"Zaydeh, soon I will be going out into the world. I'm worried that I am not ready. Can you give me advice for living in this world?"*
>
> *"Ah yes, my son...listen!"*

The book of Proverbs is assigned to the genre of the Wisdom tradition because of its "imparted wisdom" that is delivered from father to son. Other examples of Wisdom literature in Hebrew Scriptures include the book of Ecclesiastes and Job. In addition, there are elements of the Wisdom tradition found in the Psalms and the Apocrypha. Its influence is also found in the writings of the New Testament.

This "collection of collections" probably reflects the sustained work of the postexilic community of scribes which was evolving after the destruction of the Temple. However, there are absolutely no references to Israel in the book of Proverbs nor does there seem to be a desire to place it within a firm historical context. While the book of Proverbs is attested to King Solomon, son of David, it's content reflects that of numerous authors and editors over an extended period.

The context for the book of Proverbs is that of a father handing over wisdom to his son. This fits the general aim of the Wisdom tradition, namely that the young be educated to discern the world rightly. Deeds have consequences. HaShem pays close attention to the connection between actions and destiny, he hurries it along and completes it when necessary. Good or wise behavior will bring blessings, whereas wicked or foolish actions will bring disaster. This moral teaching seems to be consistent with other Wisdom traditions throughout the Near East during this time.

The teachers of this tradition do not produce a system of moral calculation; rather they attest to a relationship between humanity and HaShem that is characterized by inscrutable mystery but that has immense concrete implications. We shall see this in more detail as we look at the book of Job. Thus, they speak of foolishness and not sin. They ponder the stupidity of living against the grain of creation ordered by the creator. The God of Proverbs is clearly the Creator God who in hidden ways has ordered the world and presides over it. Wisdom thinks resolutely within the framework of creation.

Wisdom in Proverbs is personified as a woman. She is contrasted from the very beginning of the book with the forbidden, or literally "strange" woman. It is clear from the context of the book of Proverbs that this forbidden woman is adulterous and as such a threat to social order. The message of the book of Proverbs also offers a symbolic interpretation of this woman as a representation of anything that deviates from the way of

Wisdom. While there is no explicit connection in Proverbs one cannot help but be reminded of the relationship of Hosea and Gomer. If Wisdom is walking in the relationship with HaShem, than to do otherwise is not only foolishness but adultery. Given this, it is understandable why in later traditions Wisdom is connected closely with Torah even though the book itself makes no such reference.

We will also find this way of Wisdom developed by the New Testament writers in the teachings of Jesus and the Way of the early Christians. In the Gospel of John, the Logos, or Word, is personified as Jesus in much the same way that wisdom is personified in the book of Proverbs.

Job

Job is one of the most often recommended books to those who are dealing with significant losses in their lives. Rabbi Harold Kushner utilizes the book of Job as the centerpiece of his bestseller, **Why Do Bad Things Happen to Good People?** Countless Jewish and Christian saints of all ages find in Job a kindred spirit and inspiration amid crisis. However, theologically this book challenges the basic premises of Israel's faith (as well as much of Christian belief), and refuses any easy resolution of the most difficult theological questions that appear on the horizon of Israel's faith such as the cause of suffering and evil in the world (Theodicy).

In a dialog of lament and hymn, Job navigates the disputed testimony between traditional explanations and lived reality. In the end, there is no way in which to accommodate settled orthodoxy to the wretchedness of Job's plight.

The structure of the book includes a prose introduction (1:1-2:13), the dialogues between Job and his friends (3:1-37:24) followed by a powerful narrative epilogue (38-42). The introduction reveals a deal between the Satan (the Accuser or District Attorney in the Divine Court and HaShem). We meet Job, who by the way is not a Jew but rather an Edomite, in the opening verses. He has it made! He has it all: money, wife, sons, livestock the full Monty! In addition, he is virtuous and devout in his practice of the cult even to offering additional sacrifices… just to be on the safe side. HaShem is extolling Job's virtues to the Satan who retorts, "Why wouldn't he be virtuous and devout, he has everything!" HaShem retorts that he would be virtuous and devout even if it was all taken away. To which the Satan responds, "You have a bet!" Soon Job has everything in life taken away from him and he is left in misery questioning his fate, "Should we only accept good from HaShem and not evil as well?" This then becomes the question threading its way throughout the book.

Job's three friends, Eliphaz the Temanite, Bildad the Shuhite and Zophar the Naamathite, hear of his plight and come to console him. They bring with them the prevailing theologies of the day concerning suffering and obedience (particularly as it applies to Job's circumstances). The three friends engage Job in dialog one at a time with Job offering a rebuttal after each: Eliphaz (4-5), Bildad (8), and Zophar (11).

Job offers an opening lament where he expresses his righteousness and at one point prays that it might have been better had he never been born. Eliphaz' response is basically to question Job's righteousness… "Can mortals be righteous before HaShem?" If that is not bad enough he stirs the pot by saying, "Happy is the one whom HaShem reproves!" Yeah, right! Job responds with anger towards his friend, the system and HaShem holding fast to his righteousness. Rather than appeal to be absence or neglect on the part of HaShem (as do the Exiles) Job instead complains of HaShem's presence. Why should HaShem think so highly of him that he would visit Job? (A similar complaint is made by the widow of Zaraphath to Elijah in 1 Kings.) Instead of being above human sin, HaShem is a "watcher" of the human condition.

In Chapter 8 Bildad enters the fray. The issue for Bildad is, does HaShem pervert justice? Bildad appeals to the theology of the day that says you get what you deserve. There are direct consequences to your actions. In essence Job must be guilty and HaShem's cause justified. Job's response is a key question considering the end of the book, how can a mortal be just before HaShem? The key issue is that HaShem is both accuser and judge so who can stand before HaShem? Job maintains his innocence. (His speech anticipates the conversation that Jesus has with those who ponder recent disasters). Job's conclusion from this line of thought is that HaShem must be responsible for justice as well as injustice on the earth. Job complains that there is no arbitrator between HaShem and himself. A fair trial is impossible. On the other hand, Job was concerned that HaShem would need to inflict such suffering on mere human beings.

Zophar, is the final of Job's three friends to take a crack at Job. Essentially his argument is that between Job and HaShem there is really no contest. HaShem is so superior to humanity that his ways cannot be fathomed. Job's response makes it clear that Job does not want to waste time debating with his friends but rather wants to take his case to HaShem. Again, as he brings his speech to a close, Job raises the wretched state of humanity and asks why HaShem should inflict more suffering upon it.

In chapters 29 through 31 we have Job's final speech. In the speech Job recalls life when it was clear that HaShem was with him in blessing. But as the speech goes on he becomes more and more disillusioned. In his concluding statement Job seems to move from being righteous to being self-righteous.

Elihu serves in chapters 32 through 37 as a way of restating the arguments of the earlier three friends. The end of his speech extols HaShem's role in nature and creation which in many ways anticipates what is coming next.

The dialogues of dispute concern the mismatch between traditional explanations and lived reality. In the end, there is no way in which to accommodate settled orthodoxy to the wretchedness of Job's plight.

The climax of the book of Job is to be found in chapters 38 through 41 with what is commonly known as the whirlwind speeches. Demonstrated in the speeches is what Job and his friends had assumed all along, that HaShem is simply overpowering. Claiming his power in the creative enterprise, HaShem questions where Job was when he was doing his creating. It is clear that the whirlwind speech from HaShem is about perspective and the question becomes for Job and for us, "Who do you think you are?" Job's response at the end of the speech is almost whimpered in contrast, "See, I'm a small account."

The whirlwind speeches of HaShem portray him with massive power as sovereign creator. There is also an element of artistic appreciation for the beauty and wonder of the creatures that HaShem has created. The rhetoric is that of a courtroom (read 38:1ff). From the perspective of HaShem the earlier dispute is about nothing important. To quibble about suffering and guilt or innocence is of no significance to the inscrutable mystery of life with God that enwraps the entire human endeavor.

Essentially Job is crushed. While he does not cave on his innocence he does repent before HaShem for his arrogance and thinking himself capable of playing the role of HaShem. The question posed by Job and his friends, "Does HaShem pervert justice?" is dismissed in favor of the judgment that HaShem is not compelled to comply with human conceptions of justice.

Like a Shakespearean comedy the end of Job concludes on a happy note with Job's fortunes restored. However, despite this restoration Job is forever changed. Never again will he possess the self-righteous confidence to question the work of HaShem.

I raise the question; Does Job speak on behalf of corporate Israel? In some sense does the voice of Job echo the voices of the Exiles of a generation earlier?

THE FIVE SCROLLS

The books of Ruth, Song of Solomon/Song of Songs, Lamentations, Ecclesiastes and Esther are referred to collectively as the Five Scrolls or Megiloth (literally translated, "scroll"). These five scrolls have been linked by tradition and utilized in the five festal celebrations of the Jewish calendar:

Passover: Song of Solomon/Song of Songs
Festival of the Weeks: Ruth
The Ninth of Av: Lamentations
Festival of the Booths: Ecclesiastes
Festival of Purim: Esther

Ruth

Ruth is the story about the careful negotiation between a vulnerable outsider woman and a man of substance in the community, a negotiation that has to do with honor and shame, and a self-consciousness reflection about economic issues in the exchange.

The story of Ruth is set in the period of the Judges and so in the Christian Old Testament we find it nestled between Judges and Joshua. Elimelech and Naomi and their two sons sojourned to the land of Moab from Bethlehem because of a famine. Both sons take Moabite wives one

Ruth and the other Orpha. Naomi's husband and two sons all die leaving only her and her daughter-in-laws.

Naomi decides that her best course of action is to return to her homeland. Her two daughter-in-laws accompany her. After they had gone some ways, Naomi releases them to stay in their homeland for she has no more sons for them to marry. Orpha returns but Ruth is intent to follow Naomi. Ruth offers a touching sentiment of fidelity, saying, "Your people shall be my people and your god my god."

Naomi and the foreign girl, Ruth arrive in Bethlehem at the time of the barley harvest and immediately the town starts buzzing. It so happens that one of Naomi's relatives by marriage is a wealthy and prominent man by the name of Boaz.

One day Ruth goes out into the fields to gather barley that is left by the harvester. Boaz notices her and inquires of her identity. Boaz approaches Ruth and instructs her to glean only his fields and he will provide for her. Ruth is astonished that a foreigner would be treated in this manner.

When Ruth returns home that evening she tells Naomi about Boaz. "Well bless my soul he has not forgotten us," replies Naomi, "He is a relative of ours." Stay and glean his fields with the other women. So, Ruth spent her days in Boaz' fields until the harvest was finished.

Naomi decides to play matchmaker between Boaz and Ruth. When Boaz falls into a stupor at the harvest festival Ruth lies at his feet. When he awakens she informs him that she is available for marriage which Boaz declares is a great honor for him.

In a convoluted economic exchange Boaz acquires a piece of property from Naomi and Ruth is included in the deal. Boaz marries Ruth and they have a son, Obed who will become the father of Jesse who in turn will father David (yes, of king fame).

In the context of the festival's threshing floor (the festival's defining venue) the book of Ruth speaks of radical newness and opens the future for Israel.

Song of Songs or Song of Solomon

The Song of Songs is unrestrained love poetry. Similar poetry is found in Islamic texts and may reflect a dimension of the Persian tradition. It is an erotic interaction between a man and a woman who are brought to daring and imaginative speech. It speaks of a redeemed love which stands in contrast to Genesis 2-3 where man and woman failed to actualize this creaturely delight.

The Song of Songs is a favorite book of the mystics throughout Judaism and Christianity. It is a vehicle to talk about the unbridled passion of God. It is a poem of courtship and pursuit, erotic passion and commitment. It is a sensory invitation into the delightful nature of HaShem and his "courted" people.

The Song of Songs is utilized in Passover as a resource to mediate the unmitigated joy that arises from HaShem's profound commitment to Israel in the act of the exodus.

Book of Lamentations

The book of Lamentations is constituted by 5 poems of lament and grief over the destruction of the city of Jerusalem at the hands of the Babylonians in 587 BCE. The deep sense of displacement evoked by the loss led to the conclusion in some quarters that all the old promises of HaShem to Israel – and consequently Israel's status as HaShem's people and Jerusalem's status as HaShem's city – were placed in deep jeopardy. "We is in deep doo doo"!

The poetry is offered in the voice of a suffering, dying, abandoned woman who speaks with the voice of the city. She is a woman who is dying and who continues to die, but who does not die fully – in order that her voice of bereavement may be kept continually alive as the city suffers and dies without relief. Lamentations is a dirge for the dead and a lament for the living. (Jesus weeping over Jerusalem is a New Testament lament.)

I believe that the book of Lamentations and the genre of the lament is critical for dealing with the angst and displacement that occurs after a major tragedy whither personal or national. It provided a vehicle for asking the tough questions without necessarily arriving at a conclusion. The failure to express these questions only results in them going underground. Repressed they surface and influence us in many unhealthy ways such a violence, discrimination and divisiveness.

I believe it was this failure to adequately express lament following 9/11 that has led us in many ways to the situation we face almost 15 years later. We jumped from tragedy to war, from terror to patriotism, without ever dealing with the difficult questions raised by the destruction, not the least of which was the question of the young college student that night on the front porch, "Where the hell was God this morning?"

Walter Brueggemann cites that the 5 poems of Lamentations raise the themes of: truthfulness, impassioned hope, wish for justice, political action, resistance and the power of newness.

- **Truthfulness:** The speaker in Lamentations delivers a no holds barred assessment of what has happened to Jerusalem. There is inherent distrust of HaShem's intentions in all of this. Still they pray anyway on the hope that HaShem is still listening and may be open to being persuaded.

- **Impassioned Hope:** In their prayer there is a tenacious attempt to engage HaShem. The writer places claims on HaShem and calls for a future for Jerusalem and her people. Even when it appears HaShem is silent to their cries the speaker perseveres. The broken still dare to hope for HaShem to return to his senses and remember.

- **Wish for Justice:** A lament creates space to not only grieve the heavy losses sustained but also to see and name injustice… not what is wrong with us but rather what wrong has been *done* to us.

- **Political Action:** The lament is an expression of resistance to the way things are. As such they can become a communal emptying and catharsis. In that emptying out and cleansing, a space for hope is carved out from the rock of despair and sorrow.

- **Teaching of Resistance (defiance):** Blatant truth-telling before HaShem takes on the air of defiance. It is in the act of coming to terms with our passions that we become capable of being true moral agents in the world.

- **Power of Newness:** The tears of lament are not powerless but powerful agents of change and new life.

In chapters 1-3 the author lays bare the situation of the devastated city of Jerusalem and the devastated condition of the author. *"Bitterly she (Jerusalem) weeps in the night, her cheeks wet with tears." "Zion's roads are in mourning, empty of festival pilgrims; all her gates are deserted. Her priests sigh… She is utterly disconsolate!"* (Lamentations 1:2-4). It is clear to the author that HaShem is the author of this drama… he has left the building. It is HaShem that destroyed his Tabernacle. HaShem ended Zion, king and priest. *"HaShem has done what he purposed, has carried out the decree that he ordained long ago; he has torn down without pity. He has let the foe rejoice over you".* (Lamentations 2:17). In chapter 3 the lyric becomes personal. *"I am the man who has known affliction…all around me he has built misery and hardship"* (Lamentations 3:1). The speaker reaches the conclusion that for him it is finished and HaShem is a lost cause.

Midway through chapter three the mood shifts to one of hope. In the midst of wormwood and gall, distress and misery, the author comes to the recollection that HaShem couldn't have withdrawn his lovingkindness. It is not in the nature of HaShem. Now is not the time for foolish questions, now the time to withdraw, pray and hope. Even in the face of HaShem's perceived absence/silence the speaker is relentless in his pursuit of HaShem. *"The kindness of HaShem has not ended and his mercies are not spent. They are renewed every morning…ample is your grace"* Lamentations 3:22-23).

In chapter 3:55-58 we hear the cry for justice and accountability from the lamenter. *"I called to you, HaShem…called from rock bottom (the Pit/ Sheol) …Don't shut your ears to me!" "Give my enemies their just deserts according to their deed. May their hearts burn with anguish. Curse them… pursue them…destroy them."* It is time for not only hope and restoration but retribution as well.

Chapter 4 continues to lay bare the present condition of utter destruction and deprivation. HaShem's fury and blazing wrath however, have burnt out as well. HaShem will exile his people no longer.

Chapter 5 is a call for HaShem to remember. To remember what has befallen his people. It is a reminder that this poem is also a prayer. "HaShem, do not forget us… *Take us back to yourself, and let us come back; renew our days of old!"* (Lamentations 5:21). May we once again see the good old days.

The book is linked to the Ninth of Av, the commemoration of the day when Jerusalem was destroyed. That day is a weighty day of remembering and of synagogue celebration. For that event – through which many other events of loss are voiced – lingers as the supreme act of candor in Judaism. It must be enacted over and over yet again because Jews continue to live in a world where silence is not fully answered and where absence looms up daily in many forms of violence.

The Book of Ecclesiastes

The name, *Qoheleth*, given to the narrator of this book, is a feminine participle referring to "an assembly" or the one who "assembles" the "assembly" thus it is often translated, "the preacher". It is conventional to place this material in the late Persian or Hellenistic periods, perhaps in the context of economic failure or disillusionment (perhaps national disaster), when affirmation is difficult if not impossible.

The substance of the book is a collection of wisdom sayings and teachings that ponder the mystery of creation and life in the world. We find that mystery much more inscrutable and much less "user friendly" than the old affirmative wisdom teaching of the Book of Proverbs.

Ecclesiastes opens by introducing the narrator as the Qoheleth, the Assembler, son of David, king of Israel. Tradition assigns his identity to an aged and wise Solomon; however, the dating makes this impossible.

"Utter futility! All is futile!" declares Qoheleth in his opening speech. Eugene Petersen in his *Message Bible* translates futile/futility with the word "smoke" which, in some ways I believe, captures the mood well. Life is smoke and mirrors. Creation goes through her paces and in the end, there is nothing new under the sun. Yet some will still come offering a new and improved version of reality and all will flock to it forgetting what has come before.

Qoheleth admits that he himself had played the "Grab the Gusto Game" … accumulating property, slaves, wealth, beautiful women… "sucking the marrow out of every task." In the end, however he had nothing, nothing but smoke… "smoke and spitting into the wind."

It matters little if you are smart or stupid the same fate awaits us all. So Qoheleth's question is, "Why bother being wise?" Qoheleth determines that he hates life on this earth because it is all pursuit of wind. So, he calls it quits. He gives up on the pursuit of wealth, for what use is it to work your fingers to the bone? The best you can do, he surmises, is essentially to eat, drink and be merry.

In chapter 3 Qoheleth quotes from the Byrds' song of the early 1960's, *Turn, Turn, Turn* as he meditates on the nature of time. Again, it is pointless to try to figure HaShem out, we have no clue what HaShem is up to so we might as well enjoy the gifts of HaShem and eat, drink and be merry.

As Qoheleth reflects on HaShem's judgement he concludes that HaShem is testing us. In the end HaShem's judgment is this, our fate is the same as the beast so we are in the end no better than the beasts of the field and the sooner we figure that out the better off we will be. Party time!

Qoheleth then turns his attention to oppression and violence. His conclusion is that those who are dead are the lucky ones because their miseries have come to an end and luckier still are those who never lived.

Rather than working like a dog, which Qoheleth concludes is just bad business, we should find someone to share our wealth. Friendship will not only keep your bed warm at night it will sustain you in times of trial.

Chapter 5 briefly describes how you should deal with HaShem… listen, learn, keep your mouth shut and do what HaShem tells you to do. In the end too much dreaming, speculation and idle talk is just so much wind and may anger HaShem (remember Job?).

Poverty and injustice is the way of this world. Have no fear though, the earth will judge. The lover of money will never be satisfied nor will the thief be far from his door.

After this reflection, Qoheleth concludes that the only appropriate course of action is to eat, drink and take pleasure in his work for as long as he lives. He should also bear in mind that all he has is a gift from HaShem. "Because such a man will not brood much over the days of his life, because HaShem keeps him busy enjoying himself."

Chapter 7 contains a collection of short pithy wisdom sayings that might be gathered under the heading, "Don't Take Anything for Granted". Qoheleth returns to his assessment of his worthless life asking the big question, "Why do bad things happen to good people?" and the more troubling corollary, "Why do good things happen to bad people?" While he doesn't posit an answer Qoheleth does say that the key to navigating this morass is to keep the big picture in mind. Reflect on both sides of an issue and remember that while we only deal with a piece of reality HaShem holds the totality in his hands.

Wisdom, is, stronger than human strength. This Wisdom is, however, elusive. In fact, Qoheleth claims never to have been able to discover it. All he has managed to discover is that HaShem's creation was good and wise and we've managed to royally screw it up.

Qoheleth concludes with another collection of Wisdom sayings. Succinctly put, in the end all is smoke!

A postscript extols the work of Qoheleth but then ends with this sage advice: "*The making of many books is without limit. And much studying is wearying of the flesh. The sum of the matter, when all is said and done: Revere HaShem and observe His commandments! For this applies to all humanity: that HaShem will call every creature to account for everything unknown, be it good or bad*" (Ecclesiastes 12:12-13).

The sum of the matter: Fear HaShem and do what he tells you to do.

Ecclesiastes is linked to the Festival of Booths/Succoth (Tabernacles) (sic. Transfiguration), a day of deep rootage and joy. It speaks of a constant righting of balances. Set against the gaiety and plenty of the holiday, which commemorates the ingathering of the harvest, the shadows cast by the book of Qoheleth lengthen and darken. The jaded wisdom of Ecclesiastes warns the reader not to absolutize either the buoyancy of the book of Proverbs or the eroticism of the Song of Songs. Time moves and time bears away every season. The eternal one, in silent indifference, brings closure to every scene. Soberness belongs in Jewish usage of the book in the context of the festival. Translated into Appalachian: If it is good…it will only get worse.

The Book of Esther

"Zaydeh, my friend Itzhak got beat up on his way home from the yeshiva last week. He said this happens to our people all the time because we are Jewish. Is it dangerous to be a Jew in this world?"

> *"Oh, yes, Jakob, it has been that way for a long time. Let me*
> *tell you a story…"*

The book of Esther is a tale of Jewish courage amid the threats and risks of the Persian Empire. (5th and 4th Centuries BCE). It is a *tale* for both entertainment and instruction. It is preoccupied with the status of Jews in the empire who at the same time (a) maintain an intense self-consciousness as Jews and (b) with pragmatic wisdom come to terms with the reality of imperial power.

Set in the time of Xerxes who ruled from India to Ethiopia we enter the story as the king is giving a banquet. His queen commits a royal *faux pas* by refusing the king's invitation to the party. The king bans his queen from his presence. A search for beautiful young virgins to replace the queen commences in Susa.

There is a Jew in the palace complex of Susa by the name of Mordecai who is the guardian of one Esther (who is blessed with a good figure and beautiful face). Mordecai turned Esther over to Hegai who is collecting the young virgins for the king. After a year-long beauty treatment the girls were to be presented to the king. The king fell in love with Esther more than any of the other women and made her queen.

Sometime later, Xerxes appoints Haman as the highest-ranking official in his court. Xerxes decrees that all people should bow down before him and all the people knuckled under except Mordecai (who we are told did not bow because of religious objections). Haman is notified and when he himself sees that Mordecai refuses to bow declares that not only Mordecai, but all Jews in the land should be eliminated.

When Mordecai receives the news, he rends his clothes and puts on sackcloth and ashes, as do the Jews of the land, and a loud lament was heard over all the country. Word finally comes to Queen Esther about the decree.

She schemes up a dinner party for Xerxes and Haman. At dinner Xerxes offers her anything in the world. Her request is her life, and the lives of her people. This perplexes Xerxes. She informs him that she and her people have been sold and are to be massacred. The king is outraged and demands to know who would do such a thing. Then Esther drops to bomb, it is Haman!

Haman is hung on the gallows that he had prepared for the Jews. The king gives Esther all of Haman's estate which Esther entrusts to Mordecai's care. The city of Susa celebrates. The Jews are now honored throughout the countryside and many non-Jews become Jews now that they are no longer in danger.

On the dark side, the Jews of Susa went on a pogrom of their own killing Haman's sons, leading officials that had sided with Haman and in time another 300 men. Later outside of Susa another 75,000 were killed.

Haman cast the *pur* (lot) condemning the Jews but Queen Esther had intervened saving her people. On the 14th day of the month of Adar a festival is established to celebrate with much food and laughter the change of fortunes for the Jews of Susa. This is the Festival of Purim, an occasion of joy and elation over the sheer Jewishness of life and faith. It is a carnival performance of misrepresentation that prevents powerless Jews from being cornered and trapped in conventional power relations. The result is that every generation of Jews has opportunity to engage again in the daring task of Jewish particularity in the public life of the world. To be a Jew is to live both *as if* and also *here and now*.

DANIEL

"Zaydah, if this world is so dangerous for our people, how do we continue to believe?"

"My son, HaShem will save us. The world is scary and it feels we are losing ground all the time but he will ultimately triumph and save us."

Daniel is one of the most mysterious books of the Tanakh. Written in two languages, Aramaic and Hebrew, in the Tanakh. We find in the Greek translation of the book several major additions. Its composition is in two distinct divisions which do not coincide with the difference in language. While set in the time of the Exile it probably reflects a final editing in the time of the Maccabees. Finally, it is the only example of apocalyptic writing in the Tanakh. As with most apocalyptic rhetoric it is linked to a historical reality. In this instance the crisis of faith to be faced is the onslaught of Hellenism through the initiative of Antiochus IV (Epiphanes – God Himself) of the Seleucid regime of Syria who sought to establish his political as well as his cultural domination over Jerusalem by overriding and eradicating Judaism (Hitler was not the first!). It is perhaps because of this apocalyptic thrust that the Christian Old Testament includes Daniel among the prophets whereas the Tanakh includes it with the Writings.

The structure of the book is in two parts: chapters 1-6 narrative about the hero of the story, Daniel, and his compatriots; chapters 7-12 form the apocalyptic section in the form of Daniel's visions. The language division is roughly chapters 2-7 in Aramaic and chapters 1, and 8-12 in Hebrew. This has led scholars to treat chapter 1 as an introduction to the unit that circulated separately, and probably earlier, comprised of chapters 2-6. Scholars also tend to assign the remainder of the book to the period of the Maccabean Revolt. The Greek edition includes poetic material (Prayer of Azariah and the Song of the Three Young Men) inserted into chapter 3 and free-standing stories appended to the work (Bel and the Dragon and Susanna).

In most of the Tanakh the term Chaldeans is used synonymously with that of Babylonians but in Daniel, as in the rest of the material emanating from the Hellenistic period, it is used for a class of astrologers, sages and diviners. As such they would be seen as similar to the magi of the Persian/ Zoroastrian tradition.

The opening chapter sets the time as early in the time of the Exile. It seems that King Nebuchadnezzar has ordered that some of the young nobles (without blemish, handsome and proficient in all wisdom) would be trained for three years in the ways of the Chaldeans and then enter into the king's service. Among them are Daniel, Hananiah, Mishael and Azariah. They are given new names: Belteshazzar, Shadrach, Meshach and Abed-nego. The first test of their enculturation is their refusal to eat the king's food (an act of defilement under the Torah). They not only thrive but become superior physically and in wisdom and understanding to their Babylonian counterparts.

Like the Pharaoh from the Joseph cycle of Genesis, King Nebuchadnezzar is also beset with troubling dreams. When the wise men of the Babylonians were unable to interpret his dream, he orders their execution (including Daniel and his boys). Like Joseph, Daniel manages to get an audience with the king and satisfies his conditions of interpretation and interprets the dream. The king in thanksgiving pays homage to Daniel.

One of the more humorously told stories in the Tanakh is to be found in chapter 3. (It is often read as one of the readings at the Easter Vigil where I have heard it accompanied by the wide variety of musical instruments mentioned as well as articulated with the dripping satire intended). The storyline is simple: the king sets up a golden (remember the calf!) stature of himself and then orders everyone to bow down before it (this strategy would later be instituted by the Seleucids and the Romans as they occupied Jerusalem). Of course, Shadrach, Meshach and Abed-nego refuse and are turned into the court Gestapo by slandering Chaldeans. As per the royal threat they are thrown into the fiery furnace which had been stoked seven times hotter than is customary. It is reported that not only do they appear not to be consumed but that there is a fourth figure with them. Nebuchadnezzar orders them released, and like Lazarus is called forth in the tomb in John's gospel, he calls them forth by name to, "Come out!" This miraculous experience causes Nebuchadnezzar to decree that they should be allowed to worship their Most High God if they wished and that no one could do them harm for so doing. The trio is also promoted. The section ends with Nebuchadnezzar issuing a statement of faith in the Most High God in the form of a royal decree.

Chapter 4 finds King Nebuchadnezzar again plagued by a troubling dream. As in earlier chapters Daniel is called to interpret the dream and he reassures the king that all will be well. Once again, this prompts Nebuchadnezzar to bear witness to Daniel's god.

Chapter 5 presents us with King Belshazzar, son of Nebuchadnezzar, throwing a royal banquet in which he brings forth all the Temple accoutrements that his father had confiscated when the Jerusalem Temple was destroyed, and then proceeds to drink from them. When mysteriously the finger of a human hand begins to write on the wall, Belshazzar begins to mess his britches in fear and trembling. Unable to explain what any of this means once again Daniel is called to interpret. Daniel's interpretation is not good news for Belshazzar as the inscription signifies that his kingdom will come to an end, that he is been weighed and found wanting, and that his kingdom will be divided between the Medes and the Persians. In response, they clothe Daniel in purple, place a gold chain on his neck, and proclaim that he should rule as one of the three in the kingdom. That very night Belshazzar is killed and Darius, the Mead succeeds him.

Darius indeed appoints Daniel as one of the three to oversee the 120 satraps (governors) within the kingdom. Once again, the other ministers and satraps are overcome with jealousy and force Darius to issue a decree that no one should address a petition to any god or man except for Darius himself. Daniel receives word of the ban and immediately goes to pray. Daniel is turned into the authorities whereby he is reminded of the law of the Medes and Persians that has established the ban and is summarily thrown into the lions' den. A rock is placed over it and the king seals it with his signet. Unable to sleep the king goes to the lions' den first thing in the morning to confront Daniel. Daniel informs the king the dangers of trying to shut the mouths of the lions and that he was found innocent before his God. Relieved, the king orders those who brought charges against Daniel along with their children and wives to be thrown into the lions' den in Daniel's place. Again, the story ends with Darius offering a confession of faith in the god of Daniel.

Chapter 7 introduces Daniel's series of visions. While this first apocalyptic vision is written in Aramaic it is felt by scholars that the editors have done so to make a smoother transition between the court drama of 2-6 and the apocalyptic material of 7-12. The setting of this section also shifts from the Exile to Jerusalem under persecution. It is generally assumed that the time in question refers to the Maccabean Revolt against the Syrian king Antiochus IV Epiphanes roughly around the mid 160's BCE. Antiochus sets himself up as a god (Epiphanes – "god manifest") and engages in the desolating sacrilege (Daniel 11:31) where he erects a pagan altar over the existing altar in the Jerusalem Temple.

This first vision features four beasts representing four kingdoms that will arise somewhat reminiscent to the king's vision of chapter 2. However, rather than signifying the coming of an age of promise these kingdoms will arise from the chaos of the primordial seas. The scene quickly shifts to a courtroom trial presided over by the Ancient of Days. His description explains many of the anthropomorphized depictions of HaShem and later the Father of the Christian Trinity. Charges are read and the fourth beast is destroyed in the flames because of his arrogance and dominion is removed from the other three beasts. The power and dominion of the four beasts is then handed over to "one like a human being." Translated also as "one like the Son of Man" it is easy to see how this figure is appropriated by later Christian writers to speak of Jesus. Verse 15 and following introduces the explanation of the vision to Daniel by one of the attendants present. All this leaves Daniel shaken.

The second vision comes to Daniel two years later and features the fortress of Shusshan by the Ulai river. Daniel then witnesses a battle between a ram (Persia) and a goat (Greece). While the goat emerges victorious it is at the cost of its "great horn" possibly pointing to the early death of Alexander the Great. Out of it grows fours horns representing the successor kingdoms following his death: Greece, Asia Minor, Syria and Egypt. Again, it is the "small horn" (Syria/Antiochus IV Epiphanes) who assaults the god of gods and his heavenly host. It is the angel Gabriel this time who brings the interpretation to Daniel. In the end this small horn, this upstart Day Star (sic. Isaiah 14:12-15) and his assault of heaven (assault on the Jerusalem Temple) will crash and burn. In his hubris and arrogance, he will bring about his own defeat.

The third "vision" brings us to the first year of the reign of Darius. In a departure from the earlier visions this one finds Daniel consulting the ancient manuscripts concerning the prolonged desolation of Jerusalem over and against that spoken of by Jeremiah (25:11-12; 29:10-14). Daniel's conclusions will reverberate into modern apocalyptic calculus – in short you can explain or explain away almost any discrepancy in apocalyptic literature through reinterpretation. Reminiscent to the prayers in Ezra and Nehemiah, Daniel prays for understanding. Gabriel, once again, brings the necessary understanding. Verses 25-26 introduce an anointed one who will disappear and vanish. This anointed one is not to be confused with the Messiah but rather is a reference to the "anointed" High Priest Onias III who was murdered in 171 BCE.

The final vision (chapters 10-12) are set in the third year of the reign of Cyrus of Persia. We find Daniel during a three week fast. Similar to Ezekiel's vision (8:2) Daniel is encountered by an angel of epic proportions. He informs Daniel that he is an answer to his prayers. Assisting this angel is Michael who appears to be his Second Lieutenant and in charge of occupying the Persians so that he can do his work. The angel informs Daniel that in the first year of Darius, the Mede, he made his appearance.

In language familiar to Game of Thrones viewers, the Kings of the North (Syria) and the Kings of the South (Egypt) are introduced. These kings will at first engage in an alliance but eventually will war against each other. Antiochus IV Epiphanes rears his contemptable head in Chapter 11 (vs. 21ff). He invades the Kingdom on the South twice and while initially successful on his second invasion he encounters the Romans (Kittim) and is sent packing. His frustration is taken out on Jerusalem who is engaged in revolt. His campaign will be violent, destructive and successful until he meets Michael and his doom. While the ensuing *time of trouble, the like of which has never been seen"* is attributed to the Maccabean revolt, Daniel makes no mention of the Maccabees. Instead Daniel refers to the Maskilim or wise ones as the true champions of the people. The vision and the book conclude with a final scene at the river with two men standing, one on each bank. The question of the day is, "How long will this last?" For the author of Daniel, the end comes not with the Maccabean victory but points to a time in the future. It is HaShem alone who gives futures.

EZRA AND NEHEMIAH

Modern scholarship refers to these two books collectively as the Ezra/Nehemiah movement. This movement, born in the days following the Exile, is one of Torah purification that was exclusionary, not only toward non-Jews, but towards other Jews (People of the Land) who were thought to be "less Jewish" than the small group of returnees who presented themselves as "real Jews" and who were qualified in pure Torah obedience. This work is explicitly anti-Samaritan. The themes of this movement are clearly pedigree and purity.

In bringing these two books together you bring also the two major personalities of these books together in juxtaposition. In Nehemiah you have the self-glorifying entrepreneur who is credited (with Persian help) as the decisive force in rebuilding the city of Jerusalem. In Ezra, you have the self-effacing teacher of Torah who reconstitutes Judaism as a community committed to Torah obedience. The dates for Ezra and Nehemiah are 458 BCE and 444 BCE, respectively.

Ezra opens with a proclamation from Cyrus, King of Persia, that he has been commissioned by HaShem to build a temple for him in Jerusalem.

In addition to underwriting the project, Cyrus also garners the support of the neighboring countries as well as those who were left behind at the time of the Exile. He also released all the religious vessels and accoutrements confiscated by the Babylonians.

Chapter 2 includes a detailed genealogical roster of those who return from Exile. This roster was obviously designed to establish pedigree and purity, separating those who were exiled from those who were not. Also included are listings of servants, chiefs of clans, priests and Levites.

In the seventh month of the return from exile the people builds an altar in accordance with the Torah of Moses and offered sacrifices there for they were in fear of the people of the land. These sacrifices continue with regularity. By the second year of their return the foundation of the new Temple had been laid and dedicated. It was an occasion marked by both tears and great joy.

Seeing that the temple project is moving ahead the people of the land offer to assist. Their offer is rebuffed. This sets off a campaign by the people of the land to undermine the building of the Temple which in turn prompts a letter to Darius, the new King of Persia, to enlist his aid. In the sixth year of the reign of King Darius the Temple is finished and dedicated, celebrating for seven days the feast of Unleavened Bread.

Following this, Ezra, a scribe expert in the teaching of Moses, comes up from Babylon to Jerusalem. King Artaxerxes of Persia authorizes Ezra to set up a provisional government which is outlined in chapter 8.

When all this was over attention is turned toward the purity of the community. While the Temple is being built there has been laxity in maintaining a separation between the exiles and those who remained, including intermarriage. Efforts now begin to restore the land to religious purity. The book of Ezra concludes with a list of those who had brought foreign wives and after acknowledging their guilt are forced to offer the appointed sacrifice. It is clear by the details of this listing that offspring from these relationships would be seen as tainted into the future and not constitute the purity of the newly formed land.

Nehemiah was the King of Persia, Artaxerxes', cup-bearer. In the 20th year of king Artaxerxes reign Nehemiah requests that he be sent to Judah to assist in the plate of the exiles who have returned to rebuild Jerusalem. His efforts then are described in the first four chapters of the book.

In the fifth chapter we hear of the uprising of the opposition which results in sanctions being placed upon them by Nehemiah. Commissioned by Artaxerxes, Nehemiah is appointed governor of the land of Judah. The rebellion continues but so does the rebuilding of Jerusalem.

As with Ezra, Nehemiah includes a detailed list of those who came up out of exile from Babylon in chapter 7. Chapters 7-9 present the dedication of the new Jerusalem. Again, in chapter 10 detailed listing of officials, Levites, and priests is found as is a careful listing of the commandments, rules and laws of HaShem regarding the purity of the city. Chapters 10 - 12 include yet another listing of those deemed pure enough to assume positions of leadership. The final chapter describes how Nehemiah purged the foreign element within Judah.

1 & 2 CHRONICLES

"Zaydeh, tell me the story of our people once again...please...I need to remember!"

The *divrey hayyamim,* literally translated "the events of the day," is the title given in the Hebrew Bible for the work of the chronicler. With this book the Tanakh is brought to a close or should I say opened up to a future. It is a highly stylized and carefully edited second account of the history of the world from Adam to the brink of the post-exilic restoration in 539 BCE.

Whereas the Deuteronomic Historian was writing in the time of the Exile and concerned with explaining how the Glory Days of Israel and Judah deteriorate into the deportation and diaspora the Chronicler is writing a revised version of Israel's memory in the context and under the impact of the Persian Empire over Judah as a dependent colony of the empire. The chief observation of the Chronicler is that Judaism's only chance for freedom of thought, faith and action is through the maintenance of a liturgical practice and sensibility. The centerpiece of the Chronicler is the establishment and maintenance of the Temple. While the focus of the book is on the First Jerusalem Temple, the context for the Chronicler and his audience is the Second Temple.

The structure of this two-volume work is:

1 Chronicles 1-9: Introduction
1 Chronicles 10-2 Chronicles 9: Material related to the monarchy of David and Solomon
2 Chronicles 10-36: The history of the Southern Kingdom following the destruction of Israel.

The introductory material consists of lengthy genealogies and lists of those who returned from Exile. (The lists definitely slant toward those in the priestly class.)

The reigns of David and Solomon are viewed as seamless lacking the intrigue of the Deuteronomic Historian. It is also of note that the emphasis of their reign is the establishment of the Temple. Sheer volume of material makes this clear with the organization of the Temple cult taking up four chapters alone. As we have discussed earlier, the centralization of the Temple Cult (with the destruction of non-Jerusalem sites) under Josiah placed the Levites under the supervision of the priests of Aaron. Also included in this material is the rotation of priests in the service of the Temple which was a post-Exilic development to try to deal with the glut of priests in Jerusalem.

The Chronicler is more concerned with an ideal history than a factual one so that the Temple worship found here is more ideal than accurate.

The covenant that HaShem makes with David is foundational for the Chronicler and Israel's failure to remain faithful is reason for its downfall. The covenant is not focused on kingship however, but on the Temple. As long as things are kosher in the Temple life is good. In essence then, while there are Messianic overtones to this history, it is the Temple and proper worship that will lead to the people's deliverance.

Herbert Tarr, rabbi, novelist and humorist, makes the statement of Chronicles: *"This is not history, it is grand opera!"* It describes a history as it should have been and not necessarily as it was. To carry the opera image, the nation of Judah is a choir that sings its way through historical crisis, no doubt at the behest of various postexilic temple musical guilds. As we see in the narrative, it is the Levites who emerge in chapter 6 as the "Temple Singers." This view of Judaism centered on the Temple cult is legitimized by a history that is supported by divine retribution for failure to maintain the proper Temple cult practices. The Chronicler hopes that through his history this Judaism is legitimized and given proper authority.

The culmination of the book and hence the Tanakh is an act of defiant faith in the midst of occupation and crisis. Jewishness may suffer but it has not been defeated, attested to here by the capacity of HaShem to move empires on behalf of Judaism. It is HaShem, who has kept the people alive and productive all these millennia, fulfilling his part of the covenant... as promised!

> *One distinctions between the Tanakh and the Christian Old Testament is the closing of the respective books. The Christian Old Testament ends with Malachi and the expectation of the Messiah whereas the Tanakh concludes with the Chronicler and a call to faithfulness to the covenant and worship. The response given in light of the crisis of the destruction of the Temple and Exile in the Tanakh is clear – faithfulness to Torah.*

New Testament

Unless otherwise noted, all Scripture quotations are taken from **The New Interpreter's Study Bible**: **New Revised Standard Version with Apocrypha.** Abingdon Press, Nashville, 2003.

Those references cited "The Message" refer to **The Message: The Bible in Contemporary Language** (Numbered Edition), Eugene H. Peterson. NavPress: Colorado Springs. 2005

"Zaydeh, I met a new friend at the gymnasium today. His name is Crispus and he said that he is a Christian. What is a Christian?"

"That is a good question, Jakob, but not an easy one to answer. They were a movement within Judaism during the final terrible days under the Roman rule of Palestine. They were followers of a prophet, Jesus who came from Nazareth. They proclaimed him as messiah, the deliverer, and there were hopes that he would drive the Romans from the land but the Romans crucified him around the year 33. The movement continued through the time of the revolt and the destruction of the Temple. They would gather with us in the synagogue for Torah study. Things got tense after the destruction of the Temple. With pressure from the Romans we eventually expelled the Christians from the synagogue. They continue to meet in people's houses, eating and drinking together and remembering the stories of Jesus."

As we turn to the New Testament it will do us well to remember where we left off. Whereas the Hebrew Scriptures leave us at the doorstep of the exile the Christian Old Testament leaves us anticipating the coming Messiah. This is a very important distinction to keep in mind. The followers of Jesus to not constitute a separate religion until almost the end of the first century. In addition, the only Scriptures available to them are the Hebrew Scriptures in both the original Hebrew as well as in Greek translation commonly known as the Septuagint. Finally, we need to recognize that those early followers of Christ were seen within the context of the Jewish family of parties such as the Sadducees, Pharisees, Essenes and Zealots. They are distinguished within Judaism by the belief that Jesus was the Messiah and a profound apocalyptic view of history. The early followers of Jesus attended synagogue with their other Jewish brothers and sisters until the late 80s and early 90s when they were expelled.

These close ties to Judaism as well as the ensuing tensions between the parties provide a not-so-subtle undercurrent throughout the writings of the New Testament. The writings of Paul will often speak to the distinction between the teachings of Jesus and the keeping of Torah. In the Gospels we find the probing's of the Sadducees and Pharisees trying to identify and categorize Jesus within the proper Jewish party. The later New Testament writings reflect the growing unrest, the expulsion as well as early anti-Semitic teaching.

In addition to this Jewish context the New Testament also is highly influenced by the larger Hellenistic culture in which it finds itself. We see this in the philosophical tendencies of Paul (trying to validate his claims and teachings in a language that will be understood by the learned Hellenists). There is also an attempt to convey Christianity as a continuation of Judaism in an effort to convince the Romans that this new religion is actually very old (criteria which is paramount for a religion to be taken seriously by the Romans). Christianity in its infancy is forced to argue its credibility with both the Jews and Romans. The Jews saw them as diverging from the Torah and the Romans saw them as just another mystery cult. Finally, the movement of Christianity into that larger Hellenistic culture is reflected not only in Paul's letters but also the Gospels and particularly in the later writings of the New Testament including the Pastoral Epistles.

As we have noted, Early Christianity is shaped dramatically by the historical and political context of Hellenization and Roman occupation of the Palestinian region. Beginning in 334 BCE when Alexander the Great invades the Persian Empire the Greeks undertake a comprehensive process of turning the world on to being Greek. Through urban planning, language and religion they thoroughly imposed the Greek culture on the world which they conquered.

As we see with the Maccabean Revolt (167-142 BCE) this process of acculturalization did not play well with the Jews. In 142 BCE the Jews under Simon Maccabee gain full independence from Greek rule. His son, John Hyrcanus, expands the territory of Judah north into Samaria and Idumaea and parts of the Transjordan, destroying temples and encouraging the population to be circumcised and to observe Jewish law. In Idumaea, John permitted only those residents who agreed to be circumcised to be allowed to remain all others were forcibly deported. One of the most famous of the circumcised was Antipas, the grandfather of Herod the Great. John, in turn is succeeded by his son, Aristobulus who is the first of the Hasmonean (Maccabee) family to call himself king. He conquers

Galilee and converts the population to Judaism resulting in that region that was mixed with "converts" and Jews from Judea. Aristobulus is not a nice guy and has all his brothers as well as his mother imprisoned. When he dies his widow, Salome, frees his brothers (his mother had died of starvation) and marries one of them, Alexander Jannaeus. During his reign the Pharisees organize a revolt over the many abuses that Alexander had committed. In the end they abandon the revolt but Alexander has 800 of them crucified anyway, raping and slaughtering their wives and children in front of them. Alexander is succeeded by his wife, Salome who rules while her son, John Hyrcanus II, serves as High Priest. When Salome dies there is a bitter battle between her sons, John Hyrcanus II and Aristobulus II. Both brothers appeal to Rome for help in solidifying their claim to the throne. Rome is more than happy to oblige and simply takes over the Hasmonean kingdom.

Rome dismantles the Hasmonean kingdom and when Jerusalem falls (37 BCE) they set Herod up as king. Herod, while a loyal supporter to Rome, is ruthless, murdering most of his own household. Upon his death Herod's kingdom is divided between his three sons, all named Herod. They all were eventually removed by Rome and the territory is placed under direct Roman administration under the Roman Legate of Syria. Local administration was assigned to the prefect or procurator in Judea. This was a low-ranking official in the system. Pontius Pilate serves in this position from 26-36 CE and is renowned for his corruption and cruelty, he is eventually dismissed from his post.

It will be helpful for us to keep this larger historical and political context in mind as we enter into the literature of the New Testament. We will find both accommodation and reaction against Judaism as well as Hellenism in these writings. As with the Old Testament/Hebrew Scriptures the most significant historical event within the New Testament timeline is the destruction of the Second Temple in 70 CE during the Jewish/Roman revolt. While Paul's letters are written prior to this destruction the remainder of the New Testament is drastically influenced by that event. In many ways much of the New Testament writings comprise a Post-Temple-Destruction hermeneutic. Put more simply, "What do we now?"

One of the pressing questions of the post destruction era both for Jews as well as Christians is, "Are we looking at the end of time/Day of the Lord?" This question can already be seen in the writings of Paul but finds full expression in the apocalypticism of Revelation. How Jews and Christians live into these latter days will account for the divergence in teaching and practice that will eventually lead to their separation.

As we turn to the writings of Paul we will see better the struggles that are encountered in the early church not only between the followers of Jesus and the Jews but also with non-Jews alike. Paul's letters and the letters attributed to Paul provide us with the earliest of the New Testament writings.

Paul (still referred to as Saul) first appears in the New Testament narrative in Luke's *Acts of the Apostles* at the stoning of Stephen. The dates often associated with Paul then are (c. 5-68 CE) the latter date being his martyrdom under Nero (54-68 CE). He is reportedly born in Tarsus, a very large Hellenistic city at the time in the province of Cilicia (present day southern Turkey). Tarsus is a center for Stoic philosophers and many mystery cults of its day.

Paul claims a notable Jewish pedigree as a member of the Pharisee Party. He is also a Roman citizen which on more than one occasion saves his life. He is probably a tentmaker by trade. We read in the *Acts of the Apostles* that Saul was a persecutor of the Christian movement who undergoes a spectacular conversion experience. Because of this experience he receives a new name, Paul, and begins an evangelical ministry to the world outside of Jerusalem and Judea.

Paul is not only influenced by his education as a Pharisee (often reactionary in his claims) but is also heavily influenced by the Greek philosophical movements of his day. The three most influential of these being Stoicism, Cynicism and Epicureanism.

[Excursus]

Stoicism holds that Nature is rational. The universe is governed by the law of reason. One can't escape its inexorable force, but they can, uniquely, follow the law deliberately. A life led according to rational nature is virtuous. Wisdom is the root virtue. From it springs the cardinal virtues: insight, bravery, self-control and justice. Since passion is irrational, life should be waged as a battle against it. Intense feeling should be avoided.

Pleasure is not good. (Nor is it bad. It is only acceptable if it doesn't interfere with our quest for virtue.) Poverty, illness and death are not evil. Virtue should be sought, not for the sake of pleasure, but for duty. It advocated an ethic of self-discipline and control to achieve virtue regardless of one's life circumstances. A modern-day version of Stoicism is the Serenity Prayer: Abba, grant me the serenity to accept the things I cannot change, courage to change the things I can, and wisdom to know the difference.

Cynicism is a school of philosophy which holds that the purpose of life is to live a life of Virtue in agreement with Nature (which calls for only the bare necessities required for existence). This means rejecting all conventional desires for health, wealth, power and fame, and living a life free from all possessions and property.

Cynics aimed to be quite indifferent in the face of any insults which might result from their unconventional behavior. They saw part of their job as acting as the watchdog of humanity and to evangelize and hound people about the error of their ways, particularly criticizing any show of greed, which they viewed as a major cause of suffering. Many of them were later absorbed into Stoicism.

Epicureans believed that the main reason for studying philosophy was practical: to make a happy life for yourself. They said that you would be happy if you had more pleasure in your life and less sadness. But sadness is caused by not getting what you want. The Epicureans said that the best way to be happy and not sad was to not want anything. It's wanting things that leads to pain. If you're always wanting more things, then you can't enjoy the things you do have, because you're always suffering the sadness of not having things. The Epicureans advised people not to make close friends or fall in love, because it could lead to sadness if your friend went away or died. The less you want, the happier you will be.

The Epicureans also taught people that when they died, their soul would die with their body, because both were made of atoms that would be broken up and made into other things when you died. They said that therefore people should not be afraid of dying or worry about what would happen to them after they died.

The Epicureans also claimed not to be afraid of the <u>gods</u>, because the gods did not interfere with people's lives. When things happened, it was just because of natural causes, and nothing to do with the Abbas.

[***Note***]

As with the case of our discussion of the Hebrew Scriptures I am intentionally substituting the word Abba (Father/Daddy) for God. I do this for several reasons: First, the term God comes loaded with much categorical baggage that is not Biblical (i.e. omniscient, omnipresent etc.); Secondly, I would like to make a distinction between how the Jews view HaShem and how the early Christians view Abba; and finally, in the New Testament we come to God through Jesus and so I find it appropriate to refer to God with the name that captures that unique relationship.

PAULINE LITERATURE

The Pauline Literature is arranged in the New Testament according to length from Romans to Philemon. However, I will deal with these letters in order of chronology (as best as we can determine). The literary form of the Pauline corpus is that of the "letter" (*epistulae*). It was a common form among the learned including politicians, philosophers and poets alike. They were moral and aesthetic rhetoric intended as much for the ages as for the addressee. In contrast Paul's correspondence (except for *Romans)* bears a more personal tone rather than universal suggesting his priority is addressing the situation at hand. Regardless, these are not hasty e-mails, texts or tweets but well-developed works of art.

The basic form of a "Letter" is: Greeting, Prayer, Reason for Correspondence, Farewell. The great difficulty that faces us in dealing with the Pauline Literature is its occasional nature. These letters deal with specific issues within the life of the churches that he is addressing. Like a detective we must decipher Paul's letters to determine what the issue may have been. Sometimes this is clearer in some than in others.

I do not want to spill a great deal of ink on authorship of the various letters as scholars have laid out the arguments far better than I. The key is that these letters had an authoritative nature within the life of the early church and in the process of forming the New Testament canon. It is usually agreed that Romans, 1 & 2 Corinthians, Galatians, Philippians, 1 Thessalonians and Philemon can be attributed to Paul and that 1 & 2 Timothy and Titus are not. The remainder, 2 Thessalonians, Colossians and Ephesians are up for debate but the scholarship leans heavily to these not being from Paul's hand.

1 Thessalonians

"Where are you going in such a hurry?"

"Got mail to deliver to the church!"

"What's so special?"

"This letter is from Paul!"

"Who's Paul?"

"He was here in the early days and worked with us in sharing the good news of Jesus."

1 Thessalonians is the oldest of Paul's letters probably dating to around 50 CE. This makes the earliest New Testament literature written some 20 years after the death of Jesus. There were other collections of writings, stories etc. but in terms of the New Testament this is the oldest book.

Paul commends the Thessalonians for their accepting the message of the gospel and their conviction in acting out the gospel's ethical claims. They've also been faithful in their witness to the regions around them including Macedonia and Achaia. At the end of chapter 1 Paul provides a reminder to them of the kind of faith they have demonstrated in in so doing outlines the key issues for the rest of the letter. The Thessalonians have turned from idols to worship and serve the living and true Abba and they wait confidently for Jesus's return.

Paul calls upon them to remember the early days of their ministry when Paul was among them: Paul brought the good news to them and how they labored and toiled together with the sake of the gospel. He commends them for their imitation of the churches in Judea who were suffering the same type of persecution which the Thessalonians are experiencing (persecutions at this time were sporadic, localized, and driven by a mob mentality).

Paul desires to return to the church but since his way has been thwarted he sends Timothy to "strengthen and encourage" them. Paul offers high praise to the church in Thessalonica as they are his glory and joy as he awaits the coming of the Lord. He is also heartened by Timothy's report of what he is found among the Thessalonians.

In chapter 4 Paul gets down to business and expresses his concern that there might be some good old-fashioned backsliding going on among the Thessalonian community Paul admonishes the community to live a life of purity and holiness. This strong ethical demand of the gospel on the part of Paul may reflect his education as a Pharisee with overtones of the holiness and purity tradition (Leviticus).

The final issue for the Thessalonians seems to be the delayed return of Jesus. This concern is heightened by the fact that some of the early converts are now dying and what will their fate be in light of the final resurrection at Jesus return. Paul assures the community that they too will be included in the resurrection. In fact, they will be raised first and those living will be gathered with them to be with the Lord forever.

Paul concludes his letter with an apocalyptic discourse and an admonishment that will sound familiar when we get similar sections in the Gospels. Paul raises two directives concerning the end times: do not to try to form a timeline for Jesus's return but rather be faithful and diligent in your work. Paul's final admonishment is to have peace, to pray without ceasing and to always give thanks.

2 Thessalonians

Scholarship views 2 Thessalonians as modeled after 1 Thessalonians but probably not from the pen of Paul. The letter lacks the intimate language of Paul's first letter. Rather than commending the Thessalonians for their faithfulness this letter focuses more on issues of concern.

Again, the major concern is for the end times. The letter admonished the Thessalonians that the persecutions which they are experiencing are signs that the end is near and should not be a change in the divine agenda. They are also warned of those who will come with a deceiving word to the contrary such as the "Lawless One" who is placing himself over and against Abba by taking his seat in the temple and declaring himself to be Abba. Reminiscent of Antiochus Epiphanes and the desecrating sacrilege this could reflect the Roman attempt to establish the Caesar as Abba. One of the issues of great antagonism was Rome's placement of an eagle standard in the temple precinct. The fate of this lawless one will be death.

The author reminds the Thessalonians that they have been chosen by Abba to proclaim the good news, that they should stand firm and hold fast to the traditions that they had taught them by so keeping them they would obtain the glory of our Lord Jesus Christ. The letter closes by reminding the community to continue to work. It seems there were some among the community that in the light of the imminent return of Jesus had stopped working altogether. It is in this context that the often-quoted line in Welfare debates that you should earn your bread is to be seen. There is also a closing request for prayer, that the mission of the apostle might spread rapidly.

1 Corinthians

"Arcalades, did you hear Appolos is coming to town?"

"Big deal!"

"But I thought you were Christian? Petros down the street makes a big deal that he was baptized by Apollos. Don't you follow Apollos too?"

"That's the problem these days everybody's following somebody. You got the Jewish synagogues, the Greek temples, mystery cults and clubs and on top of it all these people claiming to be Christian who follow every Apollos, Petros and Paulos! It's

like everybody's trying to figure out who they are and how they fit into this wondrous port."

"I'm confused. I thought Jews and Christians didn't get along and yet in the Christian church there both Jews and non-Jews alike."

"As I said everybody's trying to find their place. In a world like we live in these days with everybody moving around sometimes it's helpful to have a group to belong to the especially when you move into a new city. In the end were all Hellenists!"

Written between 53 and 54 CE 1 Corinthians is part of a larger body of correspondence perhaps involving upwards of five or more letters. Unlike the Thessalonians the Corinthian church could not be accused of being "lukewarm". If anything, over exuberance in using the powers gained through the Spirit is causing problems within the community. What develops is a spiritual elitism… "My gift is better than your gift!"

First Corinthians is often viewed, even by himself, as Paul's "Dutch Uncle" talk to the wayward Corinthians. While the tenor of the letter is stern and forceful we cannot lose sight of Paul's fatherly love for the people of Corinth. It is this love that compels Paul to step in and address the current situation. That situation? It seems that the members of the church cannot get along with each other. Imagine that!

Paul, appeals to his appointment as their spiritual father as authority for his not so gentle admonition of the congregation. He has sent them Timothy to remind them of what he taught them while he was there. Paul informs them that he himself will be coming to them soon and so asks, *"Should I bring a stick or come with love and a spirit of gentleness?"* (1 Corinthians 4:21).

In the opening lines Paul appeals to the unity we share in one baptism. It is obvious that in Corinth even baptism has become an occasion for division. What is important for the Corinthians is not the baptism but rather who presided over the baptism: was it Apollos, Peter or Paul? Paul is insistent that in the end it is only the power of Christ and the wisdom of

Abba that matters in baptism. The ministry of the apostle is to be a steward of the mysteries of Abba. Human leaders have no room to boast - they are only agents of Abba.

As agents are stewards of Abba the apostles proclaim the message in such a way that it points to the cross of Christ. While this cross is mere foolishness for many, to the faithful it reveals the way Abba is always operated by flipping all the world's categories upside down. It is the cross that distinguishes Christian from non-Christian, whether Jew or Greek. The Jews want proof and the Greeks get wrapped up in philosophical arguments the Christian appeals only to the cross. It is this "proof" of a failed Messiah that ultimately makes no sense on the world's terms. The bottom line is that this is not about us (Apollos, Paul or Peter) but about Abba so if you want to blow somebody's horn, blow Abba's.

Paul appeals to his credentials, or lack thereof, to disarm those who would appeal to their own power or wisdom. In a rather tongue-in-cheek way he informs the Corinthians that he's kept the message simple so that they might understand that it is always about Christ and Christ crucified. It is only through the gift of the Spirit we receive in baptism that we can even begin to comprehend this mystery.

In chapter 3 Paul gets down to the point – he's frustrated by the way the Corinthians are dealing with one another – they are simply behaving like spiritual children. In light of the competing claims to this leader or that, Paul uses gardening images of planting and harvesting as well as architectural images such as blueprints and building materials to explain how one leader only builds upon another and all build upon what Abba has done in Christ. Paul then reminds the Corinthians not to get uppity and think themselves better than the Master.

It seems that there is an attempt by the Corinthians, at least some of the Corinthians, to impress the larger community by portraying Christianity in high and lofty terms. To this Paul replies with a description of the apostle's work, "*It seems to me that Abba has put us who bear his message on stage in a theater in which no one wants to buy a ticket. We're something everyone stands around and stares at, like an accident in the street. We are the Messiah's misfits. You might be sure of yourselves, but we live in the midst of frailties and uncertainties. You might be well thought of by others, but we're mostly kicked around. Much of the time we don't have enough to eat, we wear* patched in threadbare clothes, we get doors slammed in our faces, and we pick up odd jobs anywhere we can to eke out a living. When they call us names, we say, Abba bless you. When they spread rumors about us, we put in a good word for them. Were treated like garbage, potato peelings from the culture's kitchen. And it's not getting any better." (The Message, 1 Corinthians 4:9-13).

Before launching into the specifics and meat of the letter Paul takes one more shot at the Corinthians: *"I know there are some among you who are so full of themselves they never listen to anyone, let alone me. They don't think I'll ever show up in person. But I'll be there sooner than you think, Abba willing, and then we'll see if they're full of anything but hot air. Abba's way is not a matter of mere talk; it is an empowered life... So how should I prepare to come to you? As a severe disciplinarian who makes you toe the mark? Or is a good friend and counselor who wants to share heart-to-heart with you? You decide.* (The Message, 1 Corinthians 4:18-20).

It appears that within the Corinthian church community there is a sense in which now that they have been saved by the grace of Abba they are free to do whatever they desire. This leads Paul to raise several topics for discussion.

Paul appears to lead with the most sensational of topics – sex. Although as the letter continues what he sets up in his discussion on sexuality it will eventually translate into a discussion of the church as the body of Christ. It appears that there have been scandalous sexual affairs of the inappropriate kind happening with in the church body. It also appears that these matters have been taken lightly by the leadership. Paul extends his attack to include fornication, idolatry, adultery, male prostitution, sodomy, thievery, greed, drunkenness, reviling and robbery. When the community responds by saying everybody else is doing it Paul reminds them that they are not everybody else. Appealing to the image of the body of Christ Paul reminds the Corinthians that their bodies have been redeemed by the resurrection of the body of Christ and are therefore now holy and sacred. What one does with one's body, or someone else within the community, is to do it also to Christ's body. This line of thinking sets up the conversation about the body of Christ in chapter 12.

Paul also admonishes them for seeking legal resolution to disputes instead of resolving them in-house within the congregation. Matters such as those outlined above should be dealt with by the congregation. They should not let their dirty laundry hang out for the whole world to witness.

The question of marriage and singlehood for Paul is to be seen in the context of the Parousia, or the end of the age (sic. the great and terrible day of the Hebrew Scriptures). Marriage and singlehood are not to be compared to one another as one being more desirable within the life of the church. For Paul the issue is whatever you are, married or unmarried, remain in that state. Paul also deals in this section with mixed marriages – Christians married to non-Christians. If one finds themselves in that situation they should remain in it for they extend the holiness of Abba even unto their spouse. On the other hand, if a non-Christian spouse walks away from the marriage they should be let go. The bottom line with all of this is to keep life simplified considering the future. Do not get your life so complicated that it is difficult for you to carry on your service to Jesus and the community.

Chapter 8 deals with a topic that is foreign to us as 21st Century readers namely, eating meat offered to idols. What Paul is referring to is the pagan practice of sacrifice where only a portion of the offering was sacrificed and the remainder was sold in the market. While there was nothing wrong with the practice of a Christian buying and eating such food if it raises issues within the congregation, particularly among the newer members of the congregation for those interested in joining the congregation then you should refrain. Matters of the Law/Torah must always be adjudicated in the context of the community. If something is lawful but not helpful to keeping community then it must be avoided.

Chapter 10 is an interesting piece of Pauline writing. In it he equates the passing through the sea and the sojourn from Egypt as akin to being baptized (into Moses not Christ). Here is the clearest understanding of the relationship (for Paul) between Jews and Christians as that of brothers and sisters. The Jews simply are living with their heads in the cloud and unable to see clearly that this Jesus is the Messiah/Son of Abba. In chapter 10 Paul informs us that they had all the same advantages as Christians for Christ was the rock from which they drank the supernatural drink. The Israelite problem was they succumbed to idolatry and sexual immorality (as is what is happening in the Corinthian community as Paul writes). Verse 13 is probably the source for the mistranslated but often quoted, "God never gives you more than you can handle." What the text does say is that Abba does not test us beyond our capacity and always provides for us a way out so that we may endure and persevere.

Paul moves to one of the key issues in the Corinthian congregation namely the abuses around the communion table. The practices of the community expose the issue of socio-economic inequality. The rich in the congregation, who do not work, show up to the meal early and gorge themselves as well as get drunk while the poor working class come late and get the scraps. Paul attacks this by recalling the institution of the Lord's Supper which will call us back into the body of Christ until Christ returns. Paul furthermore admonishes the Corinthians that are irreverently receiving the body of Christ as being like part of the mob that cursed and spit upon Christ and his crucifixion. Finally, Paul makes it clear that there are consequences to such irreverent behavior: *"even now many of you are now listless and sick and others have gone to an early grave"* (The Message, 1 Corinthians 11:30). Mmm… The implications are pretty clear!

In chapter 12 Paul turns to the issue of spiritual gifts. There appears to be an issue over the spiritual gifts, or charisms, that the members of the Corinthian church possess. It appears that they were comparing and grading certain gifts as more desirable than others. Paul in what I consider a stroke of genius introduces the body as an illustration of how the church functions. With the precision of a skilled surgeon Paul cuts to the heart of the issue – we are the body of Christ and individually members of it each possessing a unique gift that is necessary for the body to function. This integrated life means that not only is it impossible to grade the parts of the body but that one cannot remove oneself from the body as well. *No part is important on its own. Can you imagine Eye telling Hand, 'get lost; I don't need you'? Or, Head telling Foot, 'you're fired; your job has been phased out'?* (The Message, 1 Corinthians 12:22). All the charisms/gifts within the life of the church are integrated in equal measure.

Chapter 13, which has nothing to do with marriage but everything to do with being the body of Christ, reminds the church that it is in love that we live and function as the body of Christ. Without such love the church is bankrupt. The characteristics of this love are as follows: *love never gives up. Love cares more for others than for self. Love doesn't want what it doesn't have. Love doesn't strut, doesn't have a swelled head, doesn't force itself on others, isn't always "my first", doesn't fly off the handle, doesn't keep score of the sins of others, doesn't revel when others grovel, takes pleasure in the flowering of truth, puts up with anything, trust Abba always, always looks for the best, never looks back, the keeps going to the end.* (The Message, 1 Corinthians 13:4-7)

Chapter 14 continues the discussion particularly around the gift of prophecy, its interpretation and the right use of the gift. The gift of prophecy was especially contentious in the community. This "speaking in tongues" has been deemed by the community as a special gift. Paul reminds the community that it is only a helpful gift since it leads to the building up of the community. In and of itself it is nothing. I was painfully reminded of this passage when I was doing my clinical work in a mental hospital in West Virginia. One of the patients was afflicted with a mental illness that consisted of a six-week cycle from going from catatonic to lucid and back to catatonic. When she was in her lucid phase she confided in me that she was certain that Abba had abandoned her because she no longer was able to speak in tongues. So sad. It is always about building up the body of Christ.

As in Thessalonians, Paul picks up the issue of the resurrection of Christ and of the dead. The issue here is whether there is a resurrection which as we have seen was a bone of contention between the religious parties of Jesus day. In this discussion Paul lays forth the witness of the apostles to Christ's resurrection. Paul also includes himself in that line of witnesses as the resurrected Christ revealed himself to Paul on the road to Damascus. Paul's logic is that if Jesus was raised from the dead how can one say there is no resurrection? We then as the extension of the resurrected body of Christ shall enjoy the fruits of the resurrection. Besides, Paul comments, do you think if there was no resurrection I be risking my life preaching that there was? Paul concludes his discussion on resurrection with one of the most beautiful descriptions of resurrection in all of Scripture: *"But let me tell you something wonderful, a mystery I'll probably never fully understand. We're not all going to die – but we are all going to be changed. You hear a blast to end all blasts from a trumpet, and in the time that you look up and blink your eyes – it's over. On signal from that trumpet from heaven, the dead will be up and out of their graves, beyond the reach of death, never to die again. At the same moment in the same way, will all be changed. In the resurrection scheme of things, this must happen:*

*everything perishable taken off the shelves and replaced by the imperishable,
this mortal replaced by the immortal. Then the saying will come true: death
swallowed by triumphant life! Who got the last word, oh, Death? Oh, Death,
who's afraid of you now?"* (The Message, 1 Corinthians 15:51-57).

In chapter 16 Paul concludes with an issue he will return to in many
of his letters: the collection for the church of Jerusalem. The church in
Jerusalem is experiencing especially difficult times. The church in Corinth,
like Galatia, is asked to set aside the excess of their weekly collection for
the Jerusalem church and Paul will pick the collection up on his way back.

2 Corinthians

The second letter to the church in Corinth is actually a combination
of two letters. The earliest portion 10:1-13:10 and then a fragment of a
later letter is found in 1:1-9:15 written probably somewhere around 55-
56 AD from Ephesus and/or Macedonia during Paul's third journey.
The purpose of the letter in its present form was to reestablish a good
working relationship. Because of an undisclosed affliction Paul has had
to postpone his planned visit back to Corinth hence this letter. Paul has
already had an earlier painful visit so he is somewhat relieved that this
visit has been postponed so that the Corinthians wouldn't have to endure
another painful visit from him.

Chapters 1-9 reflect the reconciliatory tone of this letter. The opening
section, 1:8-2:17, offers an autobiographical portrait of Paul including the
anxiety he experiences when he travels to Troas and cannot find Titus
there.

The section from 3:1-6:10 is a defense of his ministry. Paul claims that
the strength of his ministry is only in his confidence in Christ. Once again,
he compares the Corinthian church with Moses and the Israelites. In this
case he refers to the veil that covered Moses as reflective of the veil that
keeps the eyes of the Jews from seeing Jesus. Cannot the Corinthians see?

Chapter 4 uses the image of a treasure in a clay jar to make it clear that
the power is from Abba and not from us (a concept the Corinthians seem
to be having difficulty with). It is this extraordinary power of Abba that
will enable the community, collectively and individually, to withstand the
present and future events. In the same way that Abba supported Christ

during trial and torture, mockery and murder so will Abba support us. Paul reminds the Corinthians that these things are fleeting and insignificant when compared to the glory that awaits us in the resurrection.

One of the growing issues within the Pauline church is a falling away from, or denouncing belief in Christ. Under the Romans it was customary to offer potential martyrs the opportunity to renounce Jesus and live. Here in chapter 6 Paul issues an invitation to reconciliation for the apostate backsliders and a reminder that perseverance in suffering leads to endurance.

Chapters 8-9 are devoted to the collection for the Jerusalem church. It seems Paul has been talking the Corinthians up around his travels as exemplars of contributors to the collection – "Now don't make me look like a liar… step up and make this contribution a big one!"

In chapters 10-13 (fragment of earlier letter) Paul writes in a tone of pain and defends himself against charges leveled at him by those in Corinth. It appears that Paul is being painted as a pushover when he is present with the Corinthians and a harsh critic of them when he is away. Unfortunately, these accusations bring out the side of Paul that often lends itself to characterize him as egotistical: *I've worked much harder, been jailed more often, beaten up more times than I can count, and at death's door time after time. I've been flogged five times with the Jews 39 lashes, beaten by Roman rods three times pummeled with rocks once. I've been shipwrecked three times, and immersed in the open sea for a night and a day. In hard traveling year in and year out, I've had to ford rivers, fend off robbers, struggle with friends, struggle with foes. I've been at risk in the city, at risk in the country, endangered by desert sun and sea storm, and betrayed by those I thought were my brothers. I've known drudgery in hard labor, many a long and lonely night without sleep, many a missed meal, blasted by the cold, naked to the weather. And… That's not the half of it.* (The Message, 2 Corinthians 11:23-27).

Galatians

"Hey, Mikos, were you in church this week?"

"Yeoh, why?"

"I heard those folks from Jerusalem were stirring things up again."

"They were... telling me I had to be circumcised if I was going to be a 'real' Christian!"

"Sounds a bit extreme if you ask me."

"All I know is that this is not the Christianity that Paul introduced here when he taught among us. We were nothing but a bunch of misguided pagans in those days but I do remember Paul talking about freedom from this kind of stuff."

Galatians was written in 51-52 AD on Paul's Second journey from Corinth or Antioch or Ephesus or Corinth on his third journey. The Galatians came to Christianity directly from paganism but there seems to be a counter movement at work pulling them toward Judaism. Some scholars have wondered if the James Party or the Judaizers might have been at work. Regardless, the question confronting this new Christian community seems to be: "Did they need Torah as well as Christ?"

Paul is royally ticked off by what has happened to the church in Galatia since he had been with them. He is quick to inform the Galatians that anyone who comes and preaches another gospel contrary to the one that they had received from him is accursed. There is only one gospel and that is the gospel of Christ.

Paul wastes little time getting to the heart of his detractors' assessment of his ministry namely, his inadequate credentials and his deficient message. At the heart of the credential issue is the fact that Paul was never a disciple of Jesus while Jesus walked on this earth, this issue constituted the heart of the apostles' authority – they were witnesses of Jesus in flesh and in blood...they were there! As a result, Paul must appeal to a higher authority namely, Jesus himself. Paul claims that his message comes directly from Jesus without the need of it being handed down from "the experts." Paul then recounts in autobiographical detail and lacking in humility the details of his early life as a follower of Jesus.

What Paul concludes from his early life is that if you make Torah observance what you will follow then you are seeking to live as a perfectionist because only one who can keep Torah perfectly stands a chance of earning their way into heaven. Paul recognizes within his own self the inability to do this. No matter how hard he tried he couldn't keep the rules. It is only after he gives up on being a "Law Man" that he finds himself able to be an "Abba's Man". In a rather shocking, if not questionable revelation, Paul announces that his ego has been crucified and is no longer central in his life but has been replaced by Christ. To fall back on a life of Torah/Law is to repudiate Abba's grace. If you could enjoy a relationship with Abba based on keeping the Law then Christ died unnecessarily.

After Paul berates the Galatians for their backsliding he questions if it is their intention to continue in this chasing after the Torah. It is a matter of which comes first the cart or the horse. Do we live a moral life because we have a relationship in Abba in Christ? Or do we seek to earn a relationship with Abba by living a moral life and keeping the Torah? Paul's argument is that the latter is simply impossible to do.

The argument of Paul's opponents is that the Messiah is a Jewish savior. Being in the Messiah therefore demands becoming part of an historic people, the Israel of Abba as well. Paul appeals to Abraham who did not receive the Law but only its promise. Paul argues that the Torah was an addendum (430 years after the fact) to the covenant that Abba made first with Abraham. The promises of Abba were contained in the covenant with Abraham. The purpose of the Torah was to keep people in line with the way of salvation until Christ arrives. The Torah is not a first-hand encounter with Abba but with his middleman, Moses. We are surrounded and protected by this Torah until we are mature enough to respond freely to the living Abba. This maturity is not of our own making but of Christ's. Baptism is not only a washing but also a dressing in the wardrobe of adult faith. Christ is the fulfillment of Abba's initial promise. In short, they needed the Law before Christ came (the Law was disciplinarian) but now that Christ has arrived we no longer need a disciplinarian. As long as we are under the Law we are no better than slaves or children but now that Christ has arrived we have received adoption as children of Abba and may call Abba, "Abba, Father.

Beginning in chapter 4 Paul lays out the implications of this freedom and mature faith. There are no distinctions either between Jew and non-Jew, slave or free, male or female all are equal.

Paul returns to the issue of backsliding into the Torah mindset. He appeals to the Galatians love for him and asks that if they cannot keep from backsliding because of their being enamored by the Torah could they please refrain from it for their love for him. He drives his point home once again by using the illustration of Abraham's two children, Isaac and Ishmael. Paul claims that Ishmael, conceived by faithless connivance harassed Isaac who was from the faithful promise. Ishmael, as a slave, is unable to inherit from Abraham so the Galatians must be careful in their choices. Paul reminds them that they are not children of the slave woman but rather of a free woman.

This freedom comes from Christ and enables us to live a free life. Because of this we must be careful not to allow ourselves to be enslaved by anything including the Torah. This includes a life of law keeping as well as circumcision. The minute we allow ourselves to be circumcised we've traded in our free life for a life of slavery. The issue of circumcision is at the heart of Paul's letter to the Galatians and throughout the early church. For Paul it is clear that baptism is enough to initiate one into the life of Christ. Circumcision is not only unnecessary it can be an impediment to experiencing the grace of Abba.

In the latter part of chapter 5 Paul warns that there are dangers inherent with this life of freedom. When we are free it is tempting for us to believe that we can now get our own way all the time and do whatever we wish to do. Paul reminds the Galatians and us that this leads to *"repetitive, loveless, cheap sex; a stinking accumulation of rental and emotional garbage; frenzied and joyous grabs for happiness; trinket Abbas; magic show religion; paranoid loneliness; cutthroat competition; all-consuming yet never satisfied wants; a brutal temper; and impotence to love or to be loved; divided homes and divided lives; small-minded and lopsided pursuits; the vicious habit of depersonalizing everyone into arrival; uncontrolled and uncontrollable addictions; ugly parodies of community"* (The Message, Galatians 5:19-21).

This kind of behavior however is crucified among those who belong to Christ in their call and who live a new life, the life of the Spirit. One of the implications of this life in the Spirit is that we do not spend our time comparing ourselves to one another for the truth is we all are originals of Abba's creation.

The final chapter of Galatians centers around the cross, and nothing but the cross. It is the love of Abba as revealed in the cross of Christ that draws us into a new life. Those living in that new way should forgive; not be impressed with themselves; to take responsibility for doing the best they can; be generous; and should not grow weary doing good.

Paul concludes by reminding the Galatians that we have nothing to boast about but the cross of Christ. Because of the cross *"we've been crucified in our relationship to the world in set free from the stifling atmosphere of pleasing others.* Paul then applies this one final time to the issue of circumcision. *"It is not what you and I do – submit to circumcision, recheck circumcision. It is what Abba is doing, and he is creating something totally new, a free life all who walk by this standard are the true Israel of Abba – his chosen people. Peace and mercy on them!"* (The Message, Galatians 6:15-16).

Just in case the Galatians haven't quite figured out how worked up Paul was he leaves them with this parting shot: *"Quite frankly, I don't want to be bothered anymore by these disputes. I have far more important things to do – the serious living of this faith"* (The Message, Galatians 6:17).

Romans

"Junia, I was just talking to the church secretary and she said that a letter came in from that church planter, Paul."

"What did it say?"

"She didn't go into details but it seems that he's planning a trip here to Rome."

"We already have a church here! What does he want with Rome?"

"It sounds like he wants money for some new mission out West. You know how those evangelists are!"

"That's for sure!"

Paul's letter to the Romans is unique in that it is addressed to a church that Paul did not found. There also is no crisis that Paul is addressing. Written from Corinth during Paul's last journey (56 CE), the letter seems to be preparing a way for the church in Rome to become a new base of operations for Paul's mission west and his continual collection efforts for the church in Jerusalem. Since Paul has never visited Rome prior to this the letter to the Romans serves as a letter of introduction and recommendation for Paul. As such it provides a clear and logical statement of Paul's beliefs: sin, grace, freedom, baptism and the Christian community. (Romans could be called Paul's Greatest Hits album). Embedded in this letter is also Paul's attempt to address the growing tensions between Jewish Christians and Gentile Christians.

Paul's letter opens with a note of thanksgiving for the faithful witness of the congregation in Rome. Also included in these introductory comments is Paul's intention to finally visit the congregation in Rome that he may proclaim to them the gospel for both Jew and Greek.

Picking up where he left off in Galatians Paul uses the first three chapters of Romans to lay out his argument concerning justification by faith through grace. He begins with Abba's judgment on those who suppress the truth. While this truth is not explicit at this point it becomes clear in the argument that what Paul is referring to is justification by faith. This failure to grasp Abba's grace has been with us from the beginning of creation. Paul then begins to set the trap by laying out all manner of sin and perversion. Beginning with those sins that society would almost surely condemn. He then tightens the noose to include the envious, gossips, slanders, haughty, boastful, foolish, heartless, and ruthless. Paul reminds the Romans that Abba's decree is that such practices deserve death.

In chapter 2 Paul springs the trap announcing that those who would pass such judgment as in chapter 1 have already condemned themselves and deserve the same punishment. Paul reminds the Romans that it is not Abba's intention to condemn but rather to bring to repentance.

This leads Paul into a discussion of the place of Torah/Law in the Christian community. It is not the hearing of the Law but rather the doing of the Law, which even the Gentiles do instinctively, that is critical. Therefore, The Jewish/Christians cannot rely on the Law *and* boast on their relationship with Abba. If they break the law circumcision will not save them. The Jew then has no advantage over the Christian. The Law does not save but rather condemns. If we rely on the Law we miss the faithfulness of Abba. Paul's argument draws intensity until he reaches the end of chapter 3 with the indictment, *"since all have sinned and fall short of the glory of Abba; they are now justified by his grace as a gift, through the redemption that is in Christ Jesus, whom Abba put forward as a sacrifice of atonement by his blood, effective through faith"* (Romans 3:23-25). In short, now that we all stand condemned let me tell you about justification by faith.

Paul now turns to the example of Abraham as a model of such faith in the face of the world's idolatry. Because Abraham predates the Law Abba's promise that he would inherit the world did not come through the Law but through the righteousness of faith. The promise rests on grace and is guaranteed to Abraham's descendants because of Abba's faithfulness.

The results of this justification by faith are peace, shalom, and wholeness with Abba and Jesus Christ. Again, Paul makes it very clear that this gift comes through Christ and not in our own works of righteousness. Christ dies for the ungodly that we might be reconciled to Abba. At this point Paul introduces the image of Adam and contrasts him with that of Christ. Through Adam condemnation came into the world whereas Christ brings justification with Abba.

What does all this mean? Reverting to his earlier discussion with the Corinthians where Paul asks the question, *"Should we continue in sin in order that the grace may abound?"* (Romans 6:1). The answer is no. Paul reminds us that in baptism we have died to sin so why should we go on living in it? Rather baptism sets us free to walk in newness of life. Our old way of sin is crucified in Christ that we might be made alive in Christ. Sin brings death but Jesus Christ offers eternal life as a free gift.

Paul offers marriage as an analogy of this being set free from the Law. If a woman is married she is under the law of marriage and bound to her husband. If she lives with another man she commits adultery. If her husband dies she is now set free from the Law and if she chooses to marry another than she is not an adulteress.

Justification does not mean that we are free to disregard the Law as some have been known to do. The Law is holy, just and good. This leads to an inner conflict between what we know is right and what in our human sinfulness we feel compelled to do. On our own we tend to do what we know is not right despite that knowledge. It is for that reason that we can only be justified by Christ and not by our own works of the Law.

Abba has done in Christ what the Law could not do because the Law is ultimately bound by human flesh and desire. Therefore, when Christ sets us free we are no longer in the flesh but in the Spirit and as such children of Abba. This is not a spirit of slavery but rather one of adoption. We are now heirs of Abba and joint heirs with Christ.

Paul goes on to address the relationship of the persecutions and other calamities to our new life in Christ. What we experience in our earthly life is but preparing us for the glory that awaits us in the life yet to come. The present age is a time of travail. As a woman in labor, creation groans for adoption and redemption.

Paul brings this section to a close at the end of chapter 8 with a beautiful summary statement. *"What then are we to say about these things? If Abba is for us, who is against us? He who did not withhold his own son, but gave him up for us all, will he not with him also give us everything else? Who will bring any charges against Abba's elect? It is Abba who justifies. Who is to condemn? It is Christ Jesus, who died, yes, who was raised, who is at the right hand of Abba, who indeed intercedes for us. Who will separate us from the love of Christ? Will hardship, or distress, or persecution, or famine, or nakedness, or peril, or sword? No, in all these things we are more than conquerors through him who loved us. For I am convinced that neither death, nor life, nor angels, nor rulers, nor things present, nor things to come, nor powers, nor height, nor depth, nor anything else in all creation, will be able to separate us from the love of Abba in Christ Jesus our Lord"* Romans 8:31-39).

In chapters 9 through 11 Paul homes in on the relationship between Jews and Gentiles in this new relationship in Christ. Paul bemoans the fact that his own people, the Israelites, have it all: adoption, glory, covenants, the law, worship, promises, patriarchs and finally the Messiah but fail to understand. The Jews' continual unbelief will prevent them from receiving what the Gentiles already have obtained in righteousness through faith. Even so Paul continues to pray for his brothers and sisters that their ignorance might end and that they might see in Christ the righteousness of Abba. Paul puts a positive spin on the Jews failure by saying that through their stumbling, salvation has come to the Gentiles. Paul makes it very clear that the Gentiles have no room to boast because like a wild olive shoot they have been grafted to the true root. At issue for Paul is not the Jews unfaithfulness but rather in their pursuit of the Law. They have failed to see the mercy of Abba in Christ Jesus.

Paul now turns his attention to the ethical imperatives of this grace in Christ Jesus. In chapter 12, Paul uses body language to talk about how we are to live in this new life of Christ with a more positive spin than in First Corinthians.

Paul then lays out the identifying marks of those who enjoy this new relationship in Christ: their love is to be genuine, they are to hate evil, hold fast what is good; to love one another with mutual affection; and to outdo one another in showing honor. They should not lag in hope, be patient insuffering, persevere in prayer. They should contribute to the needs of the saints; extend hospitality to the strangers. They should bless those that persecute them; rejoice with those who rejoice, weep with those who weep. They are not to be haughty, but to associate with the lowly. They are not to repay anyone evil for evil, but look to what is noble in the sight of all. They are to live peaceably with all. They are not to avenge themselves for vengeance is the purview of Abba alone. They are to be subject to the ruling authorities for all authority comes from Abba. This includes paying taxes (it seems even then some were looking for loopholes!). Paul summarizes the law and the Commandments in: love your neighbor as yourself. Paul admonishes the Romans to recognize what time it is and therefore lay aside all works of darkness and desires of the flesh.

In chapter 14 Paul returns to where he began with the admonition that we must not judge one another. We are called to not put stumbling blocks or hindrances in the way of one another. As in First Corinthians he speaks of adhering to dietary regulations for the sake of weaker brothers and sisters. All that we do should build up our brothers and sisters rather than to tear them down or to cause them doubt. First and foremost, we should please our neighbors and not ourselves. This includes how we should treat Jew and Gentile.

Paul concludes on a personal note. While he admits that this letter has been rather bold he dares speak in this way only because of the grace given to him by Abba. This boldness has gotten him in trouble in other places and is the reason that he is hindered from coming to Rome. He announces his intention to go to Spain and hopes that Rome can become a base of operations for him to that end.

His final word is to avoid dissension and falling away from the teachings that they have learned. While the reputation is for obedience Paul admonishes them to be wise and do what is good. Paul summarizes his letter in the final and moving doxology: *"Now to Abba who is able to strengthen you according to my gospel and the proclamation of Jesus Christ, according to the revelation of the mystery that was kept secret for long ages but is now disclosed, and through the prophetic writings is made known to all the Gentiles, according to the command of the eternal Abba, to bring about the obedience of faith – to the only wise Abba, through Jesus Christ, to whom be the glory forever! Amen"* (Romans 16:25-27).

Philippians

"Euodia, Euodia, come quickly."

"What is it Syntyche?"

"The church just got a letter from Paulos!"

"Is he still in prison"?

"It sounds like it and thing are getting desperate for him. The letter sort of sounds like a last farewell."

"Paulos was always good to us here in Philippi."

"I think we were his favorites. Come on I'll let you read the letter!"

Paul founded the church of Philippi, his first in Europe. The church was a faithful supporter of Paul's work. Paul writes this letter from prison most likely in Ephesus or Rome. (If Rome 56-58 CE or if Ephesus 54-55 CE).

From the outset we get the sense that Philippians is a very personal letter. Paul opens with the greeting that every time he thinks of the church in Philippi he finds himself breaking out in thanks and prayer for their faithful service. These are not fanciful thoughts and prayers but based on the conduct of the Philippians. He prays that the love they have demonstrated so far amongst themselves will continue and bear fruit in the greater community.

In reflecting on his imprisonment Paul is encouraged that rather than the gospel message being squelched it is instead flourishing. It is true that some have stepped into the spotlight because of the void left by Paul's imprisonment but this does not bother Paul (much!). It is the proclamation that is critical regardless of how misplaced their motives might be. Whether he lives or dies, Paul is now convinced that the message will continue to be preached (so he might as well hang around for a little while longer).

Paul encourages the Philippi community to continue its unified stand, side by side proclaiming the gospel even in the face of their opponents. They should do this whether or not he is able to be with them for even in prison he hears of their powerful ministry.

Chapter 2 contains a beautiful and ancient hymn which Paul appropriates to drive home the fact that their proclamation is to be done in humility as an imitation of Christ's humility as demonstrated in the incarnation, *"though he was in the form of Abba, [he] did not regard equality with Abba as something to be exploited, but emptied himself…being born in human likeness. And being found in human form he humbled himself and became obedient to the point of death – even death on the cross"* (Philippians 2:6-11). So, the message should be proclaimed without whining or fighting.

Paul is hoping to be able to send Timothy, who is like a son to him, to them soon. It is his desire to come in person but his imprisonment prevents that at the present. So, for the moment the Philippians must be content with Epaphroditus whom the Philippians had sent to care for Paul. They are to receive him back joyously because he has risked his very life in the service of Paul.

It wouldn't be a Pauline letter without a little admonition, even though Paul himself says it is not warranted by the Philippians conduct. Like the pastor with a great sermon he preaches against backsliding whether it's needed or not (after all, it was a really good sermon!). It is the Judaizers with their reliance on Torah Law who must be avoided.

Paul turns to athletic language as he speaks of his work being like a race. Even now he is pressing towards the finish line. His call is for the Philippians to continue to imitate him remembering that their true destiny is in a heavenly citizenship and that our humble mortal bodies will be transformed into glorious resurrection bodies.

In concluding, Paul lifts up the work of Euodia, Syntyche and Clement. Citing their faithful service, he calls the community to rejoice. The return of the Lord is near so do not lose heart. They are to ponder on "*whatever is true, whatever is honorable, whatever is just, whatever is pure, whatever is pleasing, whatever is commendable, anything of excellence or worthy of praise*" (Philippians 4:8). They are to continue in the way of Paul's teaching and as such will be a reason for his rejoicing. All of this is an offering, fragrant and acceptable, to Abba to whom be glory forever and ever.

Philemon

"Linus, I hear Philemon has finally found out what happened his runaway slave."

"You mean Onesimus?"

"Yeah. It turns out he's been hanging around the apostle Paul."

"What is Philemon going to do?"

"I don't know for sure. I do know that the Roman Marshall just dropped off Onesimus to Philemon with a letter from Paul."

"I bet that's some letter!"

"Yeah, knowing Paul it's a real piece of diplomatic wordplay."

The occasion for the writing of Philemon, or perhaps more accurately, *to* Philemon, is that Paul has been in possession of one of Philemon's runaway slaves, Onesimus. Paul walks a delicate balance in the letter because technically Philemon, the slave owner, has Roman law to back up his claims, and since Paul is the cause of Onesimus' defection, he is legally to blame.

Paul's argument is that, Onesimus, now that he is a Christian, should not be treated as mere baggage or property. He is now an "equal before the Lord" and a "brother," Paul says. By accepting Onesimus, Paul has brought some financial harm to Philemon, which he promises to repay. At the same time, Paul is Philemon's benefactor: through the Pauline mission, Philemon has been given life in Christ, so that Paul can say to him, "You owe me even yourself." Paul may owe Philemon monetary compensation, but Philemon owes Paul much more. Paul thus trumps Philemon in the hierarchy of obligation.

Paul does not want to lose the assistance of Onesimus, so he would like Philemon to send Onesimus back. Although Paul's position may be tenuous from a legal standpoint, he states that "in Christ" he can indeed command Philemon's compliance. Paul will not demand Philemon's submission on the issue but will "appeal" to him on the "basis of love".

The Letter to Philemon shows us the close network of fellow workers. This fellowship (*koinōnia*) of Christian community is one of faith that is active in sharing, service and reciprocity. This fellowship "in Christ" supersedes natural kinship relationships and social conventions. In Philemon we begin to see how this new sort of fellowship will cause strain within the ancient social structures, so that not even tact and diplomacy will resolve the tension between these statements: "There is neither slave nor free" and "Slaves be submissive." In the concluding lines we see again the paradox of Paul, who, while in chains, is giving freedom to both slaves and masters through the "good news."

Colossians

"Teodora, I've been looking for you all over the place."

"Why Sophie, what's up?"

"I hear they've imprisoned Epaphras… You know the leader of the Christ cult."

> *"Really? I would've thought with all the cults that are already here that this Christ cult would blend in without any problems."*

> *"It seems that there are a growing number of Christ cult members they were getting dissatisfied with the way things were being run. They found some of the other cults more attractive because they were offering greater "perfection" than their own cult. It seems that Epaphras was getting all riled up and causing trouble among some of the other cults."*

> *"That's a surefire way getting into trouble. We don't like troublemakers around here that's for sure."*

Written late in Paul's life, or shortly after his death, or perhaps a combination of Paul and a later editor, Colossians describes Paul's ministry in the context of Abba's reconciling work in Christ. Of particular concern is the presence of an abundance of mystery cults as well as unorthodox Christian communities such as the Montanists.

In typical Pauline fashion, this letter opens with the thanksgiving for the ministry of the Colossian faith community and most especially for its founder, Epaphras. Their faithfulness is not only an occasion for thanksgiving but also for continual prayers by Paul and his cohorts.

The letter then moves into the central theme, that of the supremacy of Christ. For the author Christ is the centerpiece of creation and he is to reconcile all creation to Abba. Even now the community of faith in Colossae has been reconciled through Christ's death. They will be presented to Abba, holy and blameless, providing they don't backslide or go chasing after other gospels. Using the language of mystery, the author continues to describe this reconciling work in Christ as it is being handed over to the Colossians. Paul reminds them of how much he has been struggling on their behalf even though he is not physically present with them. Once again there is an admonition not to be deceived by the plausible arguments of philosophers or mystery cults.

Centering his arguments around the baptismal font and its promises in Christ's death and resurrection, Paul takes aim at those who would call into question their spiritual discipline. Citing these spiritual junkies as self-deluded charlatans, he critiques their commands and teachings as having the appearance of wisdom but lacking in any true value. In Christ, the Colossians already have "all the treasures of wisdom and knowledge" even though these riches are hidden. The seducers, in contrast, dangle before their eyes shiny coins, seeking to "defraud" them and, if they succeed, the Colossians will become their booty. The monetary metaphor running through this section is unmistakable in the Greek. Paul's point is that the Colossians have the true wealth that comes from Abba; they should not be taken in by counterfeit coinage. To illustrate how the attempt to achieve spiritual maturity based on human accomplishment is illusory, Paul uses another metaphor: it is like reaching after a "shadow" when the "body" (*sōma*) that casts that shadow is present (2:17). This image is very similar to Plato's famous cave metaphor, in which people settle for the shadows on the wall when the ideal and real is just outside the cave opening. For Paul, the shadow is the Colossian quest; the body (or, reality) is Christ.

Paul goes on to describe the new life in Christ as putting to death all that is earthly: fornication, impurity, passion, evil desire, and greed as well as anger, wrath, malice, slander, and abusive language. Having been stripped of the old the Colossians are now Abba's chosen ones and clothed in compassion, kindness, humility, weakness, and patience. The unity of the community is once again described in body language. The community should always live in a love that binds everything together in harmony. To accomplish this, they should dwell in the Word, which teaches and admonishes in wisdom, and to lift their voices in songs of gratitude, singing psalms, hymns, and spiritual songs to Abba.

This new life also has implications for how one lives within the Christian household. Instructions are given for how wives and husbands are to treat one another as well as the relationship between parents and children. Once again, the issue of slavery is addressed encouraging obedience on the part of the slave and just and fair treatment by masters.

In closing, Paul offers further instructions as the community deals with those around them as well as it prepares itself for the end of time. "*Devote yourselves to prayer, keeping alert in it with thanksgiving. At the same time pray for us as well that Abba will open to us the door for the word, that we may declare the mystery of Christ, for which I am in prison, so that I may reveal it clearly, as I should. Conduct yourselves wisely toward outsiders, making the most of the time. That your speech always be gracious, seasoned with salt, so that you may know how you ought to answer everyone"* (Colossians 4:2-6).

The community is encouraged to watch for Tychicus and Onesimus (more on him in Philemon) who will bring further greetings from Paul. The letter closes with greetings from other faithful servants throughout the empire who are working diligently to proclaim the word of Christ. The letter closes with this blessing, grace be with you.

Ephesians

"Mikkos, you should have been in church on Sunday we got a letter from Paulos."

*"**The** Paulos?"*

"Yeah, the converted persecutor."

"Don't you realize the Paulos has been dead for almost 60 years?"

"It says it's from him!"

"Yeah, right… So, what's it say?"

"Well, it's kind of general. Some of it seems like he may be smoking something- sounded like a lot of a mystical mumbo-jumbo. I heard one of the others say it sounded like a Eucharistic prayer! I think it's about prayer and hope. Maybe you should read it yourself."

"If I could read."

It may be because of its mystical language, or perhaps it's the use of adoption imagery, whatever the case, Ephesians is one of my favorite letters in the New Testament. It consists basically of two parts: a mystical description of the salvation received in Christ (Chapters 1-3) and secondly, the implications of the salvation and daily life (Chapters 4-6). For the author of Ephesians, theology informs prayer and prayer, in turn, conveys theology.

The letter opens with the mystery of the cosmos. This is the setting for the reconciliation work of Christ on behalf of all creation. The language of this reconciliation work is adoption and inheritance. The imagery of this opening section is also highly baptismal. The pledge of this inheritance and adoption is the seal with which we were marked by the Holy Spirit at baptism.

In almost Gnostic language the author prays that the Ephesians might receive the spirit of wisdom and revelation to gain access to Christ and to Abba. The power of Abba is seen first and foremost in his ability to raise Christ from the dead and to place him at the right hand in the heavenly places. This power and authority is cosmic, placing all things under the rule of Christ.

This movement from death to life now becomes the framework for our own conversion. Again, using the imagery of baptism and justification by grace we move from death and our old way to new life in Christ. This movement from death to life, from old to new, is reflected in the understanding that the Gentiles were once called the uncircumcised. In Christ now, there is but one body. So, the Gentiles *are no longer strangers and aliens, but are citizens with the saints and also members of the household of Abba, built upon the foundation of the apostles and prophets, with Christ Jesus himself as the cornerstone. In him the whole structure is joined together and grows into a holy temple in the Lord; in whom they are also built together spiritually into a dwelling place for Abba"* (Ephesians 2:19-22). The author claims that it is for the sake of the Gentiles that he is now a prisoner. The same gospel of grace that has set the Gentiles free to be fellow heirs is also the same gospel that now has Paul imprisoned. For all of this he offers prayers of thanksgiving that the church in Ephesus may persevere and continue to walk in the light. As with the church in Colossae, they are to be filled with the Spirit, and devote themselves to the singing of psalms, hymns and spiritual songs.

The author now moves to the specific implications of this conversation on the Christian household and the relationships between family members: husbands and wives, parents and children. These relationships are seen in the context of the greater mystery of the love of Christ for his church. The author applies the same calculus to the relationship between slave and master as well.

The final image in this letter is that of the armor of Abba. Amid this cosmic battle in which the church finds herself she must arm herself for the weapons of the Spirit and the defense of sound doctrine and faith.

The posture of this community of faith always needs to be in prayer. Prayer that they may be vigilant and keep awake, prayer for the author of the letter and prayer that the author may continue to speak boldly in the face of trial. The author's injunction to keep working will be picked up in the apocalyptic sections of the Gospels. The church, like Paul, is called in this in between time to serve as an ambassador willing to speak the truth of the gospel even if she must do it in chains.

THE GOSPELS

> *"Crispus, I asked my Zaydah about Christians. He said you believe in a man called Jesus. Who is Jesus?"*

As we begin to talk about the Gospels let's look back for a moment at the front porch. As we talked at the very beginning my thesis is that both the Hebrew Scriptures and the New Testament revolve around the catastrophic events of the destruction of the Temple. If what happened on the porch at the time of September 11 was post 9/11 hermeneutics, and the same experience is encountered in the exilic works of the Hebrew Scriptures, then what we find in the Gospels is a similar attempt to make sense out of the destruction of the Temple in 70 CE as well as where do Jews and Christians go from here.

Playing heavily on the work of the Deuteronomic tradition one of the first answers to the question about the future of Jews and Christians is a focus on keeping Torah. We have already discovered the tension that this created within the Christian community in the works of Paul.

The Gnostic tradition as well influences both Jewish and Christian thought with its focus on secret knowledge. It is also hard to deny that within the works of the New Testament there is an apocalyptic thread that points to a future end time when all of creation will be subsumed under the rule of the Christ

The question which the Gospels try to answer is, "In light of all that has, and continues to, happen who is Jesus and what does he mean for our faith community and the world?" Each of the Gospels tries to do this based on their context both in terms of audience as well as historical reality. The Gospels each come from a particular historical context in terms of distance from the destruction of the Temple and the heightened escalation of the Jewish Roman revolt. And so, we have in Mark's gospel a rather abrupt account of the life of Jesus (in fact some would say it's a Passion account with the life of Jesus attached). Contrast this with John's eloquent speeches of Jesus speaking to a church some 20 to 30 years removed from the destruction of the Temple.

One of the difficulties in talking about Jesus is that we are confronted by both a pre-resurrection and a post-resurrection portrait of Jesus. Marcus Borg in his book *Jesus* tries to describe the pre-resurrection Jesus in terms of five categories:

1. Jewish Mystic: The concept of Abba was for Jesus and experiential reality, and his experience of the sacred is the most persuasive explanation of what else he became.
2. Healer and Exorcist: His activity must've been remarkable; more healing and exorcism stories are told about Jesus than about any other figure in the Jewish tradition.
3. Wisdom Teacher: Jesus uses the classic forms of wisdom like parables and aphorisms and taught the classic subject matter of Wisdom of what Abba is like, what life is like, and "the way."
4. Prophet (Jeremiah): like the canonical Jewish prophets, Jesus was a radical critic of the domination system in the name of Abba and Abba's passion for justice. Perhaps more than anything else, this led to his execution.
5. Movement Initiator: even though Jesus' mission was brief a powerful movement came into existence around him during his lifetime. Small and embryonic, including both followers and sympathizers, it embodied his vision of the character and passion of Abba.

In an interview Marcus Borg was once asked, "What was Jesus like?" The following is his answer:

Jesus was from the peasant class. Clearly, he was brilliant and his use of language was remarkable and poetic, filled with images and stories. He had a metaphoric mind. He was not an ascetic, but world affirming, with a zest for life. There was a sociopolitical passion to him-like a Gandhi or Martin Luther King, Jr., he challenged the domination system of his day. He was a religious ecstatic, a Jewish Mystic, for whom Abba was an experiential reality. As such, Jesus was also a healer. There seems to be have been a spiritual presence around him, like that reported of St. Francis or the present Dalai Lama. And as a figure of history, Jesus was an ambiguous figure-you could experience him and conclude that he was insane, as his family did, or that he was simply eccentric or that he was a dangerous threat-or you conclude that he was filled with the Spirit of Abba.

In many ways Jesus stands firmly in the Wisdom tradition of the Hebrew Scriptures such as Ecclesiastes, Proverbs, and the Psalms. One of the characteristics of the Wisdom tradition is that there are two ways of being. The first is a common way which most will take and then there is an alternative way, a way of wisdom. In fact, the earliest Christians were called people of "The Way." This way reflected a path of transformation leading from how we ordinarily live our lives to a new way of being.

The old or common way focused around family, wealth, honor, and purity. Many if not all of these values are attested to and supported by a life of following the Torah. The new, or alternative way is centered on Abba, repentance (return from exile), and the movement from dying to rising. This alternative way, the way of Wisdom, can be summed up in a movement from death to life. In modern terms the Wisdom way is found in the work of Henry David Thoreau or in Robert Frost poem, "The Road Not Taken." The Gospels use the image of the exile to often talk about a life away from that of Wisdom. This common or old way describes life as being in exile even though we think we are at home, of being blind even though we see, of being dead even as we are alive, being in bondage even though we belong to the land of the free.

A wise way demands that such a common life is not worth living unless it is examined and judged. The diagnosis of this common life is often clouded because most of society prefers and adheres to the common life. This is often seen in a pursuit of cultural values and our image of what makes up the good life. Without examination we will continue to live in the exilic world system. The common way oftentimes receives the wise way, the way of this Wisdom, as a threat because they fear anything that threatens to disturb the cultural values and the good life. Considering this Wisdom, the general cultural mood following the destruction of the Temple is that of paranoia and fear. As such Jesus' message is not only a call to a wise life but it is also a threat to the existing order of the common life.

I would argue that Jesus sees himself firmly established within the existing Wisdom tradition. That said we must also acknowledge that at the time the Gospels were being written there was a movement that was sweeping through the Middle East called Gnosticism.

Gnosticism should not be seen as a monolithic movement but rather is a description of many movements seeking to explain the realities of the world. The word Gnostic was not used by the movement itself but is a 17ᵗʰ century invention. The word Gnostic comes from the Greek word *gnosis* which means personal, direct, and immediate knowledge. Those who practice Gnosticism claim to have a personal direct and immediate knowledge of Abba. Gnosticism can be confused with the wisdom tradition in that the Gnostic claims to walk a different path than the adherents of practical knowledge. Gnosticism creeps into the Gospels over time and does this particularly in John's Gospel.

Some of the beliefs and practices of Gnosticism include:

- angels and demons
- astrology
- atheism
- death
- dualism Holy/profane, body/spirit (soul)
- Epiphany
- Jesus Christ's humanity
- mysticism
- religious syncretism
- salvation
- symbolism

- Corporate exclusive worship
- Exclusive, wisdom/knowledge,

As one looks at the list one might wonder if the author, Dan Brown, isn't a closet Gnostic of the 21st century.

One of the discoveries of biblical scholarship in the 20th and 21st centuries is the understanding of Christianity not only as a personal and ethical movement but also a political one. To look at it another way Christianity not only has a piety but it has a politics.

Again, Marcus Borg describes these two dimensions of Christianity. First, the Bible is personal. It is our relationship with Abba as persons. And this relationship is the path of personal transformation - A way of: return from exile, sight to the blind, liberation from bondage. It is a way to new beginnings and to a life centered in Abba. Abba makes all the difference in our lives as persons.

The Bible is also political it is about Abba's passion for a different kind of world - one in which people have enough, not as the result of charity but as the fruit of justice. A world in which nations do not war against one another anymore. Abba's passion is for a world very different from domination systems, large and small, ancient and modern, systems so common that they can be called normal in a world of civilization. This is no exclusive New Testament. Much of this political agenda is found in the prophetic material from the Hebrew Scriptures.

This domination system, or coercive state system, has been expanding in the Middle Eastern region since the establishment of dynasties like Babylon and Assyria. They seem to be tied with the evolution of an agrarian society.

The context of the New Testament in general and the Gospels in specific is one in which Rome ruled the Jewish homeland through native collaborators from the elite class. When Jesus begins his mission, Galilee had been ruled for about 30 years by Herod Antipas. Judea and Samaria were ruled by the Temple authorities and Jerusalem aristocracy, under a high priest appointed by Rome. He and the other Temple authorities are charged with satisfying both Rome and their Jewish subjects. The authorities in Jerusalem did not have political jurisdiction in Galilee, they sought religious jurisdiction, not through overt authority but through influence. They had a stake in how Galilean Jews behaved – an economic stake, in that they paid tithes to the Temple and a political stake, as to whether the Galileans were restive or prone to rebellion.

As in most preindustrial agrarian societies, the system created and ruled by the powerful and wealthy, serves their financial interests and is economically oppressive to the rest of the population. This has been the way things have been in most societies since the Neolithic Revolution of the fourth millennium BCE, which created large scale agriculture, cities, city states, kingdoms, and empires.

There are compelling reasons to think the conditions in the peasant class were worsening. Herod the Great and his son spent lavishly not only on their regal lifestyle, but in massive building projects, including whole cities, all of which required a larger and larger extraction of peasant agricultural production. Rome's client rulers in both Galilee and Jerusalem also need to extract wealth from peasant production to pay the annual tribute to Rome. The economic consequences for the peasant class were severe. The life had always been hard, a peasant family that had land could normally produce enough for its own sustenance. But more and more peasant families were losing their land and entering a more desperate kind of poverty. To be landless meant living on the edge of destitution, and often over the edge.

The response to this growing domination can be found in the various religious political parties of the day. Each of these parties found their own way to approach this issue. For the Sadducees it was a matter of accommodation in finding a way within the Roman domination system to thrive. For the Pharisees it was an attempt to recapture the keeping of Torah in an effort to provide an alternative way of living. With the Essenes it was a case where things have gotten so bad that the only alternative envisioned was to abandon society and move into the desert and pray. The Zealots' response was violent revolution.

This violent revolution which the Zealots preached and practiced is nothing new. Since the establishment of Roman rule in 63 BCE, Jewish resistance continually harassed the Roman occupation troops and would continue to do so until the last major Jewish revolt is crushed and 132 – 35 CE. It is this violent revolution that has led to the destruction of the

Temple in 70 CE and the continual unrest within the region in which the gospels are set.

Over and against this violent resistance to the domination system comes Jesus who brings the language of the Kingdom of Abba. Again, this language is not new but can be found in the language of the Hebrew Scriptures. What makes Jesus vision of the Kingdom of Abba different is that it is **imminent**, within his generation; it is **inevitable**, it will happen; it is **interventionist**, Abba is about to intervene in history; and it is **unmistakable**, it will be both dramatic and obvious to all. It is the language of the Kingdom that most often gets Jesus into trouble with the Roman authorities and it is for this reason that Jesus is executed as a political criminal for crimes against Rome. This is the sentence then that warrants Jesus' crucifixion as an enemy of the republic.

SYNOPTIC GOSPELS

Before we look specifically at each of the gospels I would like to talk about the gospels in general. Matthew Mark and Luke when taken together are called the Synoptic Gospels because they present us with a coherent and consistent synopsis of Jesus life and ministry. These three are also normally taken together in a group because in many ways they are dependent upon each other for the storyline.

The gospel writers had a variety of sources at their disposal as they began to create this new genre of material called the gospel. The primary source of information about Jesus in much of the early First Century comes from the oral tradition, from stories that are shared in communities and among families either firsthand or handed on by generation. The stories probably originally had a particular context within a region or city. These could be seen in a similar way to a series of campaign stops made by political candidates. What they say and do in one city may be different than in another and each location remembers what happened in their place. As time passes these stories and other collections begin to be gathered and written down. Two of these sources may be those of the Book of Signs and the Q document.

The Q document, (Q standing for *Quelle,* meaning "source" in German, is primarily teachings and miracles of Jesus that have been collected together and written down. While no copy of Q has ever been discovered scholars are convinced that such a document existed and was used as a source by both Matthew and Luke. The reason for this belief is that Matthew and Luke have material in common with one another but that is not included in Mark's gospel.

The Hebrew Scriptures were the only Scriptures available to the gospel writers and the version most likely use is the Septuagint (LXX) which is the Greek translation of the Hebrew. The Scriptures are used heavily by the gospel writers to help interpret the message and ministry of Jesus.

The final influence of the early gospel writers is that of the Greco-Roman philosophies of the Hellenistic culture that were still pervasive in this region of the world. We've already seen how these philosophies influence Paul. Their influence among the gospel writers is less evident.

The development of the Synoptic Gospels can be described by the following process: The Gospel of Mark was the first gospel written, around the year 70 CE, and was used as a source by both Matthew and Luke. It is evident by scholarship that both Matthew and Luke in addition to Mark use a common source called Q. In addition to Mark and Q both Matthew and Luke have material that is unique to each of the authors. While the arrangement of Matthew and Luke generally follows the Markan outline this material is rearranged to help support their particular emphasis on Jesus identity.

As mentioned earlier, Mark was the first of the three Synoptic Gospels to be written. There is considerable debate among scholars as to whether Mark's Gospel was written prior to or immediately after the destruction of the Temple. Most scholars today would argue that it is after the Temple's destruction. The destruction of the Temple within the Jewish community was seen by many as a sign of the final days. Mark's gospel shows signs of some of that communal anxiety. The brevity and pace of the narrative gives the book a driving character. The use of the term "immediately" gives Jesus message an immediacy in the midst of crisis. Chapter 13 of Mark's gospel, often called the Little Apocalypse, raises some of the concerns of the early Jewish Christian community. The question as to when the end will come seems to be on the lips of many and the Jesus of Mark's gospel calls the community to action rather than benign speculation. The overall goal of Mark's gospel is to communicate the good news of Jesus Christ in such a way that it may be shared as rapidly and as far afield as possible before the great and terrible day of the Lord.

I refer to Matthew and Luke as the catechetical gospels or teaching gospels. Written 10 to 20 years after Mark I believe they are created to address a new stage within the communities which they serve and with whom they are sharing their gospel. As the initial anxiety over the destruction of the Temple subsides the early Christian community faces the question as to how to instruct new converts in the faith about who this Jesus is.

Matthew, who is addressing a primarily if not exclusively Jewish audience, tells the story of Jesus in such a way that he is presented as the new Moses. This is most evident in the way Matthew treats the material within the Sermon on the Mount. Much like Moses on Mount Sinai, Jesus brings the teachings of the new covenant to light. He even provides a new midrash to the original commandments on occasion. The balance of material in Matthew rest heavily on the teachings of Jesus rather than the miraculous displays of power. The giving of the Great Commission at the end of Matthew's Gospel is highly reminiscent of Moses speech delivered from Mount Nebo to the people of Israel prior to their crossing the Jordan River to enter the promised land. There is a decidedly anti-Jewish sentiment in Matthew's Gospel belying the growing unrest between Jews and Jewish Christians that is beginning to occur in the synagogues.

In much the same way as Matthew is a Jewish catechism Luke's gospel performs the same function in a primarily Greek or Gentile community. Luke's gospel is unique in that it contains a second volume, the Acts of the Apostles, which is a narrative of the early church and the journeys of Paul. Luke seeks to portray a Jesus that is a bigger than Jewish event, an event that has implications for the entire world. Luke's gospel shows the influence of the Hellenistic culture in the birth narratives, his use of parables, and the deeds of power. At least one commentator has made the claim that the Gospel of Luke forms the basis of the early adult catechumenate process of preparing new converts to Christianity.

One of the developing themes within the gospels is that of the growing tension between Jews and Christians. This plays out in the context of the gospels primarily with the ongoing confrontation of Jesus by the political/

religious parties of the day. Before going further, I feel a need to expand on the major parties so that you might see where the tensions arise from.

The political/religious landscape is dominated by these four major parties: Sadducees, Pharisees, Essenes and Zealots. The **Sadducees** descend from a single family, the Zadokites. Since the reign of Solomon all High Priests have come from this family. Just before the Maccabean Revolt however, this family lost control of the Jerusalem Temple priesthood. At that point the family divides into three. Part of the family emigrate to Egypt, part leave and establish a community at Qumran. The remainder stay in Jerusalem and are known as the Sadducees. They accommodate themselves to the ruling powers (both Greeks and Romans). They become part of the Jerusalem elite. They literally dominate the Jerusalem landscape as their home occupy the heights of the city with the other rich and famous. They are conservative both religiously and politically. After all, they have it made and do not want anyone messing life up.

The **Pharisees** were from the lower priestly class. They recognize both the oral tradition as well the written law as constituting Torah. They are rabbis and teachers whose task is to interpret Torah considering the present circumstances. This will be the only party that survives the Second Jewish Revolt. They were largely Judean, urban and middle-class.

The major differences between the Pharisees and Sadducees were over the afterlife and free will. The Pharisees believed that there was a resurrection and afterlife whereas the Sadducees believed that there was no life after death. On the issue of free will the Sadducees believed that there was only human free will and no divine intervention and the Pharisees held that there was both foreknowledge of Abba and human free will.

The third party are the **Essenes** who believe everything is ordained by Abba. They are composed of the dispossessed Zadokite priests. They moved to the desert (Qumran) and established a community there and lived a life that mirrored officiating in the Jerusalem Temple as they saw themselves as the true priests. Their lifestyle was a practice of ritual purity and the priestly lifestyle. While they offered no sacrifice (this could only be done in Jerusalem) it is evident that they practiced communal cultic meals that substituted for participation in Temple sacrifice. This community of Qumran ceased to exist before the time of Jesus. Despite this the influence of the Essenes can still be felt in the religious life of First Century Palestine.

The party of the militants were the **Zealots.** If the Sadducees' position towards Rome was to crawl in bed with them, and the Pharisee position was peaceful coexistence, and the Essenes' reaction to life in Jerusalem was "You're all going to hell in a handbasket we're out of here," the Zealot position towards Rome was revolution and overthrow. They followed the lead of the Maccabees and became the Taliban or Isis of their day. The terrorist wing of the Zealots was the *sicarii* or the roadside bombers, assassinators and suicide attackers.

These parties, however, made up only a fraction of the Jewish population in Palestine. The rest of the Jews were known as the people of the land, (*am-ha-aretz*) and they left little or no record of their beliefs and sympathies.

The Gospel According to Mark

"Crispus, a bunch of us are gathering on the other side of town. Its secret but I think I can sneak you it. These guys are tough. They are plotting something against the Roman garrison. Do you want to come?"

"Jakob, don't you know that movement won't change anything in this world. Let me tell you about a new Kingdom and a real messiah."

Let us look now at the Gospel of Mark and examine its outline and movement.

It is always my suggestion when beginning a study of the synoptic gospels in general or Mark's gospel specifically is to sit down and read the Gospel of Mark in its totality in one setting. Only when we do this do we get the full impact of Mark's use of language and pace. Mark's gospel is designed for sharing with as many people as one can and quickly as one is able. Mark's gospel seems to develop first as a Passion narrative to which a story of the life of Jesus is appended. The drama of Mark's gospel pushes us forward to climax of the cross. There is little in Mark's gospel to distract us from that journey. The genre of the gospel is a new literary construction but it does bear some striking resemblances to the hero stories of the Greek and Roman tradition or what Joseph Campbell will later call the quest narrative.

While the narrative in Mark's gospel leads us to the cross it also has a decidedly apocalyptic tenor. The first verse serves as a thematic introduction and a synopsis of what the gospel holds in store for us: this is the beginning of the good news of Jesus Christ!

Mark's stark narrative style stands in contrast with much of apocalyptic literature that relies on vivid descriptions of beasts and visions. At the same time, however it plays heavily on the apocalyptic imagery of the Hebrew Scriptures beginning with the quote from Second Isaiah. Mark's choice of material from Malachi, Exodus and Isaiah to introduce John the Baptist places John in the role of the prophetic forerunner to the apocalyptic Messiah. The portion from Isaiah is taken from the first chapter of what we call Second Isaiah which as we remember was written in Exile and is material of hopefulness and returning home. By the time of Jesus this hope of the 8th Century BCE becomes a dim memory and will be replaced by the tyranny of the Greeks and then the Romans. Cyrus, as earthly Messiah will be replaced by the apocalyptic Messiah who will usher in the Kingdom of Abba.

The drama begins as we are rudely deposited into the world and message of John, the baptizer. The description of John provides continuity between the story of Jesus and the Hebrew Scriptures. The description of John's diet and clothing harken back to the description of Elijah in the book of first Kings. In the Jewish messianic tradition, it is believed that Elijah will precede the Messiah. It is for this reason that an empty chair is still left at the Passover Seder for Elijah each year in the hopes that this will be the year he will return. While Mark does not overtly called John "Elijah Revisited" as Matthew will in his gospel, it is unmistakable that for Mark John is Elijah. In Mark's gospel John is not only the forerunner of Jesus, his life becomes the forecast of what awaits Jesus in his ministry (as John is arrested and executed for calling the political establishment to accountability so too will such a fate await Jesus).

The baptism of Jesus and the temptation of Jesus are narrated in Mark with the barest of descriptions. In many ways the most important verse in chapter 1, if not the thrust of the whole of Mark's gospel, is verse 14. We are told first that John is arrested (the dark clouds over Jesus have begun to gather), and then Jesus delivers his first sermon summarizing the ministry that he is about to undertake, *"the time is fulfilled, and the Kingdom of Abba his come near; repent, and believe in the good news"* (Mark 1:15). This Kingdom is neither identifiable with a specific place in this world, be it a house, a town, a Temple, a synagogue, or the fields, nor is it an otherworldly entity. The Kingdom of Abba for Mark is the people, and it arrives wherever people are liberated from the forces of evil. The mystery surrounding the Kingdom is that it is still in process and not an accomplished fact. Jesus must continue his journey toward the fulfillment of his objective. Nobody knows this mystery except the privileged insiders who will join him (that's us). We as hearers are now invited on the voyage/ journey that will continue long after the final chapter of this gospel is written.

One of the narrative geniuses of Mark is that we as readers/hearers of the story are both over hearers of the story as well as active participants. We not only hear the message of the Kingdom from Jesus first sermon but it is addressed to us as well. In much the same way as Jesus calls the first disciples to the work of the Kingdom, to become fishers for people, he is also issuing a call for us to leave behind what we are working on and enter both the story and to become a disciple in the unfolding Kingdom.

Jesus' teaching in the synagogue, his healing of the man possessed, his healing of the leper and the paraplegic all serve as credentialing of Jesus as a messianic candidate. Unlike the members of the other religious party Jesus speaks with an authority that rises above the infighting and the interparty conflicts. His healing of the man possessed points to his power even over the otherworldly spirits. This healing also sets up what many scholars referred to as the messianic secret in Mark's gospel. Jesus repeatedly tells people not to reveal his true identity as Messiah. While the disciples will be portrayed as sometimes bumbling idiots who don't seem to have a clue who this Jesus is the evil spirits recognize from the very beginning the tremendous power that comes in Jesus. It is a power that threatens to undo them (as it does the earthly powers-to-be). The stories of the healing of the leper and the paraplegic again harken back to the prophets and speak of the messianic age when the lepers will be cleansed and the lame will jump like the deer. In addition, the story of the healing of the paraplegic also identifies Jesus as one who can forgive sins which to this point in Jewish tradition is a power assigned only to Abba.

By this point we may be feeling that we are totally inadequate to follow Jesus, that we too don't get it or that perhaps we are unworthy. As a result, Jesus offers us a second invitation in the call of Levi, the tax collector. The tax collector in Roman society was perhaps the most despised of all occupations. The way the system worked was that the individual tax collectors function as independent contractors who would bid on the job of collecting taxes for the Romans. The tax collector that promises to collect the highest amount was given the contract. Often those amounts were extravagantly inflated and impossible to fairly collect. Therefore, the tax collector resorted to extortion, bribery, brute force and any other method required to raise the promised amount. They were not far from characterizations of the leg-breaking loan sharks of modern time. That Jesus would choose one such as this to be a disciple meant that no one was so despicable that he or she could not be called into the Kingdom… Even us!

As we might expect all of this raises some real concerns among the good religious folk. In chapter 2 we have the first of the confrontations between Jesus and the Pharisees. This particular confrontation concerns fasting and Sabbath Law. In both cases the issue is the role of the Torah for Jesus in this Kingdom. As you may remember in a discussion of the Exile, Sabbath keeping became an identifying marker of the Jews in Babylon. It should not surprise us than that Jesus gets in trouble when he transgresses Sabbath Law. In so doing he is striking at the very heart of Jewish identity. In short, this Kingdom of Abba may be bigger than a Jewish thing and that is very troubling to the Pharisees and the faithful.

In typical Markan fashion a teaching is often followed by a miracle to illustrate the point. Jesus has just said, *"The Sabbath was made to serve us, we weren't made to serve the Sabbath the Son of Man is not a servant of the Sabbath but rather Lord of the Sabbath"* (Mark 2:27-28). The miracle to illustrate this is Jesus healing of the crippled man on the Sabbath. The somewhat pathetic question embedded in the healing is if Sabbath Law should keep one from doing what is right for one in need or to put it another way; is it more important to keep the Sabbath or to heal? This is not the final word we will hear on the topic. In fact, we are told that a strange alliance even now is forming between the Pharisees and the followers of King Herod.

As we found in the Hebrew Scriptures geography is never just about geography. This is especially true for Mark. Mark uses the Sea of Galilee, either named or unnamed, as a critical marker in his story. For Mark, it is both a place of retreat for Jesus and a place of torment or chaos. I have argued over the years with teachers that perhaps Mark's use of the sea is in some way a baptismal image. No one has been willing to accompany me that far.

In chapter 3 Jesus retreats to the sea but the crowds follow him anyway. Jesus is portrayed time and time again as being "crushed" by the needs of the people to follow him. If the sea is indeed a baptismal image than perhaps what is being said in Mark is that it is impossible to escape our baptismal calling. The world with all its problems will find you. At the same time the evil spirits want to "out" Jesus as the Son of Abba but Jesus muzzles them. His identity must remain secret until it will be fully revealed on the cross (until then it will always be misunderstood – as we shall see).

In the fashion of Moses, Jesus climbs the mountain. Remember mountains are holy places. It is there he appoints the 12 apostles. It is worthy to note that Mark uses the word apostles rather than disciples. This is a critical distinction for the post-resurrection church. The term "apostle" designates one who had first-hand knowledge of Jesus ministry and teachings and as such possessed authority within the life of the church. It is here on the mountain that Jesus gives them authority to proclaim the word and banish demons. This becomes Mark's version of the great commission with which Matthew closes his gospel.

Once again, the reaction to Jesus ministry and mission is controversy. Jesus returns to his hometown where he is crushed by the needs of the crowd. However, some in the town think Jesus is simply full of himself. Add to this the religious elite who come down from Jerusalem with accusations that Jesus is a disciple of Satan and you have a double-barreled discrediting of Jesus and his message. (The same accusation is being made of Jesus followers in the mid to late 1st Century). Chapter 3 concludes with Jesus' family, who seem to think that Jesus has gone off the deep end and come to take him away if not to the funny farm at least out of the public eye before he embarrasses them. It is this attempt that leads Jesus to redefine the nature of family based not on bloodlines (as was so important in Judaism) but rather on the obedience to Abba's will.

In chapter 4 we return to the sea where Jesus begins his teaching ministry. Jesus method of teaching is to use parables, short stories taken from daily life to illustrate a point. Most scholars believe that Jesus simply told the stories and let the hearers wrestle with their meaning. For whatever reason, the gospel writers in many instances feel compelled to provide us with an interpretation (if not a moral). This is true of the parable of the sower. As Mark tells the story those who really need to hear it are the disciples. For them, and for those will follow them, it is a reminder that the task of the proclaimer is to proclaim whether the word takes root or not. Whether people understand and accept the Good News is not a result of the proclaimer's ability but rather the power of the Holy Spirit. Jesus continues this teaching section by introducing several other pedestrian images in parable form to describe the Kingdom of Abba: a lamp, a growing seed, and the smallest of all seeds - the mustard seed.

In 4:35-8:21 Mark narrates the universal dimension of the Kingdom as well as the reality of the 1st Century church, divided, yet in the end united. Mark uses the symbol of the lake which in this case serves as a barrier between the two sides. Two storm stories punctuate this narrative demonstrating the chaotic and disruptive force caused by this division/barrier. In both stories Jesus appears to be absent, whether emotionally detached (he is asleep in the back of the boat) or physically removed (he comes walking on the water). Often in the midst of our chaotic world we find ourselves wrestling with that age-old question, "Has Abba left the building?" In both instances, the disciples appear helpless and are confronted with doubt and fear. Jesus addresses this situation with the now familiar greeting, "Do not be afraid." What occurs in both stories is that the disciples fear of the storm is transformed into fear/awe of Jesus. The sea, as we remember from the Hebrew Scriptures, is a symbol of the forces of chaos. It is Abba alone who treads on the back the serpent, Yom Suf/Levianthan, who parts the waters, and who calms the seas. What is revealed clearly in these two stories is that Jesus is none other than Abba in flesh.

When Jesus lands on Gentile territory in the country of the Gerasenes he is encountered by a man, possessed by a spirit, who lives among the tombs and the graves. When Jesus approaches the man the spirit in him begins to question Jesus' presence. Jesus asks the demon for a name to which he replies, "Legion, for he was many". Eugene Petersen in his paraphrase translates this as "Mob. I'm a rioting mob!" Both translations carry much freight as we get to the end of the gospel. Jesus cast the demon into a herd of swine which then runs off the cliff to their demise. This does not put Jesus in good standing with the swine herders who demand the Jesus leave and never come back. It raises a question about the implications of the healing that we find in Jesus upon the larger life of the community both ethically and economically. While the swine herders wanted Jesus gone the man, now healed, goes into town and spreads the good news of Jesus.

Returning to Jewish territory Jesus is encountered by Jairus, a leader in the synagogue who informs Jesus that his daughter is dying. Jesus accompanies him through the midst of the crushing crowd.

Our story, and Jesus journey, are interrupted by the introduction of a woman who has been hemorrhaging for 12 years. She sought the help of many doctors most of whom left her worse than when she first went to them. Hearing the news of Jesus' arrival, she feels that if she only could touch his robe she might get well. She touches his robe and in that moment the flow of blood ceases. At the same time Jesus recognize that power has gone from him. Jesus confronts the woman and acknowledges that her action was an act of faith.

Amid this interruption we are told the Jairus' daughter has now died. His servants encouraged him not to bother Jesus any longer but Jesus informs him not to listen to the voices of the world, no matter how reasonable they seem, but to trust him. Jesus takes with him Peter, James, and John. We will find throughout Mark's gospel that these three form an executive committee of the disciples and are often singled out for important moments not always with exemplary results. They arrive at the house only to find it in the throes of public grief. Jesus goes in and commands that the little girl rise. Upon arising Jesus instructs them to feed her. This command reinforces the teaching of the early church that resurrection was not just a spiritual resurrection but a bodily one.

When Jesus goes on to teach in his hometown synagogue he is again confronted with critics. The script is a familiar one: hometown boy makes good; hometown boy returns; locals want to know who does this punk think he is? we know his family; he's not all that special; Jesus can't work any miracle under these conditions.

In chapter 6 Jesus sends the 12 out on a trial mission. While the mission appears to be a success Mark makes it clear that the work of the disciples can have dangerous consequences as he follows this sending with the account of the death of John the Baptist. In uncharacteristic detail Mark recounts, the death of John the Baptist which has as many political overtones as it does religious. This account casts a shadow over the gospel's success driven narrative. The mission of Jesus, as well as that of the disciples, and as well as those of us who will follow is always carried out in the shadow of the cross and death.

The apostles return checking in with Jesus. He invites them to get away from it all with for a little break from the crowds to debrief. So, they get into a boat and go off to a remote place by themselves. However, the crowds figure out where they have gone and the next thing you know Jesus has a new crowd forming. After days of teaching, and as it is getting late, the disciples remind Jesus that he should dismiss the crowds while they still have time to get dinner over at the McDonald's in Jericho before it closes. Instead Jesus instructs the disciples to feed the people. The disciples find the idea preposterous since all they have between them are five loaves and two fish. Jesus takes the loaves, blesses them and breaks them and gives them to the disciples to distribute. When all eat their fill, the leftovers are taken up and 12 basketfuls are collected… enough to feed the 12 tribes of Israel. The feeding miracles in all four Gospels not only point to Abba's providential care of people in need but also to the abundance of the apocalyptic meal that is first spoken of in Isaiah.

Following the story of the walking on water Jesus resumes his mission at Gennesaret. The religious leaders waste no time to once again catch the disciples in a breach of kosher law. It seems that some of them are not being careful with the ritual washings before meals (I hadn't realized my mother was a Pharisee). Jesus response is a rather graphic reminder that it is what comes out of a person that pollutes.

From here Jesus sets out for the district of Tyre. In perhaps one of the most disturbing stories involving Jesus in the gospels that he encounters a Syrophoenician woman with a sick daughter. When the woman asked Jesus to heal her child Jesus response is harsh, "It is not fair give the children's bread to the dogs." Jesus ministry was to the Jewish people and not the Gentiles (which was one of the great controversies in the early church as we saw in the writings of Paul). The woman's response is just as forceful, "Yes, but even the dogs gather the crumbs from under the Masters table." I've always viewed her response as a head slap that jars Jesus back into focus. This whole section of Mark's gospel has been about a Kingdom and a ministry that is bigger than just the particular people that we know as the Jews. For an instant Jesus falls back into the racist rhetoric of the day. His use of the term dog is equivalent to the "N" word as referring to African-Americans today. The woman's brutal come back makes him recognize what he has just done and his response then is to reverse his position and heal her daughter.

Jesus returns to the Decapolis and there heals a man who is both deaf and dumb. When Jesus cures him, it is remarked that even the deaf hear and the dumb speak. This testimony once again points back to the Hebrew Scriptures as a credentialing of Jesus as an appropriate candidate for Messiah. This is followed by a parallel feeding, now on Gentile territory. This time there are seven loaves and a few fish with seven basketfuls of leftovers (the complete/perfect amount).

When Jesus returns to Jewish territory the Pharisees are waiting there to rough him up a bit. Not surprisingly Jesus gets back in the boat and heads to the other side. While they are crossing the sea, the disciples recognize that they have forgotten to pack a lunch and are now hungry. As they are discussing whose fault it is that they have no food Jesus questions if they had learned anything on the journey having witnessed not one but two miraculous feedings.

Mark closes this section and transitions us into the next section with the story of the healing of a blind man. Mark will also transition out of the next section with a similar story. These two healings frame the journey from Caesarea Philippi to Jerusalem. As Jesus travels his way he attempts to open his disciples' eyes to the reality of his suffering, dying and rising. At the end of the journey, as at its beginning, the disciples are still blind while the two blind men now see. Mark accentuates this incongruity as he concludes this section with the statement that the once blind Bartimaeus "followed him on the way." The haunting and humbling pall that hangs over the disciples and us, is that those who are closest to Jesus and claim to know him best are often the furthest from the truth.

We also have in this central section of Mark's gospel the key question for all the gospels, "Who is Jesus?" Two thousand years later I will be asked the same question by a young man who is inquiring about baptism.

Jesus initiates the inquiry with his question, "Who do people say that I am?" The disciples reply with the latest poll results to which Jesus sharpens his question by asking, "Who do you say that I am?" Impetuous Peter responds, "You are the Messiah." Jesus' response is to tell him to shut up about it and tell no one.

Jesus then describes the agenda awaiting him as said Messiah. Jesus is providing a corrective to Peter's answer that Jesus as Messiah will not adhere to the popular versions of what is expected of the Messiah but will need to die (which is a portrait of a failed Messiah in terms of the messianic expectations). At this news Peter tries to dissuade Jesus from his journey to Jerusalem and death which results in a royal chewing out of Peter by Jesus and a reiteration of the dangers that await those who will follow Jesus. The final answer to Jesus' identity question in this discussion is provided in the Transfiguration. Joined by Moses and Elijah, Jesus is portrayed in almost resurrection garb and it is Abba that provides the answer to the pressing question, "This is my son, the beloved; listen to him!" It will be the centurion at the foot of the cross that will restate this identity in his declaration, "Truly, this was Abba's son!" For Mark, it is in the crucified Jesus, and only in the crucified Jesus, that we can truly understands who Jesus is.

[As one studies the Greek and Roman hero narratives one finds that in the middle of those narratives the hero generally enters the underworld and in that experience, gains important self-knowledge which transforms and informs the character for the remainder of the journey. I find myself wondering if there are similar overtones to the Transfiguration narrative.]

Coming down the mountain Jesus and the disciples are greeted by a commotion. A man has brought his son who was possessed by a demon to Jesus to be healed. It seems that the man had asked the disciples to perform the healing but they were unable to do so. Jesus performs the exorcism and the disciples are left wondering why they were unable to perform such an exorcism.

Once again Jesus informs the disciples of their pending itinerary that will include his suffering and death. This time the disciples' response is sheer ignorance… They don't have a clue! This is made clearer when Jesus asks what they were discussing on the road and he finds that they were arguing over which one of them was the greatest. Jesus reminds them that to be great in the Kingdom is to be a servant.

Chapter 10 ushers in a midrash or commentary on a variety of subjects from divorce to the criteria for entering the Kingdom. It is clear in this commentary that it is not by performance that one will enter the Kingdom for no one can fulfill the Torah as Jesus lays it out. This section of commentary is closed once again by the announcement of Jesus impending passion and death.

Mark now juxtaposes two stories to close out this section of his gospel. The first is reminiscent of the discussion about who is the greatest disciple. James and John come asking for the good seats in the Kingdom. Perhaps what we have here is a little jockeying to see who might replace Jesus following his death. Jesus reminds them of the cup that he will drink and once again that to be great in the Kingdom is to be a servant of all even to the point of giving one's life away. The second story is the story of blind Bartimaeus. The contrast is clear. The blind see and those who should see remain blind.

The section of 11:1-13:37 could easily be entitled, "The End of the Temple." The entire activity of Jesus' three temple journeys is designed to drive a wedge between the Temple and the Kingdom of Abba. While the surviving Jewish party, the Pharisees, will replace Temple sacrifice with Torah observance the Christian response is to replace it with Jesus and the Kingdom of Abba.

During the Jewish/Roman War the Temple increasingly served as the focal point of messianic hopes of liberation. These hopes literally went up in flames in 70 CE. By having Jesus predict the war, the temple destruction, and the nonarrival of the Kingdom in Jerusalem, Mark enables his readers, living after 70 CE, to come to terms with the Temple crisis in the context of the Jesus story. Jesus' mission in Jerusalem was primarily designed to make the point that the Temple was not the site of the Kingdom of Abba, neither in Jesus' or Mark's time. Instead, Jerusalem was to become the site of a double trauma, the death of Jesus and the death of the Temple.

Chapter 11 opens with Jesus' entry into Jerusalem which ushers in the passion narrative. This scene is dripping with apocalyptic and messianic trappings. Jesus enters Jerusalem as a Jewish king riding in kingly fashion on a donkey and heralded by the triumphant cry, "H*osanna! Blessed is he who comes in the name of the Lord! Blessed is the coming Kingdom of our father David! Hosanna in the highest!*" (Mark 11:9-10). Marcus Borg, in his book, ***The Last Week,*** maintains that there were two parades to usher in the high holy days of Passover in Jerusalem. The first was Jesus triumphal entry. The second was the return of Pilate from his summer headquarters. Looking much like a Russian May Day parade, Pilate would lead the Roman troops, with all the red banners and Roman tunics, back into Jerusalem as a show of force prior to the beginning of Passover. It was felt by the Romans that if trouble was to break out with the Jewish resistance it would be during the Passover festival. Given these contrasting parades it would not be hard to miss the message, 'Pilate, there's a new king in town!" Following Jesus' entry into the city he and the disciples retreat to Bethany a few miles away.

When Jesus arrives the second time in Jerusalem he enters the Temple and cleans house. Under Roman occupation the Temple had become not only the religious but also the political and economic hub of the city. At one point the Romans even erect a statue of the Roman eagle within the temple precinct. Jesus cleansing of the Temple is a direct attack on Roman occupation. Not surprising, Jesus' credentials are called into question again by the religious leaders.

In chapter 12 Jesus tells the story/parable of the Vineyard. Its language and imagery are unmistakably connected to the Song of the Vineyard from Isaiah. Like the Song of the Vineyard this parable is a parable of judgment on the nation of Israel for failing to understand and trust Abba. It is no wonder that the leadership wanted to kill Jesus on the spot after hearing these words.

In an attempt to discredit Jesus, the Pharisees raise the questions of paying taxes to Caesar and the Roman government. Jesus catches them when he asks for them to produce a coin and the coin they produce is a Roman coin rather than the Temple currency. Given that the Roman coin bears the image of Caesar, Jesus issues the famous line, "Render unto Emperor what is Emperor's and to Abba what is Abba's."

Not to be outdone the Sadducees weigh in with a complicated question about the resurrection. Jesus sees through their attempt to embroil him in a three-way debate on the nature of the resurrection with the Pharisees and informs the Sadducees that they are totally off base with their question. In in the resurrection such issues as marriage will become irrelevant.

In response to this obsessive reading of the Torah, which was probably reflective of the day, Jesus pares Torah down to one commandment. Quoting the Shema from Deuteronomy Jesus informs the Pharisees and Sadducees that the greatest commandment is: "Hear, O Israel, the Lord your Abba is one; so, love the Lord Abba with all your passion and prayer and intelligence and energy... and others as you yourselves."

Jesus continues by admonishing the crowd to be wary of the religious scholars of the day who are enamored with themselves, their knowledge and their positions. Again, to drive his point home, a living example! Jesus points to the poor widow who was placing her offering the collection box. He holds her up as an example of what he is talking about because while her offering may have been meager it was all that she had. As a wise mentor of mine once said, "If you're giving does not hurt then you are not really giving."

Chapter 13 of Mark's gospel is often known as the "Little Apocalypse." It deals with the destruction of the Temple and its aftermath. As I've mentioned earlier the destruction of the second Temple raised serious questions about the end of the world. For the Jews if the Temple was destroyed could the Great and Terrible Day of the Lord be far behind? For the early Christians the destruction of the Temple raised great expectations about the return of Jesus. Such speculation seems to be part of our human DNA. As I write this the country is recovering from two major hurricanes (Harvey and Irma), devastating wildfires in the Northwest, threats of nuclear war issuing from North Korea, continued terrorist attacks throughout the world, massive genocide and much much more. It is hard not to speculate on the end of days. However, Jesus instructs the disciples and us not to get caught up in such speculation for it only distracts from the work that is at hand. Continue to focus on what lies ahead: the continual proclamation of the good news of Jesus Christ, the Son of Abba. (I got a sense of the futility of such speculation several years ago when a group of clergy were invited to make presentations on each of their denomination's understanding of the end times. The Roman Catholic priest and I got up and quoted from Mark 13 and sat down. The remaining pastors spent the next three hours embroiled in a knockdown drag out fight over it the details and timing of the end of days. Three hours that could much better been served).

With chapter 14 the Passion of Jesus intensifies. The chapter begins with the announcement that the Passover is at hand and that a plot to arrest Jesus is being discussed by the political and religious authorities of the day. The great concern is that if they arrest Jesus during the festival it will cause a public uprising so they shelve their plans.

The scene turns to Bethany where Jesus and the disciples have been staying in the house of Simon the Leper. While they are eating, a woman enters and pours a bottle of costly perfume over Jesus head. As one can imagine this causes quite a stir among the guests. Anger and indignation abound especially at the waste of such precious resources (after all, the money could have been given to the poor, or could be used to buy weapons for the revolt, or perhaps improve the infrastructure, or offer tax breaks to the rich). Once again, those closest to Jesus demonstrate that they don't really have a clue about what is about to happen

This seems to be the straw that breaks the camel's back, or at least Judas Iscariot's. It is at this point that Judas goes to the high priests and offers his services to hand Jesus over to the authorities.

On the first days of Unleavened Bread Jesus sends his disciples out to prepare the Passover meal. That night as they are sitting around the table he announces that one of them will betray him. Again, this arouses great speculation. Such betrayal to the religious and political authorities will become commonplace for Christians throughout the region in the coming decades. As Jesus was betrayed, so will those who follow him be betrayed. During the meal Jesus provides a new midrash/commentary on the ritual bread and cup – this is my body, this is my blood. Following supper, they go out to the Mount of Olives which overlooks the city of Jerusalem. (Perhaps such a relocation offers a better perspective to watch the fall of Jerusalem from. The Christians in Jerusalem will make a similar move to the neighboring town of Pella before Jerusalem is destroyed)

It is there amid the tombs that Jesus tries to prepare his disciples for the future. He explains to them that the days will soon be upon them when they will feel like the entire world is falling apart but this too will be in accordance with Scriptures. He urges them not to worry for he will go ahead of them to Galilee after he has been raised up. Good old impetuous Peter announces that even if everyone else runs away he will not. Jesus points out the irony of Peter's statement by saying that before the rooster crows in the morning Peter will deny ever knowing Jesus three times. Again, this denial of Jesus will become commonplace in the future as the Romans and Jews exert more pressure upon the early Christians to denounce their faith in Jesus.

Jesus takes them to the area of the Mount of Olives called Gethsemane. There he takes the Inner Circle, Peter, James and John into the garden to keep watch while he prays. It is there in Gethsemane that Jesus experiences the full weight of what the days ahead hold in store for him. In abject agony, he prays to the Abba pleading that perhaps another way might be found (sounds a little like Peter…us?). If not, Jesus is willing to go through with the plan. Three times he goes to check on the disciples and three times he finds them asleep.

It is interesting for me to see in this section that is often viewed simply as a prelude to the real action of the Passion, concrete examples of the temptations that will face Christians in the decades and centuries to follow. The church will always be tempted to betray, to deny and to fall asleep.

At this point Judas Iscariot shows up with a mob that has been sent by the high priest. The Judas kiss identifies Jesus as the one to be arrested. In the ensuing melee, the high priest's servant loses his ear. Jesus reminds those who surround him that all of this is done to fulfill what the prophets had foretold. At this all the disciples desert Jesus. During this heightened drama the disciples' character remains consistent: they fall asleep, they betray, they deny, they contradict and in the end abandon Jesus. In so doing they miss the most important event in the journey of the Kingdom. It will fall to a pagan centurion, not the disciples, who in the end will witness and confess Jesus as the Son of Abba… Heir to the Kingdom. In a sense the disciples have been disqualified as leaders in the Kingdom… They have forfeited their chance to be witnesses.

An episode only to be found in Mark's gospel tells of a young man who as he is running away is grabbed but escapes by leaving his captors literally holding his clothes. He runs away naked. It is an interesting point that the word that is used to describe what the young man is wearing. The only other time that word shows up in the Greek New Testament is to describe the burial clothes found in Jesus' tomb. (No, I still have not figured this one out).

Jesus is taken to the High Priest where a kangaroo court has been assembled to bring charges against Jesus. Obviously ill rehearsed, the witnesses can't even agree on the testimony. Finally, the question of Jesus as Messiah is raised to which Jesus replies, "I am, and the days are coming when you will see it for yourselves." At this point Jesus is condemned for blasphemy and sentenced to death. While all of this is going on Peter is in the courtyard denying that he is ever known Jesus not once, not twice but three times. When the rooster crows he collapses in tears.

Because under Roman law it was illegal for the Jewish authorities to carry out a death sentence Jesus is taken Pilate, the local Roman authority, for sentencing. Pilate interrogates Jesus but Jesus refuses to answer his questions. We are told that Pilate is impressed. It was customary practice that during the festival of the Passover Pilate would release a prisoner. He asked the crowd who he should release Barabbas or Jesus. Barabbas was an insurrectionist or political prisoner who was condemned because he had killed someone (probably a Roman solider) during a recent uprising. Pilate figures the crowd's choice is easy and is shocked when they ask for Barabbas instead of Jesus. In a move that belies his political inabilities (the historical record backs this up), Pilate calls upon the mob to pass sentence. Their verdict – crucify Jesus.

Barabbas is released and Jesus is taken away to be whipped and prepared for crucifixion. It is there in the Praetorium that the Roman soldiers dress him in a purple robe and place a crown of thorns on his head (the garb of a would-be king). When they have had their fun with him they march Jesus off for crucifixion.

Jesus is led away to Golgotha, Skull Hill, to be crucified. A passerby, one Simon of Cyrene, is compelled to carry his cross. Jesus is offered a mild painkiller but he refuses. We are told that it is 9 o'clock when Jesus is lifted up on the cross. It must be noted here that crucifixion was a means of execution reserved for political prisoners. This explains the inscription over Jesus head, "King of the Jews." As king of the Jews Jesus becomes a threat not only to the puppet Jewish king, Herod, but also to Roman authority. Jesus' crucifixion appears to have been the entertainment for the day with the crowds gathered mocking him and inviting him to climb off the cross. Other ancient authorities attest to this public gathering around crucifixions which often was accompanied by the rape and murder of the crucified's followers. It was a brutal form of execution designed to dissuade any attempt to overthrow Rome. It was a slow death, often taking days, and the bodies were left on the crosses in prominent sight until their bones had and picked clean by the birds and bleached by the relentless sun.

In contrast to this, Jesus' crucifixion appears almost merciful. At noon the world turns dark. Three hours later Jesus cries out, "My Abba, my Abba, why have you abandoned me?" and with a loud cry breathes his last. Our modern, post-Enlightenment sensibilities have great trouble with Jesus final words.

At his death, the Temple curtain that separates the sanctuary from the Holy of Holies (where Abba himself dwells) is torn in two from top to bottom. Abba is now on the loose and accessible to all.

It is at the moment of death that the true identity of the Messiah is revealed for public consumption. The irony is that the announcement comes not on the lips of the disciples, nor of the religious authorities of the day, not even the political movers and shakers of mighty Rome but rather from a lowly soldier who recognizes in that death that here is the son of Abba.

The Passion's dénouement occurs in the burial of Jesus. We are told of the women's presence at both the crucifixion and now here at the burial. They are named in detail. We might even assume that they will replace the disciples as the proclaimers of the good news.

Joseph of Arimathea, who is all but described as a follower of Jesus, goes to Pilate and askes for Jesus' body. Pilate is shocked to think that Jesus might already be dead after such a short amount of time and asks for confirmation. When confirmation arrives, he turns the corpse over to Joseph who wraps Jesus' corpse in a shroud and places it in a rock- hewn tomb. A large stone is rolled to cover the opening.

When the Sabbath is over the women come to the tomb to finish the burial preparations for Jesus' body. They speculate on their way how they are going to roll the stone back and are shocked when upon arriving at the grave to find that it is already rolled away. Walking in they are encountered by a young man dressed in white (the traditional garb of a heavenly messenger). The women are assured by the young man that Jesus has been raised and that they need to go and tell Peter and the other disciples that he will meet them in Galilee as he had arranged earlier.

The Message captures well what happens next, *"[the women] got out as fast as they could, beside themselves, their head swimming. Stunned, they said nothing to anyone"* (The Message, Mark 16:8).

This abrupt ending caused many in the early church to wonder if the ending of Mark's gospel had been lost. Later manuscripts of the gospel include a longer ending describing the women's testimony to the disciples as well as appearances by the risen Jesus. This addition also includes a forecast of what awaits the early church.

Rather than having the last page of the manuscript torn from the gospel I believe Mark fully intends to end his gospel in this abrupt manner. With the disciples running away and the women failing to report there is no one but us left to tell the story. The question left for us to ponder is, "Who will tell the story?" Will we?

As the story began… *the **beginning** of the Good News of Jesus Christ…* so now the beat goes on…the "conclusion of the Good News of Jesus Christ" … only now…in, with and through us.

Gospel According to Matthew

"Hey Levi, want to go play hide and seek in the old Temple precinct?"

"No, I've got catechism class."

"What's that?"

"It's for the church. It's where we learn about who Jesus is."

"So, what have you learned so far?"

"Not much, he sounds a lot like Moses."

While Matthew's gospel follows Mark's outline it is very clear that Matthew is moving through the material at a slower pace. Matthew's approach is more methodical, more intent on linking the Hebrew scriptures with the Christian scriptures as well as being concerned with the question: "Who is this Jesus in relationship with the prevailing winds of Judaism?"

As I mentioned earlier I believe Matthew's gospel is addressed to a Jewish/Christian community and that it is designed as the catechetical tool to introduce Jewish converts to Jesus and Christianity. Matthew's intention is to portray Jesus and his teachings in continuity with the Hebrew scriptures. For Matthew, Jesus is to be the new Moses or new Lawgiver. The connecting of Jesus with the messianic tradition of the Hebrew Scriptures is also much more pronounced in Matthew. Matthew accomplishes this connection by using portions of the Hebrew scripture as being prophetic, in the sense of foreshadowing the ministry and personage of Jesus. One of the scandals that the early Christian movement needed to get past was that by Jewish scorecards Jesus is a failed Messiah – he dies and ignominious death on the cross. You can't blow Messiahship in any worse way.

Matthew, in addition to Jesus as Lawgiver, also plays heavily on Jesus as prophet. I've often suggested that one of the best ways to prepare oneself to read Matthew's Gospel is to read the books of Numbers and Jeremiah. While Matthew does not directly tie his gospel narrative to these two books they form the underpainting for his work of art.

Matthew uses the Torah/Law is a connecting device between Jesus and Moses I believe he also makes a case for the failure of the Law, or perhaps our keeping of it, as a way of maintaining a faithful relationship with Abba. In most instances when Jesus refers to the Torah he gives it a new midrash or interpretation that is much stricter and virtually impossible to keep than the common interpretations of the day. As such one might argue that Matthew is a good Lutheran in that the Torah/Law drives us to the cross and Abba's grace.

Matthew's gospel begins with what should now be a recognizable Hebrew device, namely, the genealogy. As with genealogies in the Hebrew Scriptures this is to establish Jesus pedigree and authority. It is an unusual genealogy in that it includes the names of several women. These women are all involved in some controversy in the Hebrew scripture narrative.

Their inclusion may be a somewhat backhanded way of paying tribute to the prominent role that women played the early Christian movement, particularly as benefactors. Or, as evidence that even "tainted" ancestors can be used by Abba as part of Abba's plan for salvation (sic Jacob). Matthew's genealogy traces Jesus' roots back to Abraham. As we have talked throughout our discussion of the Hebrew scriptures, Abraham is the doorway to a more universal understanding of the Jews place in the world. As such, while addressing a primarily Jewish audience Matthew uses Abraham to prop the door open for future expansion of the Jesus movement into non-Jewish territory.

Matthew and Luke are the only two Gospels to include birth narratives of Jesus. While distinct in the material they are often conflated in such a way as to produce those beautifully bucolic nativity scenes complete with animals, shepherds, *and* Magi. Matthew approaches the news of Jesus pending birth through Joseph, not Mary. It is Joseph who must be convinced to follow through with this drama. With it we have the first of the fulfillment quotations in 1:22-23 (*a virgin shall conceive and bear a son, and they shall name him Emmanuel).*

Following the birth of Jesus, we have the visit of the three Magi. Magi come from the Zoroastrian tradition and were holy men or magical practitioners. It is Martin Luther in the 16th century, as he translates the New Testament into German, that first introduces the term Wiseman in place of Magi. These magi stopped first at the court of King Herod in a scene that is highly reminiscent of the emissaries of Naaman the leper and the king of Israel and 2 Kings. The news of a new king in town is not good news to Herod and when his attempts to elicit the aid of the Magi fails he launches a pogrom upon newborn males that takes us back to the Exodus narrative. By inserting the narrative of the Magi Matthew accomplishes not only a tie to the massacre of the innocent in the time of Moses (and Rahab) but also develops the movement that enables Jesus to be one who also comes out of Egypt (Mary and Joseph flee to Egypt to seek sanctuary from King Herod).

Much of the remaining material in Matthew's Gospel is an expansion of the Markan narrative with material that solidifies Matthew's claim that Jesus is the Messiah/Lawgiver and material that he takes from the Q source material. The exception to this is a rather lengthy section the runs from chapter 5 to 7 commonly referred to as the Sermon on the Mount. Like Moses, Jesus is depicted as delivering the "Law/New Torah" to the people from the Mountain of Abba. This section depicts Jesus in continuity with the Torah (and so he is in step with the developing Pharisee movement of first century Judaism) and yet in many cases Jesus reinterprets that Law in a much stricter sense. In this way, he both stands in solidarity with the Pharisees and critiques their misplaced dependence on the Law.

The sermon begins with a reaffirmation of the covenantal in material that is commonly referred to as the Beatitudes. The Beatitudes are more descriptive than they are prescriptive. They describe the current situation within Christianity and at the same time affirm that Abba's blessing/covenant is still intact despite what things seem to look like. This is perhaps most clearly seen in the beatitude: *Blessed are those who are persecuted for righteousness' sake for theirs is the kingdom of heaven.* This covenant/blessing section also calls to mind the baptismal rite that moves from blessing to action. The discussion of salt and light reveal the imperative for service and witness the grows out of this blessing. In the words of the baptismal rite: "Go, let your light so shine before others that they may see in your good works the glory of your Father in heaven".

The sermon then moves into a discussion of the relationship between Jesus and the Torah and the prophets. It is a matter of fulfillment of Torah, not abolition, that is at the heart of Jesus teaching and ministry. He ends the introduction with a set up. Unless we can do a better job of keeping the Torah than the Pharisees do ow we have no hope of entering the Kingdom of Heaven either.

Following this brief introduction Jesus begins a new midrash on the Commandments: anger, adultery, divorce, oaths, retaliation, love of enemies, almsgiving, prayer, fasting, treasures, worry, judging others, and profaning the holy. While there is a rootedness in the Commandments of the Torah I would also speculate that these were the hot button topics being debated between Christians and Jews at this time. The sermon ends with the injunction that one must practice what one preaches and acknowledges that Jesus teaches with an authority unlike that of the scribes and Pharisees because he was willing to walk the walk.

In chapter 18 Matthew introduces Q material with the parable of the Lost Sheep. As with Luke, one of the issues that Matthews community is dealing with, and perhaps even more acutely, is the falling back into the old ways of Judaism when faced with the crisis of persecution. Not only does Matthew use the parable to portray Jesus as one who searches out those who have lost their way he offers a process to help them reconnect. I would argue that the injunction, if a brother or sister sins against you, has less to do with breaking the relationship between individuals as it does the community of faith. The process begins one-on-one, if that fails some witnesses are added, if that fails the matter is taken before the whole community of faith, and if that still fails to bring resolution there to be treated as a Gentile and tax collector (the interesting preaching point on this process is that we know how Jesus treated the Gentiles and tax collectors).

This then leads into a discussion on forgiveness and the question of how many times one must forgive another. Again, Jesus response is to go over and above the requirements of Torah on the subject. Matthew also introduces at this point a strictly Matthean parable of the Unforgiving Servant. Given the context this parable is not directed at the Pharisees and Sadducees as much as it is the Christian community. Forgiveness is at the heart of living in such a community.

In chapter 20 we have another parable found only in Matthew, the Laborers in the Vineyard. In contrast to the prevailing portrait of Abba as righteous judge this parable exposes a gracious and generous benefactor. Abba's grace goes against all the modern day economic conformities. In short, it is crazy to run the kingdom like Abba is proposing.

While Matthew uses Mark and Q as a basis for his Passion narrative it does begin with a rather humorous Matthew– only oops. Matthew's adherence to the Hebrew Scriptures with regards to his quotations leads him to have the disciples bring Jesus two animals, and ass and a colt, for his entry into Jerusalem. It has always conjured up images of me of the circus riders with one foot on each animal riding into Jerusalem.

Matthew is also the only gospel writer to include an account of the death of Judas. In chapter 27 he presents a repentant Judas who tries to return the blood money. When the chief priests and elders will not receive it, he throws it down and goes out and hangs himself. The money is then used to buy a potter's field to bury strangers in which is known to all, at least in Matthew's world, as the Field the Blood.

It is also Matthew who includes a conversation between Pilate and his wife concerning her dream about Jesus. This distancing of Pilate from the role of executioner already points to a growing Roman apologetic and more concerted responsibility for the execution of Jesus upon the Jewish religious leaders.

One final amplification in the Passion narrative by Matthew is that when Jesus dies and the Temple curtain is torn in two we're told that there is a great earthquake which opens the tombs and allows many of the saints who had died to exit and appear in Jerusalem. The identity of the saints, while apparently know by Matthews community, is a mystery to us today.

One of the distinctive features in all three synoptic Gospels is how they treat the resurrection. In Mark's gospel, we are left with only an empty tomb but in both Matthew and Luke Jesus appears to some, if not all the faithful. In addition, both Matthew and Luke contain some distinctive material in their respective accounts that reflect concerns of their community concerning the resurrection. In Matthew's account, the placing of the guard at the tomb and the subsequent reporting of the guards following the resurrection that Jesus' disciples came by night and stole him away, raises the question that a contentious story circulated by the Jewish community concerning the reality of the resurrection.

The gospel ends again much like the Mount Nebo scene from the book of Numbers, where Moses commissions Joshua. Jesus commissions the disciples, imparting to them his authority, and sending them out to teach what he has commanded (Commandments) and to baptize in the name of the triune Abba. They are able and empowered to do this because Jesus will remain with them to the end of the age.

Gospel According to Luke/Acts of the Apostles

O, most excellent Theophilus, how I've wanted to write to you and share these things that are on my heart. As you are new to the faith are so many things I want to instruct you about but the distance makes that so difficult. I have included my thoughts about Jesus of Nazareth, the Savior of the world, and a brief history of the early churches as I know it. I hope this helps in your studies.

"Hey, Theophilus. where you going in such a hurry?"

"Catechumenate studies."

"Cata whatchamacallit?"

"Catechumenate. It's my preparation for baptism and the Christian tradition."

"I thought you were pagan?"

"I was but then I saw the light. My friend Luke introduced me to this story of Jesus and it just makes more sense to me than all the other Abbas. He wrote it all down for me so that I can study it. Would you like to read it sometime?"

If Matthew's Gospel as the catechetical gospel for a Jewish audience then Luke's gospel is a catechetical gospel for a Hellenistic audience. While Matthew portrays Jesus as the new Moses Luke portrays Jesus more in line with a classic Greek/Roman hero figure.

Luke weaves this sense of Jesus as a hero figure with a distinct closing of an old age (Judaism) and the dawning of the new age (Christianity). With larger-than-life characters reminiscent of the opening chapters of Genesis, Luke uses the infancy narrative material to initiate this transition.

If having an exceptional birth narrative paves the way for greatness later in life as it was for Greek and Roman heroes, then Luke offers an appropriate narrative for Jesus in the opening chapters of the gospel. Not only is Jesus' birth to be exceptional but also that of John the Baptist. In classic Lucan fashion, the opening lines of the narrative place the action at a particular time and in a particular place as well as having particular characters. The introduction of King Herod; John's father, the priest Zechariah; John's mother, Elizabeth, who is of the priestly line of Aaron, set the stage.

As with Sarah and Hannah in the Hebrew Scriptures, Elizabeth, who is not getting younger has yet to be able to conceive a child. While Zachariah was performing his priestly functions in the Temple and angel appears announcing that Elizabeth will have a son and he is to name him

John. The son will have the power and spirit of Elijah and will be the forerunner of the Lord. While Sarah had laughed at such news, Zechariah questioning the angel's announcement. As a result, he is struck mute unable to speak until John was born.

In the six-month of Elizabeth's pregnancy and seclusion the angel Gabriel appears also to a virgin named Mary who is engaged to a man named Joseph who lives in a town in Galilee called Nazareth. Again, the news is of an unexpected pregnancy, this time it is not because of old age but rather because Mary is still a virgin. When she questions the angel, she is told that nothing is impossible for Abba and that as confirmation, her relative Elizabeth who is old and barren is now in the six-month of her pregnancy. Mary concludes this conversation with the standard acceptance speech from the Hebrew Scriptures, "Here am I":

This sets the scene for the remarkable visit of the two women. Mary initiates the visit and when she and Elizabeth meet the baby in Elizabeth's womb leaps for joy as a sign of fulfillment of what the angel had spoken.

This exchange causes Mary to offer a hymn of praise which we know best as the Magnificat deriving from the opening lines of the song, "My soul *magnifies* the Lord." This song captures what for Luke will be a major theme, namely, that in Jesus there will be a great reversal of fortune particularly between rich and poor. The language of the song is reminiscent of the great prophetic hymns found particularly in Isaiah. A new day is dawning that will usher in a new world. The recollection of Abraham and his descendants opens the door to a more universal fulfillment of the promises made initially to the Jews.

John's actual birth is dispensed of in one short sentence. What becomes important is what happens when the ritual Law of circumcision occurs. While the extended family insist that the baby is to be called Zachariah after his father, his mother insists that his name will be John. When questioned, Zechariah affirms this in writing and immediately he again speaks. When asked about the significance of this child Zechariah also responds with a prophetic song blessing HaShem, remembering the covenant, is establishing this child as the forerunner of the Lord and the one who will usher in the advent of a new age.

The narrative of Jesus' birth, immortalized by Linus in *Charlie Brown's Christmas*, is perhaps the best-known piece in all of Scripture. Again, the event is set within a particular timeframe, in a particular place and with a particular cast of characters: Emperor Augustus; Quirinius, governor of Syria; Joseph and Mary. They are traveling from Nazareth to Bethlehem to participate in a Roman census. Mary gives birth to the baby Jesus in a stable and lays him in its feed trough.

The first announcement of this miraculous birth is to shepherds who are tending their flocks. Much is made of the shepherd's lowly lot in life, their poverty and their economic standing but I would like to raise the possibility that the image of the shepherd also carries with it a royal connotation. In the Hebrew Scriptures the role of the King was seen as that of shepherding. As such the 23rd Psalm is a job description of not only the shepherd but of the King. In the prophets it becomes clear that the kings of Israel and Judah have failed to be good shepherds so that their flock has been scattered. At this point HaShem steps in and assumes the role of the shepherd. What if the angels' encounter with the shepherds is not a visitation to the lowly but to the royal as well? What if it is a similar prophetic message as we find in the Hebrew Scriptures that the kings of this age have failed to be appropriate shepherds and that there is a new King/Shepherd in town who will gather his flock and lead them to green pastures? Either way the shepherds go to see the things that had been told them and then like Mary and Zachariah to go forth proclaiming and glorifying HaShem.

The presentation of Jesus and the purification of Mary in the Jerusalem Temple is often portrayed as a beautiful Hallmark moment. Simeon who has waited his entire life to see the Lord now holds the baby Jesus in his arms and breaks into song: "Lord, now you let your servant go in peace, the word has been fulfilled for my eyes have seen your salvation." With his bucket list fulfilled Simeon into now free to die.

I would argue that rather than a touching moment for Simeon this storyline is of great significance for Luke and his gospel. I believe Simeon stands for all those who have waited thus far for the coming Messiah. As such Simeon is the remnant of faithful Israel. Therefore, I believe Simeon offers us the transitional moment between the old covenant and the new, the old-age and the new age.

The story addresses two of the major issues facing the early Christian community: the destruction of the Temple and the role of Torah/Law. By the time Luke is writing his gospel the Temple has been destroyed and the keeping of Torah has become the dominant form of Judaism in its place. The storyline begins with Mary and Joseph coming to the Temple to fulfill Torah. What happens is that the infant Jesus takes center stage in the drama. With Jesus now on the scene, Simeon/Temple/Torah are now superseded by the presence of the Christ child and the new age that his dawned with him. The prophetic texts of Isaiah are now embodied in the infant Jesus.

This is amplified by the presence of the strange figure of Anna, the prophet. With the touching scene of Simeon, one must wonder why we need a second version of the encounter. But if Simeon marks the embodiment of the end of the old-age Anna represents the coming of the new age and the appropriate response: like Mary, Zachariah and the shepherds, Anna praises Abba and announces the arrival of Jesus to all who are looking for redemption in Jerusalem.

Unlike Matthew there is no visit of the Magi or the flight to Egypt. Mary and Joseph uneventfully return to Galilee, to Nazareth, and we are told that Jesus grows in strength and wisdom.

The conclusion of the infancy narrative finds us in the Temple. The occasion is the celebration of the Passover (old covenant) and Jesus is 12 years old (the age of accountability). On the return trip, it becomes obvious to Mary and Joseph that they have lost track of Jesus. The search among the relatives turns nothing up and so they return to Jerusalem and the Temple and find Jesus entertaining the teachers. When asked what he was doing there Jesus seems surprised that they were upset because where else would he be but than in his father's house, educating the teachers of the Law. This leaves Mary, and perhaps us, pondering what all this means and what lies ahead.

In chapter 3 we again join Mark and Matthew with the arrival of John the Baptist. In Lukan fashion John is, like Jesus, placed in specific and detailed context. Unlike in Matthew's Gospel, Luke's censure is of the crowds, not the Pharisees and Sadducees, that have come out to be baptized. Luke wants to make very clear that this is not the latest fad to be sweeping the nation but that it has historic ties to ancient Israel (Abraham) and has serious ethical demands. Within the early church there are serious questions raised by many as to if Christianity is just another mystery religion among the hundreds that are populating the Middle East at this time. Luke wants to make very clear this is not the case.

In between Jesus' baptism and his temptation in the wilderness Luke inserts a genealogy. That the genealogies in the Hebrew Scriptures this has more to do with pedigree than information. It is worth noting that Luke's genealogy of Jesus goes in reverse and goes from Jesus to Adam rather than from Abraham to Jesus. With this Luke makes it very clear that Jesus has a universal claim and not just a Jewish claim as Messiah.

As with Matthew, Luke too follows Mark's outline, expanding it and utilizing the Q material to bolster his assumptions about Jesus. For instance, whereas Matthew depicts Jesus' sermon on the mountain Luke utilizes that same material but we find Jesus preaching on a plain (again reflecting the leveling and reversal that comes with the Kingdom of Abba) as well as changing "poor in spirit" to simply "the poor." It is clear for Luke that the arrival of Jesus carries with it significant ethical imperatives particularly with regards to the poor and the lowly. In this respect it sounds very familiar and reminiscent of the Hebrew Scripture prophets such as Amos.

One of the salient features of Luke's gospel is his use of parables particularly the section that runs from chapters 14 through 21. The use of parables/stories in teaching is a method that is consistent with Hellenistic rhetoric and wisdom. Jesus uses these parables: to critique and judge the wealthy and the Pharisaic; to introduce the nature of the Kingdom of Abba; and perhaps most importantly, to depict Jesus/Abba as one whose primary mission is to redeem the lost. The works of Robert Farrar Capon offer a provocative look at these parables as well as those in Matthew's Gospel. Capon raises the radical and often scandalous implications of the parables that provide ample thought for preaching and study. These parables were meant to be scandalous and to provoke conversation long after Jesus was no longer on the scene.

There is a strong implication in these parables that the Jews have had their chance to accept Jesus as the Messiah and that failing to do so they will be excluded from the new age. The parable of the Wicked Tenants returns us to Isaiah's Song of the Vineyard with the now decidedly final verdict upon the Jews. Another important theme for Luke is the element of lost and found. Again, embedded in this theme is that the Gentile was lost and is now found and that the Jew who was found is now lost. The culmination of this theme is the parable of the Prodigal Son. Shrewd and scandalous behavior is often rewarded in the parables and with it comes conversion (such as the parable of the Dishonest Manager, the Persistent Widow and the Unjust Judge as well as the story of Zacchaeus). The theme of rich and poor and the appropriate relationship between the two is the central focus of the parable of the Rich Man and Lazarus.

After a brief apocalyptic interlude in chapter 21 we find ourselves back on track in chapter 22 with the plot to kill Jesus. The passion narrative of Luke follows closely the narrative of Mark and the additions of Q.

We see already in Matthew and Luke an attempt to distance the Romans from being the active executioners and Jesus' death being the responsibility of the Jewish leadership. With the gulf between Christians and Jews widening following the destruction of the Temple we find Christians having to make claims of authenticity before the Romans as Christianity moves deeper into the Empire. On the one hand their association with Judaism gives them the much sought after historical character that is so important for Romans and on the other they are searching for an integrity for Christianity apart from Judaism that is more than just another mystery religion.

The most outstanding of the Lucan additions to the passion narrative is the dialogue between Jesus and the criminals who are hanged with him. Consistent with the theme of lost and found, who's in and who's out, the one criminal derides Jesus while the other one begs for mercy. It is the latter who will see Jesus in Paradise.

Luke's post-resurrection accounts offer us distinctively Lukan material. The role of the women which was so dominant in Mark's account is downplayed to the point that their words are received as mere gossip. In the appearance of Jesus to the disciples on the road to Emmaus, Luke makes the connection between the resurrected Jesus and the community's ritual of interpreting sacred Scripture (Hebrew Scriptures) and meal (Eucharist). The appearance of Jesus to the remaining disciples (24:36-49) appears to address a concern that the resurrection of Jesus was simply a spiritual resurrection and that Jesus was but a ghost, and apparition. Finally, the abbreviated account of the ascension of Jesus into heaven forms the bridge between Luke's gospel and the second volume of Luke's work, the Acts of the Apostles.

In the **Acts of the Apostles** Luke offers us a glimpse of the development of the Christian movement from a localized Jewish mission to a ministry that will encompass the Empire. Luke takes us from the witness of Peter and the disciples through the ministry of Paul and into the emerging Christian communities. The structure of this book reflects this movement as it is divided into two parts with a brief transitional introduction.

Luke begins this transition with a brief summary of the ministry of Jesus, including his post-resurrection appearances, and then picks up where he left off in the gospel with the ascension. In the slightly more expanded narrative Jesus ascends into heaven leaving the disciples on the ground gazing into the sky. Unceremoniously, they are reminded by two men, who bear a striking resemblance to the two men from the tomb, to get their heads out of the clouds and get back to work. One of their first jobs is to replace Judas among the Twelve with Matthias.

Pentecost marks the transition from the ministry of Jesus to the ministry of the disciples/apostles. On Pentecost, the disciples are empowered with the gift of the Holy Spirit which is presented much more in the fashion of the *ruach Adonai* of creation than the dove of Jesus baptism. It is this outpouring of the charism that empowers the disciples to witness to the risen Jesus.

The first major section of the Acts of the Apostles (2:1-9:43) documents the first stage of this witness to those in Jerusalem, Judea, and Samaria. Beginning with Pentecost and Peter's first sermon, moving on to the martyrdom of Stephen (which demonstrates the high-stakes of this witness), through a series of conversions it culminates with the conversion of Saul in chapter 9 and Peter's ministry to the Gentiles in Joppa. Following Saul's conversion, Saul/Paul goes to Jerusalem and is foiled in his attempt to join the disciples. Meanwhile Peter is pushing the boundaries of his ministry to the edge of the sea in Joppa. In these two scenes, and we have the stage being set for the Christian movement to begin witnessing to the ends of the earth.

This final section (10:1-28:28) begins with the conversion of Peter. Peter and James were two of the key figures in the Jerusalem Gang. They saw the tie between Christianity and Judaism as necessary. (In later debates with Rome over the legitimacy of Christianity as a religion within the Roman Empire the apologists would appeal to the connection between Christianity and Judaism in face of Rome's insistence that if your religion wasn't old it wasn't really a religion worth acknowledging). At this point, however, the Jerusalem Church's insistence that to be Christian one first had to be a Jew, hence circumcised (not a real Seeker friendly approach) was a major point of contention between them and the expanding ministry of Paul and others who insisted that baptism alone was sufficient. Through a series of visions Peter is convinced to see things Abba's way which conveniently is also Paul's way. This culminates in the Council at Jerusalem in chapter 15 and an official decree that baptism alone was sufficient for non-Jews to enter the Christian community.

The remainder of the book deals with Paul's missions to various cities throughout the Empire. Attempts have been made over the years by scholars to try to reconcile Luke's chronology and geography with that which we find in Paul's letters. The task is impossible primarily because Luke is not interested in providing an accurate description of Paul's voyages but rather a picture that moves theologically and literarily.

The book concludes with Paul's arrest and subsequent journey to Rome. We are told that Paul remains in Rome for two years welcoming all who would listen *and proclaiming the kingdom of Abba and teaching about the Lord Jesus with all boldness and without hindrance* (The Message, Acts 28:31).

"Jakob!"

"My Zaydeh says I can't talk with you anymore. Your people got kicked out of the synagogue! You don't believe in HaShem he says. He says you are not like us and I should stay away from your kind."

"But Jakob, we are friends…"

*"We **were** friends!"*

Gospel According to John

"Hey, Jakob!"

"Shhhh…. Where in church! Do you want to get thrown out of the balcony and have to sit with your parents?"

"Not a chance! What are you reading?"

"A new gospel."

"Who's it by?"

"Some guy by the name of John. It didn't make much sense when I was reading it at home but sitting here in the church I'm starting to see what he's doing."

"What do you mean?"

"He tells the story of Jesus and is very different way than the other Gospels that we hear. He uses a lot of symbolic language. It's strange, but here in church the symbols all take life… Bread and water, the meal, and the flashbacks to Moses and the people of Israel. It's not bad. I'll let you have it after I'm finished with it but you'll have to read it here if you want to make sense."

It seems strange to me that the final chapter for me to rework in this book is the Gospel of John. But in many ways, it makes sense. Perhaps more than any other book of the New Testament John's Gospel occupies the place of the church's book. Like the book of Revelation, it makes little sense to those outside of the Christian community and has its primary context within the worshiping community.

Instead of following a consistent narrative and agenda of Jesus' life as in the Synoptics, John instead paints a symbolic life of Jesus highlighting those teachings which the church most needs to keep in the forefront. John is addressing a community that is struggling not only with the aftermath of the destruction of the Temple but also with the recent expulsion of Jewish Christians from the synagogue. A benediction, called the Benediction Against the Minim (Nazarene/Christian heretics) is introduced into the synagogue liturgy probably between the years 85 and 95 CE leading scholars to see John's gospel as being written around this time with a finish date of no later than 100 CE.

John's Gospel is highly influenced by the Hebrew Wisdom tradition, if not the Gnostic tradition. We see this in particular in the preface of John's gospel. In chapter 1, the Word, or logos, speaks in ways that are very consistent with the Jewish understanding of the embodiment of Wisdom. John's community is also seen at least by itself as an exclusive community over and against the Jewish community that has just so rudely expelled them.

John's Gospel is a symbolic painting of not only the life of Jesus but also that of the church. The narrative is loosely organized around three celebrations of the Passover in Jerusalem and a celebration of the festival of Tabernacles.

The first of the Passover celebrations is found in the second chapter of John's Gospel beginning with verse 13. The unique feature of this celebration is Jesus cleansing of the Temple. John sets the cleansing of the Temple at the very beginning of Jesus ministry rather than during the events of Holy Week to dramatize the separation between Jews and Christians and perhaps even a tongue in cheek commentary to the effect: you may have thrown us out of the synagogue but Jesus threw you out of the Temple.

The second celebration of the Passover begins in the fifth chapter and continues into chapter 6. Chapter 6 is for John a midrash or commentary on the Eucharist or the Lord's Supper. In the story of the feeding of the 5000 John connects the events of the Exodus and the miraculous feeding of the Israelites with manna from heaven. This feeding however is contrasted with a celebration of the Eucharist in that the Israelites got hungry again.

The Passover celebrations are broken up in chapter 7 by the festival of the Tabernacles. Reinterpreting the purification rights of the Tabernacle festival, Jesus makes the connection between himself and living water. Also in the section is the reference to Jesus as the good Shepherd. The motif of Abba as Shepherd was ritually connected to the rededication of the Temple commemorating the Maccabean revolt. It also reminds us of the use of the shepherd metaphor with regards to the King of Israel. Unlike the kings of old, Jesus is the true and model king.

We find the final celebration of the Passover in John's gospel in chapters 11 through 19. Beginning with the anointing with costly perfume by Mary which prefigures the burial of Jesus and ending with the crucifixion (which in John's Gospel occurs on Passover, rather than the day after as in the synoptic Gospels). For John, Jesus is the perfect Passover lamb sacrificed in anticipation of the deliverance of Abba's chosen people.

Having looked at the basic structure John's Gospel let us return to the beginning. Using language that is reminiscent of Genesis, the Wisdom tradition and even Gnostic elements John opens his Gospel. It is clear from the beginning that the distance between Abba and the earthly Jesus is imperceptible. For John Jesus is Abba in flesh. He is the light which Isaiah anticipated that has now come into the world.

In the midst of this cosmic opening there breaks in a strange interruption where John introduces the figure of John the Baptist. Not only does this settled the dispute regarding the place of John the Baptist but it also grounds the cosmic mystery in the real world. John the Baptist is clearly not the light but rather bears witness to the light. The true light will enlighten everyone when he comes *into the world*. This will allow the church to boldly proclaim following baptism: Let your light so shine before others that they may see in your works the glory of Abba.

Following this brief commercial John returns to his cosmic language. At the end of this introduction John also makes the relationship between Torah and Jesus very clear: *"From the fullness of [the Word made flesh] we have received grace upon grace. The law indeed was given through Moses; grace and truth came through Jesus Christ"* (John 1:16).

John's narrative then begins with the testimony of John the Baptist. When confronted by the Jewish authorities as to his identity, John makes it very clear that he is not the Messiah, nor Elijah, nor the prophet but rather the voice of one crying out in the wilderness, make straight the way of the Lord (just as Isaiah said).

The next day John introduces Jesus to the world, and to us, as the Lamb of Abba who takes away the sin of the world. This designation of Jesus is the Lamb of Abba introduces Jesus as a new kind of sacrifice, unlike that of the now defunct Temple. John goes on then to witness to Jesus baptism (note we do not witness Jesus baptism but only get a report of it from John). From witnessing this event John makes the conclusion that becomes the basis of his testimony that Jesus is the son of Abba.

The next day as Jesus walks by, John reveals to two of his disciples that this is the Lamb of Abba. Upon hearing this they follow Jesus. When asked what they are looking for they ask in return where he is staying to which Jesus replies, "Come and see." This response of Jesus will continue to weave itself throughout the gospel and in essence becomes the invitation of the church to those outside who are looking for the Way the Truth and the Life, "Come and see."

The next day Jesus has an encounter with Philip and Nathaniel. Nathaniel serves as the stock skeptic character who wonders if anything good can come out of place like Nazareth. Upon meeting the apparently clairvoyant Jesus, Nathaniel confesses his faith in Jesus the son of Abba, the king of Israel. Jesus comment to Philip, "Very truly, I tell you, you will see heaven opened and the angels of Abba ascending and descending upon the Son of Man," is the same testimony that Jesus makes during his trial in the other Gospels. This once again reveals the Jewish leadership's inability to see the true identity of Jesus from the very beginning of the Gospel.

On the third day (if you've been keeping track you realize this is actually the fourth day which should make it very clear that were dealing not with actual time but rather symbolic time and that the third day is the day of resurrection) Jesus finds himself with his mother and disciples at a wedding in Cana where the wind runs out at the wedding reception. His mother confronts Jesus and tells him to fix the situation to which Jesus replies his time is not yet. In short, what she is asking is inappropriate because such a sign belongs to the kingdom of Shalom that will follow the resurrection. The abundance of wine that is produced in this miracle belongs to the vision of Isaiah that great feast for the wine will flow in great abundance.

We now encounter the first of the Passover celebrations and the cleansing of the Temple. Unlike the other Gospels to locate this story during the Passion, John loads it up front to again take aim at the Jewish leadership and to address the Temple crisis. Jesus condemnation of what is going on in the Temple precinct is not so much about commerce as it is the failure of the transactional relationship between Abba and the Jews that plays out in the sacrificial system of the Temple and the keeping of Torah. This transactional approach (If we make the right sacrifices or keep the Torah then we keep in the good graces of Abba) has now been cleaned out and supplanted by a new relationship based of grace. This new relationship will be sealed in the "sacrifice" of the Lamb of God on the cross. The old Temple has been destroyed (cleared out) to make way for the new Temple which is the body of Jesus, a new Temple come down from heaven.

Chapter 3 offers us both a summary to the introduction and a foretaste of what will unfold in the remainder of the gospel story. It begins with the story of Nicodemus who is a leader of the Jews and who comes to Jesus under the cloak of darkness (the Jewish leadership still walks in darkness). Jesus interrupts the customary flattery with a pronouncement that unless one is born from above one cannot see the kingdom of Abba. The Greek word for above can also be translated again which is what Nicodemus does in his outlandish response to Jesus, how can anyone crawl back in their mother's womb? Jesus makes it very clear that the birth he is talking about is one of water and Spirit, which for the Christian community is clearly baptism. For John baptism supersedes circumcision as a mark of the covenantal people.

Jesus goes on to use the image of Moses in the wilderness to foreshadow his own death and to interpret that death considering the tradition. For just as Moses lifted up the serpent in the wilderness to save his people from certain death so when Jesus is lifted up (crucified) he will draw all humanity to himself that they may not perish but have eternal life. Jesus goes on to explain that the motivation for doing this is the love of the world. But we encounter in the unfolding gospel is not about condemnation of the world but about salvation. Unfortunately, there are those who still will walk in the darkness because they preferred the dark to the light.

This is the first of four stories (Nicodemus, the woman at the well, the man born blind, and the raising of Lazarus) that will be used by the church in the preparation of candidates for baptism. These readings continue to be used in the church today in the adult catechumenate process as well is in the Roman Catholic Church's Rite of Christian Initiation of Adults (RCIA) and are the Gospel readings used during Lent in Cycle A of the Revised Common Lectionary.

In chapter 4 the ministry of Jesus begins in earnest with his encounter with a woman of Samaria at Jacob's well. In this story, we continue the church's teaching on baptism that was begun in the story of Nicodemus. In a rather comical exchange between Jesus and the woman that is akin to a similar discussion with Nicodemus, Jesus engages the woman in the discussion of water which given its context is clearly about baptism. Again, there is an element of supersession of baptism over the traditions of the Jews in the ensuing conversation as well. When the woman realizes she's in the presence of a prophet, she decides to take advantage of the moment by asking a question that is pestering her (as well as Jews and Samaritans over the centuries). On which mountain is it proper to worship? In his response, "The days are soon going to be here when it won't matter on which mountain you worship," Jesus reacts to the present question as to where you worship after both temples have been destroyed.

When the woman returns to the town and witnesses to her encounter with Jesus she is met with skepticism. Her response? Come and see. When the townsfolk have encountered Jesus' testimony they themselves believe. In the same way when those who are stirred by the testimony of witnesses to Jesus encounter Jesus in Word and Sacrament it is anticipated that they too will then believe for themselves.

During this story there is yet another comical exchange this time between Jesus and the disciples. It is not about water but rather food. What "feeds" Jesus, what is at the heart of his mission, is to do the work of Abba. It will be this mission that will be handed over to the disciples at the appropriate time.

Many scholars speculate that John had at his disposal a source often referred to as the Book of Signs which contain a collection of healing and resuscitation miracles concerning Jesus. This would explain why many of the miracles in John's Gospel are not found in the Synoptics. These miracles bear witness to the power and authority of Jesus which are constantly being called into question by the Jewish authorities.

If chapter 4 was midrash/interpretation on baptism then chapter 6 is a similar interpretation on the Eucharist. It begins with the stories lifted out of the synoptic Gospels of the feeding of the 5000 and Jesus walking on the water. But beginning in verse 22 the feeding miracle is unpacked through a conversation between Jesus and the disciples. Once again, the work of Moses and Jesus are contrasted. Moses provided manna in the wilderness which the people ate and yet eventually died. Jesus on the other hand gives the "*bread of Abba that gives life to the world and whoever eats of this bread will live forever; and the bread that I will give for the life of the world is my flesh*" (John 6:32-51).

The Jews present speak on behalf of those who accuse the early Christians of cannibalism raising the question of how can this man give his flesh and blood. Jesus response is to establish the priority of the Eucharist at the heart of Christian worship: "*Those who eat my flesh and drink my blood have eternal life, and I will raise them up on the last day; for my flesh is true food in my blood is true drink. Those who eat my flesh and drink my blood abide in me, and I in them... This is the bread that came down from heaven, not like that which your ancestors A, and they died. But the one who eats this bread will live forever*" (John 6:56-58   ).

As one might expect many of those who were following Jesus found this teaching hard to swallow. Like the murmuring motif that followed Moses through the wilderness unrest by those who follow Jesus seems to be a constant. Jesus even go so far as to ask the disciples if they too wanted defect. Even his family encourages him to abandon this foolish mission that will surely end in death.

The Festival of the Tabernacles offers the backdrop for Jesus response to this murmuring/questioning. Jesus explains that his authority is from Abba and not of his own and that their complaints about his healing on the Sabbath are misguided. Using the Torah required circumcision on the Sabbath as an example Jesus asked the authorities why healing a whole person, and not just mutilating a part, would not also be judged right and salutary. This raises again the question of Jesus identity as Messiah and also escalates the murmuring to a matter of arresting and executing Jesus.

On the final day of the festival Jesus invites everyone to come to him and receive living water. Again, the question of Jesus as Messiah divides the crowd and those in authority condemn Jesus citing that if you check the Torah you will find that no prophet ever has come from Galilee.

Chapter 8 begins with the familiar story of the woman caught in adultery. While one of the most familiar and often quoted of Jesus teaching stories it is almost universally regarded among scholars not being part of the original Gospel of John. One of the reasons for this is that it interrupts the progression of the narrative.

If the story is removed we move smoothly into a continuation of the discussion on authority and bearing testimony which were issues that the early church continually had to wrestle over with their Jewish brothers and sisters. Again, we find Jesus using a Johannine feature in this narrative, that is the use of the designation of himself with the two-word phrase, I am. In this case I am the light of the world. We may remember that when Moses asks Abba for a name he says, "I am who I am". Jesus' use of the term "I am" makes a clear statement that he sees himself as Abba. This identification of Jesus with Abba is often referred to by scholars as a High Christology (Jesus as Abba in flesh) versus a Low Christology which focuses on the connection between Jesus and humanity.

There seems to be a distinction made in John's Gospel between Jewish leadership and the ordinary Jew. We find in John's Gospel that there are those Jews who believe in Jesus, like Nicodemus. We find Jesus in chapter 8 addressing this particular segment of the Jewish population in a discussion on truth and being set free. Obviously forgetting 2000 years of Jewish history and their present-day predicament the Jews are indignant to think they have ever been slaves to anyone. Furthermore, they make claim on the Abrahamic promise/covenant, which in their minds supersedes Jesus authority. This leads into a lengthy excursus on the place of Abraham, the Samaritans and Jesus authority. In the end, they seek to stone Jesus.

As one might expect having read the Synoptic Gospels, John closes this misguided discussion and failure to see who Jesus is with the healing of a man born blind. This is now the third of the four great stories used in baptismal preparation in the early church. What seems like a pretty straightforward miracle story opens up a great debate with the Pharisees. It seems that this miracle was performed on the Sabbath bringing Jesus' authority once again into question: *this man is not from Abba, for he does not observe the Sabbath.* When they asked the man born blind his opinion he simply responds, he is a prophet. Some of the Jews, thinking Jesus is simply a charlatan, question whether the man was born blind in the first place and they drag his parents in for questioning. Fearing that they may be thrown out of the synagogue, as was happening to any who confess that Jesus was Messiah, they refer the Jews back to their son. Again, the man born blind is asked to recant and when he confronts the Jewish leadership for not recognizing Jesus they drive him out the synagogue.

The punchline of this encounter comes when Jesus questions the man born blind as to whether he believes in the Son of Man. When Jesus reveals himself as such the man born blind confesses, I believe! and then worships him. The judgment comes in Jesus response: *I came into this world for judgment so that those who do not see may see, and those who do see may become blind.* The Pharisees' response is tantamount to self-incrimination.

In chapter 10 we have another of the I Am sayings, namely, I am the Good/Model Shepherd. If you remember our discussions on the role of the Shepherd in the Hebrew Scriptures there is not so much a bucolic pastoral sense as there is a royal one. Jesus contrast of himself with thieves, bandits and hired hands picks up the discussion from the cleansing of the Temple as to the ineffective leadership within Judaism of his day. Like their ancestors in the past they have failed in caring for the sheep. This is particularly true in his discussion about the hired hands which may be a direct hit to the Sadducees who have become bedfellows with the leaders of the Roman occupation. Rather than running away Jesus is willing to die for the sake of the sheep. The crucifixion in John is not to be seen as an abortion of justice but is a willing offering of his life. This condemnation on Jesus part is met again but Jewish opposition and an attempt to stone him. Jesus again leaves Jerusalem for safety across the Jordan.

The final of the four great stories in the baptismal process is the Raising of Lazarus. We are told that Lazarus is the brother of Mary and Martha, whom we are not introduced to prior to this in John's Gospel. In fact, we are told that Mary is the one who anointed Jesus with perfume and wiped his feet with her hair - a story that will take place following this one.

Jesus receives word across the Jordan that Lazarus is ill and instead of rushing off he stays where he is. When questioned about his behavior he explains that Lazarus' illness will not lead to death but that it is for glorifying Abba. After a two days delay, two days are required for someone to be really dead, Jesus announces that they are going to Lazarus.

The disciples remind him that it was just the other day that the Jews were trying to stone him there and that it might not be too safe to return now. After another comical dialogue between Jesus and his disciples on the nature of sleep and death, Thomas (who is the disciple exemplar for John) announces that he is willing to go to Jerusalem and die with Jesus.

Upon arriving Jesus is confronted by Martha who questions Jesus' delay and informs him that if he'd showed up on time her brother certainly would not have died. In the tradition of the psalmists this lament is followed up by a confession of faith, "yet even now I know that Abba will give you whatever you ask of him." Jesus reminds her that her brother will rise again. Quoting the popular party line Martha, the responds, I know he will rise again in the resurrection on the last day. To which Jesus replies, I am the resurrection and the life.

Jesus then is encountered by Martha's sister, Mary, who confronts him with the same lament. When Jesus sees her grief and the grief of the professional mourners he too is moved to tears. Those who witnessed this sod is a sign of his deep love for Lazarus while others pondered, "Could not he who opened the eyes of the blind men of This man from dying?" This question that is now asked three times by Martha, Mary and the crowd may speak to a question within the Johannine community concerning those who have died prior to Jesus seemingly delayed return.

Jesus' request to be taken to the tomb is met with horror at the potential stench that they would encounter there. He asked that the stone be rolled away (a foreshadowing of his own resurrection?). He offers a prayer to Abba, and then with a loud cry he demands that Lazarus come out. Lazarus emerges from the tomb wrapped like a mummy. Jesus then instructs those gathered to unbind him and let him go. Of note here is that Jesus does not unbind him and let him go but rather the community that gathers. As such it will be the community of the faithful that will be responsible for witnessing to the Truth that will set people free. The work of the church is to unbind.

As one might expect this powerful display of Jesus authority leads to a plot to kill Jesus. With this we are introduced to the last of the Passover sections in John's Gospel.

The narrative begins six days before the Passover at the house of Lazarus. In a strange narrative that offers no connection with the preceding drama, we find ourselves again with Mary, Martha, and Lazarus. Mary anoints Jesus feet with costly perfume and wipes them with her hair. This sends Judas Iscariot into a tizzy about wasteful spending. We are told that

Judas' motive is not his apparent concern for the poor but rather that he might be caught in his embezzlement scheme.

When the Jewish authorities discover that Jesus has returned to Lazarus' home they seek also to put Lazarus to death because his witness is now causing many Jews to defect. This may also reflect what is going on in the community of John as the witnesses of Jesus are now being persecuted by the Jewish leadership because of the conversion of Jews to Christianity

Following this Jesus rides into Jerusalem amid shouts of Hosanna! John makes it very clear that this is a royal entry with a quote from Zechariah that the king is now at hand. His disciples don't have a clue what any of this means until after he is raised from the dead. It is the crowd that witnesses the resuscitation of Lazarus that continues to testify about Jesus to the point where the Pharisees begin to wonder if the whole world has not gone mad after him!

The question is answered in the next story where Philip is encountered by some Greeks (the whole Hellenistic world). Jesus uses the occasion of this encounter to compare his death to grain that falls into the earth and dies only to bear much fruit. Still many do not believe him. We are told however that many do believe him but for fear of the Pharisees and getting thrown out of the synagogue they do not confess their faith.

In chapter 13 we have the meal which in the synoptic Gospels is a Passover meal and occasion for the institution of the Eucharist. This meal however is not a Passover meal nor is there any mention of what has become known as the Eucharist or the Last Supper. The reason for this is twofold: first, the discussion of the Eucharist is already taken place in chapter 6 and secondly, the Passover in John does not precede Jesus crucifixion but is the occasion of Jesus crucifixion. In John, Jesus is the Passover lamb. In his death, he will save the world from death. Note that this is not a sacrifice of atonement but rather a sacrifice of identification. The blood of the lamb marked the homes of Abba's people in Egypt causing the angel of death to pass over them. The blood of Jesus, the Lamb of Abba, marks the Christians as those who will not taste eternal death. This marking will be made clear in the baptismal right of the early church as the candidates are anointed with the cross of Christ on their foreheads - a practice already attested to in Ephesians and Revelation.

What takes center stage in John's meal is the foot washing. This symbolic act amplifies the teaching to love one another just as Jesus loves us. It is by this love that others will know that we are his disciples, if we have love for one another. As I mentioned in the outset John is the church's gospel. Because of this John tends to hammer those things which the church easily forgets. It is hard to forget the Eucharist when you are celebrating it each time you gather but it is easy because of our humanity to forget to love one another. The act of foot washing is an outward sign of that love even as acts of charity proclaim that love to the world.

What begins in the meal continues in the following chapters which constitute Jesus farewell discourse with his disciples. The section is reminiscent again of Moses instructions to Joshua and the people prior to their entering into the promised land. These will be the things the church needs to remember most in the days ahead not only prior to Jesus crucifixion but also prior to his return in glory. As such these are not only instructions to the disciples but to us.

The first of these teachings deals with Jesus imminent departure. He must leave to prepare a place for those who will follow. When Thomas pleads ignorance on behalf of the rest of the disciples and us as to where Jesus is going Jesus responds, *"I am the way, the truth, and the life. No one comes to the father except through me. If you know me, you will know my father also. From now on you do know him and have seen him"* (John 14:6-7). This leads to Philip's request to show them Abba. You can almost see Jesus shaking his head at Philip's inability to grasp the reality that in Jesus we come and see Abba. This leads then into a discussion of the Holy Spirit or Advocate. We must be cautious at this point not to identify the Holy Spirit in John's Gospel with that of the third person of the Trinity. The doctrine of the Trinity is very much in process at this time. John is referring to the spirit of the resurrected Christ which will continue to dwell with the disciples. He will not leave them orphaned but rather is coming to them in a new way. It will be the Spirit that will serve as an advocate and enable them to be faithful witnesses particularly in times of trial. The sign of this will be the peace/shalom the Jesus leaves with them and which the church will later liturgically share with one another.

In chapter 15 we have Jesus discourse on the true vine and the nature of the church. The church owes its existence and sustenance to being grafted onto the true vine, Jesus. It is Abba who will attend the vine and continue to prune its branches. The task of the church is to bear much fruit. Referring to the foot washing, that fruit will be to love one another as Jesus has first loved us.

Jesus explains that he is offering these instructions so that they might not stumble or fall back into their old Jewish ways. In times of difficulty the Spirit will be guide and voice. Jesus explains that there are a whole lot of things that he would like to tell them but they simply are not able to hear them at this point which points to the ongoing revelation of the Christian witness and the teachings concerning Jesus.

John replaces Jesus' prayer of agony in Gethsemane with what is often called the High Priestly Prayer in chapter 17. This prayer, modeled after the High Priestly prayers of the Temple, is Jesus' prayer not only for his disciples but for the church. Recognizing the potential for disintegration, disagreement and defection the prayer is one of unity. It is a unity that derives its nature and strength from the unity that Jesus shares with Abba.

The Passion narrative proper in John's Gospel now follows the traditional narrative line in the synoptic Gospels with Jesus arrest, his appearance before Caiaphas, Peter's denial and his appearance before Pilate. It is in his appearance before Pilate that the narrative becomes most dissimilar from those that have preceded it. There is a distinct distancing of Pilate from Jesus death and yet at the same time a portrayal of him as an inconsequential puppet in this whole drama. It is obvious the Pilate wants nothing to do with this man's death and attempts to dissuade the Jews from carrying out their death wish. It is finally the reminder from the Jewish authorities that if Pilate releases this one who is heralded as King of the Jews that risks calling his allegiance to the Emperor into question. For everyone who claims to be a king sets himself against the Emperor. With this he hands Jesus over to the Jews to crucify him.

Two of the distinctive features of John's crucifixion of Jesus concern his mother Mary and his pierced side. In a very tender scene, which seems so out of place in the midst of the gruesome crucifixion, Jesus hands his mother Mary into the care of the disciple whom he loved. We are told from that moment on the disciple took her into his own home. Because John is who John is I'm left wondering if there is more to this scene than simply the handing on of Mary's future care. Perhaps it is also a symbolic transfer of those who are now called to bear Jesus to the world.

The second distinctive feature of John's crucifixion scene is the piercing of Jesus side. It was tradition to leave the bodies of the crucified on the cross for days (it often took days for them to die) or even weeks as a warning sign to all would be enemies of the Empire. In very uncharacteristic fashion then we are told that because of the holiday their deaths are to be hastened so that the bodies might be taken down before the Sabbath. Traditionally this hastening was done by breaking their legs which was administered to the first two of those crucified with Jesus. When they came to Jesus they found him already dead and so did not break his legs. As such he remained the perfect and unblemished Passover lamb. What the soldier does do is to drive his spear into Jesus side and at once blood and water gush forth. Blood and water are signs of Eucharist and baptism in the early church. It is also customary among the historic churches to mix water with the wine in the cup of the Eucharist.

Nicodemus shows back up at the burial of Jesus. He brings with him a mixture of myrrh and aloes of exceedingly great worth (as Mary Magdalene had previously anointed him) and he assists in the preparation of Jesus body for burial. Jesus is then laid in a new tomb in the garden *(the* Garden?).

The post-resurrection accounts in John's Gospel are unique to John. The initial encounter of the empty tomb by Mary Magdalene and her subsequent witnessing to Simon Peter and the disciple whom Jesus loved that someone had taken Jesus out of the tomb is at least in narrative like the Synoptics. But when the disciples return home Mary remains weeping outside of the tomb. Looking into the tomb she discovers two angels who ask why she's crying. While she is explaining to them how someone has taken the body of Jesus away and that she doesn't know where they have taken him (remember Phillips question earlier about not knowing where Jesus was going?) Jesus arrives on the scene and asked the same question of her. Not recognizing Jesus, she repeats her answer. Upon hearing her name, she realizes who Jesus is. Her first instinct is to try to hold onto Jesus but he reminds her that he must ascend to Abba. It is always the first instinct of the church and the faithful to want to hold on to Jesus and so we must be reminded that if his mission is to be complete we must share that good news with others and so Mary exits Stage Left.

The scene turns to later that night where we find the disciples huddled together behind locked doors for fear of the Jews and the possibility that crucifixion might be waiting for them. Jesus enters without opening the door which startles the disciples. He offers them the promised peace/shalom and shows them his hands and his side – signs of his crucifixion. He then breathes on them the Holy Spirit, the *ruach Adonai* that blew over the face of creation in the beginning. It will be this Holy Spirit that will be imparted upon the newly baptized through the laying on of hands. It is the gift of the Holy Spirit that enables the church to see the risen Christ where others see only chance, luck and fate.

Thomas is not with them on that night and is very skeptical of the report that they gave. As such Thomas stands not only with those who questioned the Christian witness of the early church but also with us who have had our moments of doubt and fear. Some days we just want proof. Thomas receives that proof the next Sunday when Jesus shows up again. Thomas's response is akin to Peter's confession in the synoptic Gospels, "My Lord and my Abba". Jesus response to Thomas' confession of faith is to pronounce blessing upon all those who have not seen as Thomas has and yet still have come to believe - which includes us.

In verse 30 John tells us: "*Now Jesus did many other signs in the presence of his disciples, which are not written in this book. But these are written so that you may come to believe that Jesus is the Messiah, the son of Abba and that through believing you may have life in his name*"(John 20:30). In many ways, this provides a fitting conclusion to the Gospel of John… But there is more…

Scholarly consensus is the chapter 21 is a later addition either by John or one of his disciples. It is perhaps best read as an epilogue to the preceding drama. The scene takes place beside the sea of Tiberius. Peter has announced that after all that they have gone through he's going fishing. As with skeptical Thomas so Peter reflects the temptation of the church to simply go back to doing business as usual and in his case, that meant fishing. The others join him but they spend the night in futility not catching a thing (they have become failures as fishermen). At daybreak, as the sun/Son rises, they see Jesus on the shore and like Mary they don't recognize him. He calls out instructions to try throwing their nets on the other side. When they do the catch of fish is so great they can barely haul it in. At this point Peter realizes that it is Jesus on the shore and jumps into the water and swims to meet Jesus (the baptismal imagery here is unmistakable).

When they had had breakfast together, fish and bread, (remember the feeding of the 5000?) He takes Peter aside for little one on one follow-up. Three times Jesus asked Peter if he loves him. Three times Peter responds in the affirmative - A threefold confession following a threefold denial. Three times Jesus tells him to feed his sheep. After this Jesus simply says, "Follow me."

Again, a good way to end. But wait... There's still more...

The final verses of chapter 21 turn our attention toward the fate of the disciple whom Jesus loved. We are briefly taken back to the supper and reminded that it was he who asked the question concerning Jesus betrayer. Peter, upon seeing the disciple whom Jesus loved standing there, asked Jesus about his fate. Jesus response is pretty much, if he still alive when I come back what concern is that of you? This leads to speculation within the community that the disciple whom Jesus loved would not die. We are then told that it is this disciple who is testifying to these things in his written down this true testimony. He also acknowledges that there are many other things that Jesus did that are not written there and speculates that if all the things about Jesus were written down the world could not contain all the books that would need to be written.

PASTORAL EPISTLES

"Thespotus, how are things going with the congregation?"

"It's a struggle. We seem to be moving through unchartered waters. Some of the issues were facing we've never had to deal with before."

"Like what?"

"Like good order. How can we be a church home? We can't even agree on right beliefs and good worship practices? We need new leadership. A strong central figure."

"I don't hear as much speculation about the return of the Messiah these days. Has that been shelved?"

"I guess. Not many people are expecting Jesus to return tomorrow. It's time to move on. We must figure out how to live in this world as Christians. It's a struggle to figure out when to accommodate the world we live in and one to stand over and against it. And then there's the whole issue of women."

"Ah, women!"

Collectively Paul's letters to Timothy and Titus are considered the Pastoral Epistles. Modern scholarship believes that these are not authentic Pauline writings but rather the work of later Pauline writers, purported to have been written even as late as the mid-second century.

The pastoral epistles point to a growing church and the beginning of church orders. At this point in church history there is an emerging genre of material being written to oversee worship and ministry. Two of the more famous of these documents are the *Didache* and the *Apostolic Constitutions.* The Pastoral Epistles show evidence of a church that seeks to address a new generation of Christians.

1 Timothy

As the first letter to Timothy opens we are greeted with the key issue that is facing the developing church namely orthodoxy or correct belief. The pressing question is how to keep the church orthodox in its teaching and belief amid a growing number of "Christian" groups purporting all manner of myth and speculation rather than sound teaching. The issue of sound teaching must always be love that comes from a pure heart, a good conscience, and sincere faith. This love is seen over and against the practice of the Law/Torah which is obviously slipping back into many Christian communities.

In the first chapter we are introduced with what will become an ongoing metaphor for the Christian life, the fight. It seems obvious that the Christian community is in for the fight of its life against the pressures of the world both secular and religious. If it is to persevere it must fight the good/correct fight.

The first weapon in the good fight is that of prayer. Prayers and intercession should be made for everybody including kings and all those in positions of leadership that all may lead a quiet and peaceable life in all godliness and dignity.

There is however a double standard emerging at this point within the life of the church between men and women. Using Eve's subordinate position to Adam as justification, women are not to teach or to have authority over men. They should remain silent. The salvation of women is to be seen in their ability to bear children so long as they also continue in faith and love and holiness, with modesty. While this understanding seems archaic in the church today the idea of women as being subordinate and submissive is very much alive in our culture. Statements like: "A woman's place is in the kitchen, barefoot and pregnant," or "I married my wife when she was 13 so I could raise her up right," attest to the presence of the ongoing struggle for women in both church and society today.

There is developing in the church at this time a threefold office of ministry: Bishop, presbyter, and deacon. These roles develop within the early church to address the increased need for order as the ministry of the church continue to expand in the world.

The role of the bishop is that of oversight and orthodoxy. The qualifications of the bishop laid out in this letter are temperance, sensibility, respectability, hospitality, the ability to teach, peaceful, and not a lover of money. He must be able to manage his own household because if he cannot manage his own household how can he manage the household of Abba. He must not be a recent convert (a rule that will be broken repeatedly in the future by such bishops as Ambrose and others). He must have a good reputation in the world as well as in the church.

Deacons, who manage the day-to-day ministry of service to the world, are to be serious, sober, not greedy, and orthodox in their faith. Before one can become a deacon, they must be tested and only then can they serve as a deacon. Women are viewed as deacons of the household and the qualities of a good deacon should be possessed by a good wife and mother.

There appears to be a growing asceticism creeping in to the church at this time. Asceticism is the belief that if you renounce the worldly pleasures it is possible to achieve a high spiritual state. The ascetics now are forbidding marriage and demanding abstinence from foods. The argument against such asceticism is that everything was created by Abba and is good. Nothing should be rejected so long as it is received with thanksgiving.

Attention is now turned toward the office of the presbyter or pastor. Orthodoxy is again the prime consideration for a good servant. While training the body may be good and beneficial one must also continue to train in godliness if one is to perform the duties of servant. One in this role should set an example and speech and conduct, and love, in faith, in purity.

Elders and widows should be held in esteem and they should be provided for by relatives. It appears at this point that there is developing a "list" of widows for whom the church has responsibility. The church should not waste its resources on younger widows because they may decide to run off and get married. Elders receive a double honor especially if they are called to the task of preaching and teaching. Slaves should be submissive to their masters especially if the master is a believer.

We return at the end of the letter to the concern for orthodoxy in teaching and practice. The church must fight the temptation to submit to those who would teach a contrary doctrine. Once again, the image of the good fight is used to speak of the journey of faith. "Fight the good fight of the faith; take hold of eternal life, to which you were called in for which you made the good confession in the presence of many witnesses."

2 Timothy

The second letter to Timothy opens with a Thanksgiving of encouragement for the community's faithfulness especially to Lois and Eunice who were leaders in the community. Once again, the example of their faithfulness and orthodoxy are used to remind us to be true to the good treasure that is entrusted to us. This same good treasure is also commended to the recipients of the letter.

The image of the fight that is used in the first letter is expanded to describe the Christian as a good soldier of Jesus Christ. Again, the author outlines the moral character of those that seek to be soldiers of Jesus Christ. Rules, good order and station are among the highest qualities of a good soldier of the faith. The example of Hymenaeus and Philetus (who claim the resurrection has already taken place) is used to remind the good soldier that they should also refrain from idle and pious chatter.

In chapter 3 the author reminds the community that the last days will be stressing times for all and that they are most surely coming. The task of the Christian is to be firm in his faith in the face of this growing lawlessness. *"In these times people would become lovers of themselves, lovers of money, boasters, arrogant, abusive, disobedient to their parents, ungrateful, unholy, inhuman, implacable, slanders, profligates, brutes, haters of good, treacherous, reckless, swollen with conceit, lovers of pleasure rather than lovers of Abba"* (2 Timothy 3:2-4). (sound familiar?).

Timothy himself is singled out and given special instructions as a leader within this community not to give in to false doctrines. The author reminds Timothy and the community that the time is coming when sound doctrine will have no hearing within the people's ears but rather they will seek teachings that satisfy them. *"For the time is coming when people will not put up with sound doctrine, but having itching ears, they will accumulate for themselves teachers to suit their own desires, and will turn away from listing to the truth and wander away into myths."*

Finally, Paul turns to his own imminent departure and encourages his example to be the measuring stick for all Christians as they wait the appearing of Christ Jesus. *"As for me, I am already being poured out as a libation, and the time of my departure has come. I have fought the good fight, I finished the race, I have kept the faith. From now on there is reserved for me the crown of righteousness, which the Lord, the righteous Judge, will give me on that day and not only to me but also to all who have longed for his appearing"* (2 Timothy 4:6-8).

Titus

Titus is reminded that he has been left behind on Crete so that he might continue what Paul has begun including the appointment of elders and bishops. We again are reminded of the qualifications for elders and bishop in terms of morality and deportment. They should be *"blameless, married only once, as children are believers, not accused of debauchery and not rebellious. A bishop must be blameless; he must not be arrogant or quick-tempered or addicted to wine or violent or greedy for gain; he must be hospitable, a lover of goodness, prudent, upright, devout, and self-controlled. You must have a firm grasp on the word that is trustworthy in accordance with the teaching, so that he may be able to both preach with sound doctrine and to refute those who contradict it"* (Titus 1:6-9).

The second chapter of Titus again returns to the issue of teaching sound doctrine and the relationship of husbands to wives and slaves to masters. The faith also must be evident in the moral conduct and good deeds of the Christian so that others may see in them the goodness and lovingkindness of Abba. *"Be obedient, ready for every good work, speak evil of no one, avoid quarreling, be gentle, show every courtesy to everyone. For we ourselves were once foolish, disobedient, led astray, slaves to various passions and pleasures, passing our days in malice and envy, despicable, hating one another. But when the goodness and lovingkindness of Abba our Savior appeared, he saved us, not because of any works of righteousness that we've done, but according to his mercy, through the water of rebirth and renewal by the Holy Spirit. The Spirit he poured out on us richly through Jesus Christ our Savior, so that having been justified by his grace, we might become heirs according to the hope of eternal life"* (Titus 3:1-7).

HEBREWS

"Did you hear that Moishe got caught up in the last round of interrogations?"

"I hear he broke under pressure, denounced the Christian walk, and went back to his Jewish ways."

"That's what I heard too. With the Temple now destroyed in Jerusalem there's a lot of confusion and uncertainty between Jews and Christians."

"Yeah, the Christians are really struggling to figure out what is their relationship with the Jews."

"You're right. It's a struggle right now trying to figure out if we hold on to the old Jewish practices or what if any is the role of Torah in our morality."

"I think that's the topic for discussion this Sunday."

The main theme of Hebrews is the supplanting of the old covenant by the new. In the opening line the author reminds the community, *"Long ago Abba spoke to our ancestors in many and various ways by the prophets, but in these last days he has spoken to us by his son."*

Following an interesting if not confusing discussion of angels, which could be a commentary on some Gnostic issues within the community, the author begins in chapter 3 homing in on his theme. He begins with a contrast of Moses as servant and Christ as Son. He sees Moses as laying the tradition that Christ will inherit and fulfill. In the very beginning of this section the author warns of backsliding in the same way that the Israelites murmured in the wilderness at the time of the Exodus.

In chapters 4 and 5 we have Jesus revealed as the great high priest who is both able to sympathize with human weakness and yet is the Son of Abba. As high priest Jesus stands in the order of Melchizedek. Note that the author does not have Jesus standing in the order of Aaron. Melchizedek, who predates Moses and Aaron, is not tied with the Mosaic covenant and presents a more universal priesthood. Again, the author warns of falling away from the central focus of these teachings. Like Paul, the author appeals to Abraham as a figure of faithfulness and is a connection with Melchizedek. The Melchizedek priesthood is contrasted with the priesthood of Aaron with the latter being seen is deficient. The priesthood of Aaron has or soon will come to an end with the destruction of the Temple whereas Jesus standing in the order of Melchizedek will be a priest forever and a guarantee of a lasting covenant. Appealing to Jeremiah 31 the author reminds the readers of the promise of a new covenant, not like the covenant he made with their ancestors when he took them out of the land of Egypt. The author also contrasts the tent that was constructed for Abba's worship in the wilderness with the tent that is the body of Christ. So, Christ's sacrifice on the cross becomes a perfect once and for all sacrifice that negates the need for sacrifice in the Temple.

Again, the author encourages the community to persevere in their faith during the difficult times in which they find themselves. The readers can do this because of faith which the author defines as, *"the assurance of things hoped for, the conviction of things not seen"* (Hebrews 11:1). The author then moves from Able, Enoch, Noah, Abraham, Moses, Gideon, Barack, Sampson, Jephthah, David, Samuel and all the prophets as exemplars of faith who yet still did not receive the promise. Unlike the reader, these giants of old would not be made perfect through the perfect sacrifice of Christ.

The author reminds us that we can persevere in faith because we are surrounded by so great a cloud of witnesses. During persecution this cloud of witnesses encourages us to run our race with perseverance. In persecution, we see the discipline of Abba. Rather than being a negative sign it is a sign of our being children of Abba. As human parents discipline their children Abba disciplines us.

At the end of chapter 12 the author returns to the subject angels and mystery. The community is encouraged once again to be found in love and to practice hospitality. Hospitality to strangers is an opportunity to entertain angels without knowing it. The author then lays out how all of this impacts the ethical demands of life particularly for leaders within the church. The final benediction is to be seen as replacement to the Aaronic benediction, a benediction not from Aaron but from Jesus the great Shepherd of the sheep and of the blood of the everlasting covenant.

JAMES

"Answer me this, Gallus, what is it about the Jewish way of life that so many Greeks and Romans find it attractive?"

"I think amid the self-indulgent culture the Torah, or their Law, offers a refreshingly simple and disciplined moral code. It also weds the religious ritual practice with the affairs of daily life. For the Jews there's no division between sacred and

secular. It seems that all life is lived in the presence of their HaShem."

"I heard their prophets were pretty hard on the notion of making high sounding religious talk in the Temple and then going out in behaving in a totally foreign way in the marketplace."

"Yes, for them it's all about the doing. Doesn't matter what you confess if you can't put it in action then how much do you really believe."

"That all sounds really good but it sounds like it may conflict with what Paul's been teaching the Christians about faith and such works."

"And there's the rub."

It is the emphasis on behavior or works in the Letter of James the causes Martin Luther to characterize it as a "straw epistle" and call for its removal from the canon. The letter is intensely Jewish and obviously is written to a Jewish Christian audience. The letter is general in nature addressed to the 12 tribes in the Dispersion.

As with the earlier writings we see in the opening of James an encouragement to endorse sufferings and trials because such trials produce endurance and a mature and complete faith. This mature faith leads one to be a doer of the word and not simply a hearer. We may think we are religious but if we continue to lead a life that does not bear fruit we are deceiving ourselves. Blessed are those who endure the temptation to backslide into former behaviors. It is not Abba who is tempting us but rather our own desires. James also raises the question of rich and poor. In language both reminiscent of the prophets and Mary's Magnificat, there will be a great reversal of fortunes for the rich and poor.

The appropriate response to the persecutions that the community is experiencing is not anger but rather meekness. It is in humility like that this community of Jesus that has power to save. This gives rise to James' main theme: Be doers of the word, and not merely hearers. If you cannot bridle your tongue in the face of persecution then your religion is worthless.

In like manner, the Christian is not to practice favoritism particularly among the rich. This deference to the rich seems to be an issue within the communities that are being addressed. The commandment to love your neighbor as yourself is to be done with no partiality. If you practice such partiality then you have failed the Law and if you fail in one point you're failed the Law in total.

In 2:14ff James provides a concise summary of the entire letter: faith without works is a dead faith. In contrast to Paul's justification by grace alone James insists that faith without works cannot save. *"Show me your faith apart from your works, and I by my works will show you my faith"* (James 2:18).

James now returns to the issue of taming one's tongue. The mouth should be checked and bridled just as horses are bridled to make them obey. The mouth should be bridled so that the rest of the body obeys. James also speaks of the two kinds of wisdom in the world; that which is heavenly and that which is earthly. The difference is revealed by the fruits that are borne by faith. The wisdom of the world is earthly, unspiritual, devilish. Whereas the wisdom from above is pure, peaceable, gentle, willing to yield, full of mercy, without a trace of partiality or hypocrisy. The community is also warned about becoming judgmental particularly about matters of the Law which is in the sense to criticize the one Lawgiver and the Law. If you judge the Law then you are not a doer of the Law but a judge. Since there is only one Lawgiver and one judge who are we to judge our neighbor?

The author closes his letter with a reminder to live each day. This is particularly true during times of suffering. One must be patient in suffering, calling upon the elders of the church to come and pray for you during your suffering, anointing you with oil in the name of the Lord. Above all else, when faced with persecution we are not to swear an oath but rather let our "yes" be "yes" and our "no" be "no."

Finally, if you wander from the truth and are brought back by another, *"you should know that whoever brings back a sinner from wandering will save the sinner's soul from death and will cover a multitude of sins"* (James 5:20).

This letter is often attributed to James, the brother of Jesus. Whether this is true or not, the letter does reflect the Jerusalem school. It is perhaps the best example outside of the Acts of the Apostles of the tension between the Jerusalem school and the writings of Paul. The relationship between the fundamentalism of keeping the Jewish Torah and the role of Christ's death and resurrection is one of the great dividing issues for the early church as well as today. Much of evangelical Protestantism has far more in common with Torah keeping than it does with grace. This tension is also reflected within the worship life in the synagogue were Jews and Christians were beginning to divide over this issue. The letter of James does provide a helpful corrective especially considering what is going on in some of the early Christian faith communities such as Corinth.

1 PETER

"Did you hear that sermon at Crispus's baptism on Sunday?"

"It was pretty awesome. I especially like the way the preacher made it sound like it was a letter from Paul."

"The part that got me was that we are a chosen race and a royal priesthood. It's important to remember in these times of persecution."

It is clear from the very beginning of the sermon that the communities to which this letter is addressed are experiencing trials and persecutions. The letter then is an address on baptismal living in such difficulties. The baptized should be prepared for action and have their hopes set on grace of Abba and this will in turn produce holiness. The source of this hope is the resurrection of Jesus Christ from the dead. This is our inheritance which is *imperishable, undefiled, and unfading, kept in heaven* for us. This inheritance will protect us even as we are moving into the latter days.

This hope leads to a new way of living. In language similar to the holiness code of Leviticus this new way of living leads to purity which is obtained by obedience to the truth and leads the baptized into genuine love for one another.

The baptized are seen as a chosen race, a royal priesthood, a holy nation (replacing the Jews) for the purpose that the mighty acts of Abba might be proclaimed through them. The baptized are to live honorably among Gentiles despite their evil intentions for the baptized. In short, they are to accept the authority of every human institution. The author then goes on to talk about the relationship between slaves and masters, husbands and wives and to those are imprisoned or persecuted. In all of this it is the example set by Christ that should be a model for the life of the baptized.

The baptized are to be good stewards of Abba's grace. Since the end is near they must be serious in their discipline, faithful in their prayers, loving one another, hospitable without complaint, serving one another with the gifts that they have received from Abba. The reason for this behavior is always to glorify Abba for to him belongs the glory and the power for ever and ever.

Finally, the author turns to the suffering of many Christians as a sign of the "beginning of the end" of Abba's judgment. Using Christ as a model, the baptized Christian is to be an exemplary shepherd. The author reminds the Christians to discipline themselves and to keep alert "*for like a roaring lion or adversary the devil prowls around, looking for someone to devour. Resist him, steadfast in your faith, for you know that your brothers and sisters in all the world are undergoing the same kinds of suffering. And after all, have suffered for a little Abba will restore, support, strengthen, and establish them in faith*" (1 Peter 5:8-9).

> *"Boy, the preacher was really wound up on Sunday!"*
>
> *"You can say that again. I wonder what got into him?"*
>
> *"I was talking to the secretary on Monday and she said he got a couple letters this week that really seem to have an effect on him."*
>
> *"The language must've been pretty strong for him to get that worked up."*

JUDE AND 2 PETER

Most scholars today believe there is direct literary dependence between the books of Jude and Second Peter. It is speculated that the author of second Peter uses Jude as source material.

The tone of **Jude**'s letter is outrage. His language is apocalyptic. His rhetoric attacks the false teachings that are appearing in the second-generation of Christianity. The fate of these false teachers and those who would adhere to their teachings is portrayed in vivid detail offering new motivation for obedience lest a similar fate await the community.

The issue of orthodoxy in the face of false teachings is at the center of Jude's letter. Calling them "dreamers," Jude accuses them of "*defiling the flesh, rejecting authority, slandering the glorious ones/angels... They are grumbler's and malcontents; they indulge in their own lusts; they are bombastic in speech, flattering people to their own advantage*" (Jude 1:8-160. As with the community at Corinth there seems to be issues with regards to the love feast. It appears that these false teachers are encouraging participants to have far too much fun at assemblies that should be solemn.

During all this the faithful are encouraged to recognize that such divisiveness is a sign of the end. Therefore, it is our job to "*build ourselves up into a most holy faith; pray in the Holy Spirit; keep ourselves in the love of Abba; look forward to the mercy of our Lord Jesus Christ that leads to eternal life. And have mercy on some who are wavering; save others by snatching them out of the fire; and have mercy on still others with fear hating even the tunic defiled by their bodies*" (Jude 1:20-23).

Second Peter, in contrast to Jude, makes it clear that the moral condemnation here is an attack against false teachers who put forth such destructive doctrines. These proclaimers of destructive heresies are they themselves heading toward destruction. While Jude leaves the judgment of these false teachers in the hands of Abba, Second Peter makes their fate explicit and emphatic.

The letter opens with a reminder of the Christian call that through Christ divine power we have been given everything needed for life and godliness. We are called upon to *support our faith with goodness, and goodness with knowledge and knowledge with self-control and self-control with endurance and endurance with godliness and godliness with mutual affection and mutual affection with love"* (2 Peter 1:5-7).

This will confirm one's call and election and entry into the eternal kingdom.

The author appeals to his being an eyewitness and not just a teller of tales when it pertains to the power and coming of Jesus Christ. It is this that gives the author authority to speak boldly on the matters of faith. Of prime concern is the interpretation of Scripture. Scripture is not a matter of human will but of men and women moved by the Holy Spirit. (This will become one of the foundational text in the inerrancy of Scripture movement that will develop in the time of the Enlightenment).

The issue at hand is the appearance of false prophets and teachers among the Christian community were bringing destructive opinions. *"Bold and willful, they are not afraid to slander the glorious ones, whereas angels, the greater and might and power, do not bring against them is slanderous judgment from the Lord. These people, however like irrational animals are creatures of instinct born to be caught and killed. They slander and they do not understand and when those creatures are destroyed, they also will be destroyed, suffering the penalty for doing wrong... They have eyes full of adultery... And hearts trained in greed"* (2 Peter 2:11-14).

The Second Letter of Peter closes with a familiar New Testament theme – the return of the Lord. It is this return that gives the content of the letter its urgency and the community it's hope. As with previous literature the stance of the faithful Christian is to hold onto to the tradition in patience, despite suffering, for a new heaven and new earth, a new home, awaits the faithful.

THE LETTERS OF JOHN

Most scholars would assign dates to this correspondence to between 90 and 100 CE. Using familiar Johannine themes such as light, Holy Spirit as advocate, and love the author writes these letters to his "little children" to remind them of the faith they have received.

"Hail, Xerxes!"

233

"Hail, Argos!"

"Did you read this morning's paper?"

"Yeah! I think the world coming to an end!"

"What are you hearing in the Christian community you belong to?"

"Mostly reassurance that it will all be okay so long as we don't lose faith."

"What's that mean?"

"We need to keep loving one another."

1 John

It is often argued that the first letter John really isn't a letter but rather a homily that was sent from church to church to be shared during worship.

The opening of the sermon begins in the same way that the gospel writer John begins his gospel, in the beginning. The author draws on the audience's initiation into the Christian community and the faith it has received. It is a faith based in the witness of those like the author who have seen and heard the witness of Jesus Christ and now declare it to those who have not so that their joy may be complete.

Again, using the Johannine and prophetic image of light in the darkness the author addresses one of the main concerns of the community namely, the issue of sinning after baptism. The author reminds us that "*if we say we have no sin we deceive ourselves and the truth is not in us. If we confess our sins, Christ who is faithful and just will forgive us our sins and cleanse us from all unrighteousness*" (1 John 1:8-9). The purpose of the letter is to encourage the little children not to sin. While the object is to avoid sin those that do sin have an advocate in Jesus Christ before the Father.

The author reminds his little children that he is not offering anything new that they have not heard before – love one another. We love one another but not the things of the world – the desire of the flesh, the desire of the eyes, the pride and riches. These things will pass away. With this the author turns his attention to the end, the last hour.

The first of his admonitions concerning the end of time has to do with the antichrist*s*. These refer to those who have removed themselves from the community and gone out on their own denouncing the Christian faith. Even now they are trying to deceive members of the community with this alternative message. The author admonishes his little children to continue to abide in the community as Christ abides in them.

The strength of this community is the love that Abba has given to his children. This love is demonstrated by the children and their love for one another and their desire to avoid sin. Using Cain is an example of how not to behave the author reminds us that our faith is active in love. What is critical are not our words or speech but rather truth and action.

There will be many spirits and prophets in these last days and the community will need to test the veracity of their witness. It is the community which is gathered by the Spirit and abides in Jesus that is able to tell what is the witness of Abba in the world. This is because love comes from Abba and that those who love must be born of Abba. While we have never seen Abba; if we love one another we know that Abba lives in us and his love is made perfect in us. It is impossible to say that one loves Abba and hates their brother or sister. To love Abba is to keep his commandments which form the basic rule for our love of brother and sister.

One of the key issues addressed in this sermon as well as elsewhere in the New Testament is the issue of the faithful renouncing their faith during difficult times. Christians are often called upon to bear testimony of their beliefs in the world court. The author reminds the faithful that those who believe in Jesus already have the necessary testimony in their hearts: Abba gave us eternal life, and this life is in his Son. Whoever has the Son has life; whoever does not have the Son does not have life.

2 John

The Second Letter of John is truly a letter which is addressed to an eclectic and unnamed woman and her children. Again, the content of the letter focuses on the theme of love for one another and the deceivers of the world. The woman is admonished not to accept into her household any persons that do not confess that Jesus has come in the flesh for they do not abide in the teaching of Christ.

3 John

The Third Letter of John is addressed to an elder of the church, the beloved Gaius. The author admonishes Gaius to provide worthy hospitality to the itinerant preachers and missionaries, his coworkers, who might avail themselves to Gaius' home. Revealed in the letter is also the prevalent issue of divisions within the life of the church as well as power struggles among the members. We are reminded through Gaius to imitate only that which is good. Whoever does good must be from Abba; and whoever does not do good has obviously not encountered Abba.

The content of these last two letters concerns reassurance that in the midst of difficulty and faithfulness we continue in the walk of Jesus Christ. The issue of false teachers has become more and more of a concern for the emerging church of the second century.

THE REVELATION OF JOHN

"Zaydeh, tell me the story again"!

"What story?"

"The story of the Great and Terrible Day. Please, Zaydeh, please."

"Why you so interested in the Great and Terrible Day?"

"Because I think it's here!"

"What makes you say that"?

"The Temple is destroyed, the tensions between Rome and us are growing, and I heard rumors that they're persecuting Christians in Ephesus."

"How about if I tell you that story in a new way, not a story about the past, but rather a story about the future?"

As I prepare to write this final chapter I've retreated to my studio. The reason for this is that I believe the Revelation of John is more art than prose. There is something about reading Revelation surrounded by Wagner and van Gough that speaks to John, the artist, who paints in vibrant, if not disturbing, images. I have often toyed with offering a course called Painting Revelation, in which participants are given a pallet of vibrant colored paints and a variety of brushes. As sections of the book are read the participants are invited to paint what they hear. In many ways I think that would be more faithful to the author's intention rather than the tedious autopsy we often give the book in Bible studies.

Also, given the structure of the book of Revelation with its patterned and mnemonic devices scholars feel certain that the context for the communication of Revelation was an oral reading in in worship. In fact, I believe that Revelation only makes sense in the context of worship. In that context, the disturbing images are balanced and illuminated by the ritual actions of worship. I would argue that reading Revelation outside of the worship context contributes to using this book as some map to the future rather than a hope filled portrayal of Abba's actions during trying times.

As a result, I would like to approach this book in a slightly different manner. After a brief introduction, followed by the first part of the book which are brief letters to the seven churches of Asia minor I will offer a pallet of images that hopefully will guide us as we read this book together.

John writes from the island of Patmos where he is in exile (like the Israelites is Babylon where this story began). Patmos is about 60 miles southwest of the mainland of Asia minor and he is writing to the seven churches on the mainland. Most scholars believe the revelation was composed during the last days of Emperor Domitian (95 CE). It is in the framework of the pastoral letter but is filled with apocalyptic content.

One thing to note about the persecutions at the end of the first century is that they were sporadic and local in nature. Sweeping persecutions of Christians would not occur until about the third century. This does not mean that those communities experiencing persecution were not experiencing intense suffering.

In addition to the destruction of the Temple in Jerusalem there is growing conflict between church and state amid the totalitarian regime, namely Rome. Like the Jews a century earlier Christians are now being forced to claim allegiance to Caesar rather than Christ. A major crisis facing the church in this time is also the delayed return of Christ. Revelation therefore offers a prophetic interpretation of this present condition of the churches and is not primarily a reaction to the persecution. The material of Revelation is highly symbolic, highly evocative, and draws heavily upon Old Testament images and themes.

The first three chapters of Revelation are like many other New Testament writings: they contain seven letters to seven churches in the Roman province of Asia. They are not real letters like those written by Paul, for they purport to come from the risen Jesus himself, and John says that their content was given to him in a vision (as was the rest of the book). But these letters deal with very down-to-earth matters and show a detailed knowledge of these people and their environment. Their churches were involved in disputes over Christian beliefs and their commitment to Christ was wavering, as a result they were in no position to face up to the challenge of sustained persecution. To do that, they needed to be wholeheartedly committed. This is a message that we find many times in the New Testament, and it is not significantly different from that of 1 Peter.

The letters addressed to the seven churches in Asia bear a striking resemblance to the prophetic oracles against the nations of the past, "Thus says the Lord". What was addressed to the nations, Israel, and Judah in former times is now the critique of the Christian churches.

The first of the churches to be addressed is Ephesus. Ephesus is the fourth largest city of the Empire. It is a commercial center and the most important seaport in Asia. It is also the center of the Imperial cult. The church of Ephesus is of high importance. The letter praises the church of Ephesus for its toil, patient endurance and confession in the face of crisis. At the same time, it is censured because it has abandoned the love that they had at first. In their zeal for orthodoxy they have become unloving, inquisitional, and censorious. The letter offers Ephesus three imperatives: remember, repent, and hear.

The second of the churches addressed is that in Smyrna. The Temple to Caesar Tiberius is found in Smyrna and as such it is the center of the Imperial cult. The church is in bitter conflict with the Jews. Rome has granted Jews the privilege of practicing their religion in any part of the Empire and the Jews perceive Christians as messianic troublemakers. At this point, Jews and Romans are colluding to put Christians into prison. The judgment of the church in Smyrna is that many are avoiding prison by offering confession to Caesar. Despite this the letter offers the promise that this tribulation pales when compared to the millennial time of paradise or Christ reign.

The third church addressed is that of Pergamum. Pergamum is the official seat of the Roman government in Asia. There is a Temple to Roma and Augustus as well as Zeus. At the center of the church of Pergamum are many who are sliding into an increased sense of patriotism and atheism. The community is praised however for its resistance against the threat of the Imperial cult. The letter calls the church to repentance in the presence of heretics.

The fourth church addressed is that of Thyatira. This is the least important of the seven cities mentioned in the letters. There is a Temple to Apollo to be found in the city. It is a center for commerce featuring craftsmen, merchants, and artisans. The presence of guilds with their mandatory membership, required meetings and practices are causing a crisis for Christians. Do they withdraw from the guild and face unemployment? The church is commended for its works of love, faith, service, patience, and endurance. It does receive censure because it has not excluded heretics.

The fifth of the church is addressed is in Sardis. This is capital of the ancient Kingdom of Lydia. It was greatly damaged by an earthquake in 17 CE, its glory days now past, it is called to wake up, to be strengthened and to remember.

The sixth church is that of Philadelphia. This city was also destroyed by the quake of 17 CE and was rebuilt under Tiberius. The Christian community in the city had little power and receives hope in the promise of a new Jerusalem.

The final church to be addressed is in the affluent trading center of Laodicea. It is a commercial and industrial center. The water supply for Laodicea is channeled from 5 miles away providing lukewarm water (contrast this with a Hierapolis' hot springs or the cool wells of Colossae). But like the water supply to the city, the accusation leveled at the church in Laodicea was that it was lukewarm. The interesting piece is that it is not even warm enough or cold enough to warrant a condemnation.

The second part of the book (4–22) is quite different. Here we come face to face with the language and imagery of apocalyptic writing. No longer do the visions seem to relate to real events and people, but instead they introduce monsters and dragons in a quick succession of terrifying events. The whole section is introduced in chapters 4 and 5 by a vision of heaven which sets the scene for what follows. This is a powerful and impressive presentation of the central importance of the life, death and resurrection of Jesus in the Christian understanding of life and its meaning. It is significant that at the very beginning of his visions, John links the future destiny of the world and its inhabitants with Abba's self-revelation in the historical events of the life of Jesus.

The chapters that follow then present a series of visions describing how justice will be served on all those forces that are implacably opposed to Abba's will. Many of the descriptions here are quite horrific, and much of the language in which Abba's judgment is described comes from the story of the plagues in Egypt in the Old Testament book of Exodus.

As I mentioned earlier the images in the second half of the book of Revelation are drawn from the Old Testament. Let us now prepare our pallet from these images that are relevant to Christian preaching and teaching today.

The Temple. The Temple represented for Jews a scale model of all creation. The early Jewish Christians would've recognized the Temple in Revelation's description as heaven. The menorah (seven golden lampstands) and the altar of incense, stood before the Holy of Holies, the dwelling place of Abba. In the Temple four carved cherubim adorn the walls, as the four living creatures minister before the throne in Revelation. In Revelation, chapter 24 elders replicate the 24 priestly divisions who served in the Temple. The sea of glass like crystal was the Temple's large polished bronze basin that held 11,500 gallons of water. At the center of both temples is the Ark of the Covenant.

According to ancient Jewish beliefs, the worship in Jerusalem's Temple mirrored the worship of the angels in heaven. In the church of the apocalypse, however, we see a movement from praying in imitation of the angels to worshiping together with the angels.

The Jews throughout the world saw the leveling of the Temple in 70 CE as a cataclysmic event that was believed to be the ushering in of the Great and Terrible Day and the destruction of the cosmic Temple at the end of time.

John's vision describes the passing away of the old order, old world, old Jerusalem, old covenant, and the creation of a new world, a new Jerusalem, a new covenant and the new worship. This is reminiscent of Jesus words, "destroy this temple and in three days I will raise it up," and "the day is coming when neither on this mountain or in Jerusalem will you worship the Father." Also in Matthew's crucifixion scene, the Temple's veil is torn from top to bottom.

Lamb. John looks for the Lion of Judah but instead he is introduced to the Lamb. Like the lamb on Mount Moriah where Abraham was asked to offer up Isaac or the lambs of the Temple this lamb is a sacrificial lamb.

Woman. For John, the woman in Revelation is Mary, the mother of our Lord, and was viewed as the new Eve.

Dragon/Serpent. The image of the dragon or serpent in Revelation is that of the Nahash, the serpent in the Garden of Eden.

First Beast. This beast represents corrupt political authority of any sort. Certainly, Rome would qualify, but the portrait is a composite of the four beasts from the vision of Daniel. In short, the seven-headed beast stands for all corrupted political power. In John's day that corruption was demanding the worship that belongs to Abba alone.

Second Beast. The second beast is the corrupted priesthood of the first century Jerusalem. This priesthood has thrown itself in with a lot of the first beast instead of with Abba. They have rejected Christ and of elevated the Caesar.

Apocalypse. Apocalypse or revelation literally means "unveiling". The word was used for the cultic wedding practice of the lifting of the veil. It also points to the cross and crucifixion of Christ – the tearing of the Temple curtain. It is a beginning not an ending. The Revelation of John speaks to the end of an old order but it also points the way to a new Jerusalem and a new heaven and earth. The church has always taught that the end is near – as near as Sunday morning as we gather around the

Eucharistic feast – and it's something that we should not be running from but rather running to.

Armageddon. Armageddon was the place where Josiah, the great Davidic king, amid his holy reform of the Jerusalem cult, was cut down in his prime for disobeying the instruction of Abba's prophet. Josiah's defeat at Megiddo weakened Israel's defenses and eventually brought about the destruction of Jerusalem by the Babylonians. For the early Christians, Jesus, like Josiah, a Davidic king and reformer, cut down in his prime, would persevere in obedience in establishing a new Jerusalem. The siege of Jerusalem brought on famine, pestilence and strife which we see in the four angelic horsemen of the apocalypse and the seven trumpeters.

Through all the strife of the Jewish War the Christians remained unharmed because the community of believers had fled to the mountain across the Jordan to a place called Pella. These Christians (144,000) from the 12 tribes of Israel, were preserved because they were sealed upon their foreheads – these are the baptized, signed with a cross and white robed.

Epiphanius reports that in 130 CE when Hadrian arrives to put down the Second Jewish revolt, Jerusalem is still in ruins "except for a few houses and the little Church of Abba on the spot with the disciples went to the upper room." The heart of the new Temple will be the meal.

With pallet prepared let us now be encountered by the visions and images of Revelation.

We find ourselves with John knocking on heaven's door. The word, which greets us like a herald's trumpet, is, "Enter, and I will show you what is to happen." (It is not all that unlike the announcement from Scrooge's three-night visitors and Charles Dickens, ***Christmas Carol***).

We find ourselves immediately in the midst of the divine worship which will be the context for the revelations to follow. The central focus of this worship is the one who sits on the throne and the nature of the worship reflects both the Temple tradition as well as the Christian Eucharist. The sevenfold gifts of the Spirit (the spirit of wisdom and understanding, the spirit of counsel and might, the spirit of knowledge and the fear of the Lord, the spirit of joy in the presence of the holy one) emanate from the one on the throne like a Fourth of July fireworks display. The four creatures prowling around the throne bear a striking symbolic resemblance to the avatars of the gospel writers: Matthew, Mark, Luke and John. For

Lutherans this setting should conjure up images of worship as Word and Sacrament. As with the vision of Isaiah in the Temple we are greeted with a trifold, Holy, Holy, Holy! (The theme song for both HaShem and Abba). The final act in this worship scene is the acknowledgment by the Elders that they stand in the presence of the one who elicits all glory honor and power. (The strains of *All Hail the Power of Jesus Name!* Can be heard building in the background… "let angels prostrate fall; bring forth the royal diadem and crown him Lord of all.").

Our attention is now focused on the one who sits on the throne holding a scroll that is sealed with seven seals. An angel addresses the crowd asking if there is anyone among us who is worthy to open the seals. There is no one in heaven and on earth deemed worthy for the task. The church's response is tears. In a scene that is somewhat reminiscent of Mary Magdalene's encounter with the risen Christ in the garden the angel's response to the church's wailing is, "Do not weep." The reason? Even now the Lion of Judah, the Root of Jesse, has triumphed and he can open the seals of the scroll. While it is a lion that we anticipate we are greeted instead by a Lamb standing amid the gathering as one who is been slaughtered. Like the one who is seated on the throne the seven gifts of the Spirit emanate from the Lamb and a new song is to be heard: Worthy! And the voices of the throngs of angels surrounding the throne echo the chorus: "Worthy is Christ, the Lamb who was slain, whose blood set us free to be people of Abba. Power, riches, wisdom, and strength, and honor, blessing, and glory are his." And the church gathered said, "Amen!"

The Lamb begins to open the seals as the four creatures gathered around the throne boom with encouragement, "Go!" There appears a rider on a white horse who rides off conquering right and left. The second seal is opened, and again with a voice like thunder, "Go!" This time a red horse comes out removing peace from the earth leaving only death and destruction. The third seal, and again, "Go!" A third horse, this one black, emerges with a rider holding a set of scales. Are these portending economic disaster and depression? The fourth seal is broken, "Go!" A pale green horse with its rider, Death, emerges with Hades following. A quarter of the earth was given to their charge to kill with sword, famine, and pestilence. The breaking of the fifth seal ushers in a vision of those who have died for the faith and who now stand lamenting beneath the throne, "How long, O

Lord, how long?" They are given white robes and told to have patience for things are about to change. The six seal opens with the force of an earthquake. The sun becomes black and the moon like blood and the stars of the sky fall and every mountain crumbles (check out Psalm 46). These events send the populace running for shelter for the Great and Terrible Day of the Lord is obviously now upon them.

Before the seventh seal is opened we are offered a vision of the four angels taking their places at the four corners of the earth holding back the winds of death and destruction. They are given instructions to hold them back until these servants of Abba are marked with seals upon their foreheads (the rite of anointing the newly baptized with the sign of the cross is seen as a branding and claiming of them by Abba). The number of those sealed are reported to be 144,000 who are called out of the 12 tribes of Israel. Again, the scene shifts and a great multitude stands before the throne and the Lamb. This great multitude elicits images of both Pentecost and that great cloud of witnesses referred to in the book of Hebrews. They are joined by angels and the elders together lifting up their voices in song with the second verse of the hymn: "Amen! Blessing and honor, glory and might be to Abba and the Lamb forever. Amen". We are questioned by the elders as to the identity of these white-robed ones. When we fail to answer he continues, "These are the ones who have come out of the great ordeal/ persecution and who now sit before the throne day and night in worship of the one who sits on the throne. They who have washed their robes in the blood of the lamb will hunger and thirst no more, the sun shall not strike them by day and the Lamb will become their shepherd and will guide them to springs of the water of life".

The response to the opening of the seventh seal is silence. The seven angels around the throne pick up their trumpets in anticipation. Another angel stands before the altar and with a great quantity of incense offers prayers for all the saints. The smoke of the incense and the prayers of the saints rise before Abba. The angel then takes the censer, filling it with fire from the altar, throws it upon the earth causing peals of thunder, rumblings, flashings of lightning, and earthquake to ensue. At this the first trumpeter blows his trumpet and there falls hail and fire, mixed with blood and a third of the earth is destroyed. The second angel blows his trumpet and a volcanic mountain is thrown into the sea and a third of the sea becomes blood. A third angel blows his trumpet and a great star falls from heaven blazing like a torch and it falls on a third of the rivers. The name of the star is Wormwood and a third of the waters become wormwood and many die from the water. A fourth angel blows his trumpet and a third of the sun the struck, as well as a third of the moon and a third at the stars so that a third of their light is diminished. At this point an eagle arrives on the scene crying a word of woe. As the fifth angel blows his trumpet we see a star falling from heaven to earth and smoke rising from the great shaft that it left in the ground. Through the smoke come locusts whose sting was like that of the scorpion. They are to spare those who bear the mark on their foreheads but their sting will lead others to wish for death. The scorpions are described like a mighty army and the king who rules over them is called Abaddon, (in Hebrew) or Apollyon (in Greek). The blast of the sixth angel signals a voice from the altar that seeks the release of the four angels bound by the great river Euphrates. The release signals the death of one third of humanity. This is carried out by troops numbering 200 million. They are described in gruesome detail bearing a striking resemblance to the army of locusts. Even with all this much of humanity refuses to repent.

At this point another mighty angel descends from the heavens wrapped in a cloud, crowned with a rainbow. He holds a little scroll. The contents of the scroll are not disclosed but the angel is charged to seal up the revelation. In the days when the seventh angel finally blows his trumpet the mystery of Abba will be revealed as it had been promised by those who have gone before him, both servants and prophets. The little scroll is handed to us and we are told to take it and eat (in the same manner the prophets of old were instructed to eat the Word of HaShem) and while it may be bitter to our stomachs it will be sweet as honey in our mouths.

We are given a measuring staff and told to measure the Temple but not the Temple precincts for they will be given over to the nations. Abba's witnesses will be given 1260 days to prophesy in sackcloth and ashes. When these prophets finish their testimony, a beast will come out from the bottomless pit and the dead will lie in the streets of a great city prophetically named Sodom and Egypt. The inhabitants of the earth will come and go for 3 ½ days because these prophets have been a torment to them. The breath of Abba will enter into them after 3 ½ days and they will stand on their feet and all will be terrified. As they are gathered up into heaven there is a great earthquake in which 7000 people are killed. The seventh angel blows his trumpet and ushers in the third and last woe. Our musical ears now need to listen for the strains of Handel's Messiah building in the background. The voices cry out, *"The kingdom of the world has become the kingdom of our Lord and of his Messiah and he will reign for ever and ever"* (Revelation 11:15). All fall on their faces worshiping Abba. The Temple in heaven is opened (as at the crucifixion) and the Ark of the covenant is revealed as a second fireworks display goes off.

Our attention is once again diverted. This time by a woman clothed with the sun and the moon beneath her feet and a crown of 12 stars on her head. She is pregnant and wailing in labor as she prepares to give birth. A great red dragon appears with seven heads and 10 horns and stands before the woman, a menacing figure ready to devour the newborn child. She gives birth to a son who is immediately snatched away and taken to Abba. The woman flees to the wilderness where she lives 1260 days in a place that has been prepared for her.

At this point we are informed that war has broken out in heaven. Michael and his angels have fought against the dragon and the dragon and his angels fought back but are defeated. The great dragon called the devil/Satan are thrown down to earth. Like Miriam at the Red Sea this too is an occasion for a song of rejoicing. When the Dragon hits the earth, he chases down the woman who had given birth. The woman is given wings like eagles to fly into the wilderness. While the Dragon sends a flood to drown her the earth swallows up the water. Frustrated, the Dragon goes off to make war on the rest of her children, those who keep the commandments of Abba and hold the witness of Jesus.

As the story turns we are introduced to two beasts. The first rises out of the sea. It looks as though he has received a mortal wound and yet it appears to have been healed. The whole earth gives authority to the beast and worships the beast saying, "Who is like the beast, and who can fight against such a force?" With a mouth, that obviously needs to be washed out with soap, the beast utters all manner of haughty and blasphemous words. It makes war on the saints and is given authority over every tribe and people and language and nation. During this war there is a call for the endurance and faith of the saints. The second beast rises out of the earth. This beast is equally as menacing as the first beast. The call this time is for Wisdom. This is the Wisdom of the later Jewish Kabbalists and the Christian Gnostics. Fraught with numbers, signs and codes (that would make even Dan Brown proud) this Wisdom assigns to the beast the number 666.

Our focus returns to the Lamb and to Mount Zion. Gathered around the Lamb are the 144,000 who have Abba's name written on their foreheads. A new song is now sung before the throne that sounds like the voice of many waters and the clapping of thunder. Only the 144,000 can sing it, no new voices are able to be added. These are the first fruits for Abba and for the Lamb.

Three angels now arrive on the scene bearing messages. The first bears the eternal gospel to proclaim to every nation and tribe and language and people. Its message is clear. *"Fear Abba and give him glory! His hour of judgment is come! Worship the one who has made the heavens and earth the sea and the springs of water"* (Revelation 14:7). A second messenger shows up announcing that Babylon has fallen! This one is followed by a third Angel crying with a loud voice that those who worship the beast will drink of Abba's wrath. Once again there is a call for the endurance of the saints who keep the commandments of Abba and hold fast to the testimony of Jesus. We hear a voice from heaven calling us to write: Blessed are the dead who from now on die in the Lord.

Our scene is now dominated by a white cloud with one like the Son of Man sitting upon it. A golden crown is upon his head and a sickle in his hand. An angel comes out of the Temple imploring him to reap the earth for it is harvest time. A second angel emerges from the Temple with a sickle in his hand and he is charged to gather the clusters of the vine, for the grapes are ripe. The grapes are placed in a great wine press outside of the city. As they are trodden, blood flows from the winepress for 200 miles.

Chapter 15 introduces us to another great and amazing vision: seven angels with seven plagues now bring an end to Abba's wrath. There is a sea of glass and fire besides which stand those who have defeated the beast and his minions. With the sound of harps, they sing the Song of Moses as he and Miriam had sung it following the victory over Pharaoh and his great army. Then appear seven angels from the Temple robed in pure white with golden sashes across their chests. Each one is carrying a bowl full of the wrath of Abba. The Temple is filled with smoke from the glory of Abba and no one can enter the Temple until the seven plagues are finished.

The seven angels are instructed to pour out the contents of their bowls upon the earth. Foul and painful sores appear upon those who bear the mark of the beast as the first angel empties their bowl upon them. The second angel dumps his contents into the sea and it becomes like blood. A third pours his contents into the rivers and they to become like blood. A fourth pours his on the sun and it scorches the people with fire. A fifth pours the wrath of Abba upon the throne of the beast and his kingdom is plunged into darkness. A sixth angel pours his contents into the great river Euphrates and the water is dried up. The seventh angel throws his into the air and a voice from the Temple announces that it is finished! A third pyrotechnics display and the city is split into three parts. It is said that Abba remembered Babylon and gave her the cup of his fury.

The great whore is now revealed. She is clothed in purple and scarlet and adorned with gold and jewels and pearls. She holds in her hand a golden cup full of the abominations and impurities of her fornication. On her head is inscribed, "Babylon the Great, mother of Horace and of Earth's abominations." She is drunk with the blood of the saints and the blood of the witnesses of Jesus. Our first reaction is amazement. Then an angel challenges us with a rather cryptic description of the woman and her activities. In the end he discloses that she is the great city that rules over the kings of the earth. Walter Brueggemann in his writings refers to this image and those like it as reflecting the concept of "Empire." He reminds us that like Egypt and Babylon, Rome, France, Great Brittan, as well as these United States would qualify under that heading.

Yet another angel descends from heaven with great authority and splendor announcing the fall of Babylon. In hymnic prose he announces both the why and the how of her destruction.

As the angel finishes his song the great multitude of heavens echo, "Hallelujah!" And the 24 elders cry, "Hallelujah!" And the great multitude cries out, "Hallelujah!" The chorus crescendos with an invitation to the marriage supper of the Lamb.

From the heavens there comes a white horse whose rider is Faithful and True. His clothing is dipped in blood and his name is called the Word of Abba. Following him are the armies of the heavens robed in white riding similar white steeds. There comes from his mouth a sharp sword to strike down the nations. He will rule with an iron rod and will tread upon the winepress of the wrath of Abba. It is written on his robe and tattooed on his thigh, "King of Kings and Lord of Lords."

Our vision is diverted by the ascending of all the birds that fly from the heavens. Again, an invitation: "Come, gather for the great supper of Abba, eat the flesh of Kings, the flesh of captains, the flesh of the mighty, the flesh of horses and their riders – flesh of all, both free and slave, both great and small." We watch the armies of the beast and their kings engaged by the rider. The beast is captured and is thrown into a lake of fire. The remainder are killed by the sword of the rider and the birds of prey gorge on their flesh.

Again, an angel comes down from heaven this time holding in his hand the key to the bottomless pit and a great chain. He binds the Dragon (Devil/Satan) for 1000 years. After that he will be let out for a little while.

As so often in the Hebrew Scriptures we find ourselves amid a heavenly court scene. Those who had been beheaded for their testimony of Jesus and the word of Abba are raised to new life and reign with Christ for 1000 years (the remainder do not come to life until the thousand years were ended). This is the first resurrection. Over these the second death has no power for they will reign with Christ for 1000 years. When that time is ended, Satan will be released from prison and will come and deceive the nations and gather them for battle. They will march over the breadth of the earth and surround the camp of the saints and their beloved city.

Fire will come down from heaven and consume them and the devil who deceived them will be thrown into the lake of fire in everlasting torment. The dead shall stand before the throne and the books will be opened as well as the Book of Life. The dead will be judged by their deeds that have been recorded. Death and Hades will give up their dead and they too will be judged. And death and Hades will be thrown into the Lake of Fire. This is the second death, the Lake of Fire, and anyone whose name is not found written in the book of life will be thrown into the Lake of Fire.

The last two chapters of Revelation provide us with a vision of the New Earth and the New Heaven. The holy city, the new Jerusalem, will come down from heaven prepared as a bride adorned for her husband. Abba will make his home among mortals. He will dwell with them; they will be his people, and Abba himself will be with them; he will wipe away every tear from their eyes. Death will be no more; mourning and crying and pain will be no more, for the first things have passed away. "See, I am making all things new," says Abba. He announces that he is the Alpha and the Omega, the beginning and the end. To the thirsty he will give the waters of new life.

Then one of the seven angels who had the seven bowls of the last plagues comes and says, "Come, and I will show you the bride, the wife of the Lamb." And the spirit carries us away to a high mountain showing us the holy city Jerusalem coming down out of heaven from Abba. It's 12 foundations are no longer only the 12 tribes of Israel but also include the 12 disciples of the Lamb. Again, the city is to be measured.

This new Jerusalem does not feature a temple for the Temple is Abba the Almighty and the Lamb. The dawn of the messianic age and city are described with images drawn from Isaiah. With illusions to Psalm 46 and Genesis the revelation is brought to a close – a return to paradise. *"The throne of Abba and of the Lamb will be in it, and his servants will worship him; they will see his face, and his name will be on their foreheads. And there will be no more night; they will need no light of the lamp or sun, for the Lord Abba will be their light, and they will reign for ever and ever"* (Revelation 22:3-5).

John attaches an epilogue and a blessing upon those who wash their robes and enter the city. The message of Revelation to the seven churches and to us is that the fate of the old Jerusalem awaits us and all who fail to recognize their mistakes – their loss of faith amid secular and political coercion. These final words echo the familiar strains of the exilic prophets.

The earthly liturgy is a foretaste of that heavenly liturgy which is celebrated in the Holy City of Jerusalem toward which we journey as pilgrims. As such, chapters 1 through 11 comprise the liturgy of the Word, chapters one through three being a penitential rite (confession and forgiveness) with the call to repent! Chapters 11 through 21 begin with the opening of Abba's Temple in heaven, and culminate in the pouring of the seven chalices and the marriage supper of the Lamb – the liturgy of the Meal.

Again, I would argue that the only proper context to hear the Revelation of John is to be seated in the sanctuary during the Eucharistic liturgy. It is only there that the signs and symbols, monsters and dragons, find their context and interpretation. It is also there as we gather, at the end of time, that we can put in its proper context not only the visions of Revelation but also the visions of September 11, 2001. Both the Gospel of Mark and Revelation leave in the hands of the gathered community the task of continuing to tell the story of Abba's love and faithfulness shown through the pages of the Holy Scriptures. Though the waters rage and foam, and kingdoms are shaken, HaShem is HaShem, and Abba is still Abba. Surrounded by that great cloud of witnesses who have gone before us we pray continually, "Amen. Come, Lord Jesus!"

> *"May the grace of our Lord Jesus be with you and all the saints. Amen. Come, Lord Jesus"* (Revelation 22:21).

Epilogue

"Papa, do you remember 9/11?"

"Yes, Savanna, I certainly do. It was one of those days you don't forget. Why do you ask?"

"We were learning about it in school."

"So, you know what happened?"

"Something about airplanes and terrorists. Is that right?"

"Kind of. On that morning terrorists flew two passenger planes into the World Trade Center in New York City destroying the Twin Towers, a third plane was crashed into the Pentagon in Washington, DC, and a fourth plane was prevented from hitting its target when passengers attacked the terrorists – that plane crashed into a field in SW Pennsylvania."

"How many people died?"

"About 3,000."

"That's a lot."

"Yes, but that day did more than kill people and destroy buildings... that day changed the world."

"What do you mean?"

*"For the first time in 60 years an enemy attacked US.
Until that day we thought we were invincible now we were
vulnerable. People were afraid. People were angry. Hatred
began to run high for all Muslims. People didn't know what
to do. We gathered as a nation to pray but were uncertain
what we were doing. We searched for words to say. Before
we knew it, we were at war. To raise questions became
unpatriotic. Homeland security became the watchdogs. New
security regulations for flying were put in place. We learned
to distrust everyone who was different. Soon when people
disagreed they chose up sides and started to scream at each
other. Before long churches started to empty out. People began
to wonder if there was a HaShem or Abba or if they had
anything to offer us... had Abba finally left the building?"*

*"Papa, that sounds like the Great and Terrible Day you wrote
about in your book. Is that why you wrote it?"*

*"I wrote it because I think there are some clues in the Bible
that might help us deal with it better or at least help us
understand why we have reacted the way we have."*

"What do you mean?"

*"Unlike our Jewish brothers and sisters who dealt with the
great disaster of the destruction of the Temple we were never
given the opportunity to lament and reflect. Such actions were
condemned and those who dared express the hard questions
were threatened."*

"That's awful."

*"It happened. It is what people do when they are afraid. Soon
we were making laws "to protect us" that we never would
have passed before because they limited our freedom. We also
started to divide people into groups that were good (those
like us) and bad (the foreigner, the stranger, the immigrant,*

the homosexuals, the African American, the Hispanic, the Asian and especially the Muslim). It soon spread to include women and people living on Welfare. Many in our churches joined the act. Soon the voices got louder, voices that were underground for many decades now surfaced. Voices filled with hate and anger. Cries to overthrow the oppressor were more and more common. Leaders rose up that were championed as new messiah's, who would save this nation and make it great again."

"Papa, what did we do?"

"The church in this country became divided. We could no longer deny that we had two distinct Christianities. Many reverted back to the old ways of the Law. Others engaged in a backlash of persecution and terror. We forgot that Jesus advocated neither a screwing down the jot and tittle of the Law nor advocate for a Messianic rebellion. Instead he embraced the outcast and marginalized and called for the healing of the nations."

"Do you think we will every return to the way it was?"

"No, Savanna... Jesus ushered in a new age... the world will never be the same again."

"So, Papa, why do you spend so much time with this old book?"

"Savanna dear, it is a story about a fragile people, in a fragile land, with a fragile hope. It is our story. It is your story. In remembering the story, we find the courage to face our fears and continue the work Abba has called us to on this earth... the healing of the nations and the reconciliation of all creation."

"Wow, Papa, we better get started... will you read it to me again!"